AUTO/BIOGRAPHY

AND IDENTITY

WOMEN, THEATRE AND PERFORMANCE

SERIES EDITORS

MAGGIE B. GALE AND VIV GARDNER

AUTO/BIOGRAPHY AND IDENTITY

Women, theatre and performance

EDITED BY

MAGGIE B. GALE AND VIV GARDNER

Manchester University Press

Manchester and New York

distributed exclusively in the USA by Palgrave

Published by Manchester University Press
Oxford Road, Manchester M13 9NR, UK
and Room 400, 175 Fifth Avenue, New York, NY 10010, USA
www.manchesteruniversitypress.co.uk

Distributed exclusively in the USA by
Palgrave, 175 Fifth Avenue, New York NY 10010, USA

Distributed exclusively in Canada by
UBC Press, University of British Columbia, 2029 West Mall,
Vancouver, BC, Canada V6T 1Z2

British Library Cataloguing-in-Publication Data
A catalogue record for this book is available from the British Library

Library of Congress Cataloging-in-Publication Data
A catalog record for this book is available from the Library of Congress

ISBN 13: 978 0 7190 6333 6

First published in hardback 2004 by Manchester University Press
This paperback edition first published 2009

Printed by Lightning Source

CONTENTS

LIST OF ILLUSTRATIONS

SERIES EDITORS' FOREWORD

This series, *Women, Theatre and Performance*, has its origins in the work of a number of feminist theatre academics from the 1980s and 1990s – a period when interest burgeoned in the part that women have played in theatre over the centuries. That interest was in its turn the daughter of the 'Second Wave' women's movement, the women's theatre movement and the women's history movement from the previous two decades. It was with some delight that women theatre workers, spectators and scholars alike discovered that women *did* have a significant history in performance, and these women – and some men – have continued to investigate, interrogate and work with their histories. Feminist performance analysis and women's theatre history has now become an established part of performance practice and theatre studies at both a university and a more popular level.

In the 1990s the journal *Women and Theatre Occasional Papers* became the host for the documentation and dissemination of contemporary research and innovation in theatre practice and scholarship in Britain. The emphasis on history and historiography was a considered decision. It was felt that at that time no consistent outlet existed for all the work that carried on the feminist retrieval project of the 1980s which was emerging from theatre and drama departments in Britain and elsewhere. This emphasis on history did not – and does not – preclude engagement with contemporary practice. On the contrary, it was felt that our history was very much part of our present and that the two could, and should, be studied side by side. This series seeks to continue that original project and to make the research and debate available on a more than 'occasional' basis. The series will consist of themed volumes and monographs that consider theatre as part of a wider nexus of social and cultural practices. Women's contribution to all areas and types of theatre and performance will be included, from opera and acrobatics to management and dramaturgy. Continuities and consistencies will not be sought, though they may be found within the transhistorical and transcultural organisation of the material.

The series is designed for academics, students at all levels, teachers and practitioners, as well as the interested enthusiast who wishes simply to 'fill in the blanks' where women have been hitherto 'hidden' in theatre histories.

Maggie B. Gale
Viv Gardner

ACKNOWLEDGEMENTS

The editors have made every effort to contact copyright holders and obtain relevant permissions. The editors would like to thank the following for permission to reproduce materials: White Cube Gallery (London), Artangel (London), Artsadmin (London), Museum of London, Henrietta Butler and Shirley Askins and family.

To Ben and Jan, our book widows ... with love and thanks.

NOTES ON CONTRIBUTORS

Elaine Aston is Professor of Contemporary Performance at Lancaster University. She has published several books and numerous articles on aspects of feminist theatre and performance. Her authored studies include *Sarah Bernhardt* (Berg, 1989); *An Introduction to Feminism and Theatre* (Routledge, 1995); *Caryl Churchill* (Northcote, 1997); *Feminist Theatre Practice: A Handbook* (Routledge, 1999); and *Feminist Views on the English Stage: Women Playwrights 1990–2000* (Cambridge University Press, 2003).

Susan Croft is Curator of Contemporary Performance at the Theatre Museum where her work has focused on video documentation, live art and black British theatre. She worked as a director, dramaturg and workshop leader in London before founding the New Playwrights Trust. She has held research fellowships at Manchester Metropolitan University and the Harry Ransom Humanities Research Centre at the University of Austin, Texas, working on women's writing for performance. She is currently completing a *Critical Bibliography of Published Women Playwrights in the English Language 1360–1914*. Her other publications include *...She Also Wrote Plays: An International Reference Guide to Women Playwrights* (Faber, 2001) and *Black and Asian Performance at the Theatre Museum: A Users' Guide* (2004).

Maggie B. Gale is Chair in Drama at the University of Manchester. Her recent publications include *West End Women: Women on the London Stage 1918–1962* (Routledge, 1996); *British Theatre Between the Wars: 1918-1939* (Cambridge University Press, 2000), co-edited with Clive Barker; *Women Theatre and Performance: New Histories, New Historiographies* (Manchester University Press, 2000), with Viv Gardner. She is co-editor with John Stokes of *The Cambridge Companion to the Actress* (Cambridge University Press, 2006) and co-editor with Viv Gardner of the series *Women, Theatre and Performance* (Manchester University Press).

Viv Gardner is Professor of Theatre Studies at the University of Manchester. Currently working on a history of early twentieth-century provincial theatre in Britain, she is the co-editor with Susan Rutherford of *The New Woman and Her Sisters* (Harvester Wheatsheaf, 1992), and with David Mayer of the journal *Nineteenth Century Theatre and Film* (Manchester University Press) and has written extensively on late nineteenth- and early twentieth-century British theatre. Viv Gardner is co-editor of *History and Histrionics* with Jacky Bratton and Gillie Bush-Bailey and of the series *Women, Theatre and Performance* (Manchester University Press) with Maggie B. Gale.

Gabriele Griffin is Professor of Gender Studies at the University of Hull. Her research interests focus on women's contemporary cultural production and on Women's Studies as a discipline. She is co-editor of the journal *Feminist Theory*. Recent publications include *Contemporary Black and Asian Women Playwrights in Britain* (Cambridge University Press, 2003); and *Thinking Differently: A Reader in European Women's Studies* (Zed Books, 2004), co-edited with Rosi Braidotti.

Jen Harvie is Lecturer in Drama at Queen Mary, University of London. Recent articles on contemporary performance and cultural identities have appeared in *Contemporary Theatre Review, Theatre Research International, Theatre Journal, Theater sans Frontières: Essays on the Dramatic Universe of Robert Lepage* and *Postmodernism: The Key Figures*. Her monograph *Staging the UK* is forthcoming from Manchester University Press, and she is co-writing with Paul Allain *The Routledge Companion to Theatre and Performance*.

Deirdre Heddon is Lecturer in Drama at the University of Exeter. She teaches and practices autobiography and performance, and her recent research has appeared in *Performance Research, Reconstructions, M/C* and *New Theatre Quarterly*. Forthcoming work on Bobby Baker, co-authored with Jane Milling, is being published in Jo Gill (ed.), *Modern Confessional Writing: New Critical Essays* and *Devising Performances: Histories and Practices*.

Catharine McLean-Hopkins is Lecturer in Drama at the University of Central Lancashire and a PhD candidate at the University of Manchester researching women's life performance.

Bella Merlin is an Honorary Research Fellow at the University of Birmingham where she lectured in Drama and Theatre before returning to professional theatre practice. Recent publications include *Beyond Stanislavsky* (Nick Hern, 2001) and *Stanislavsky* (2003) for the Routledge Performance Practitioners series. She played Wedekind's Lulu in London in 1992 which led to her research into Tilly Wedekind's relationship both with the role and with her playwright-husband, Frank.

Nicola Shaughnessy is Director of Drama at the University of Kent where she teaches contemporary performance, dramatic auto/biography and applied theatre. She has published on gender and theatre and autobiography. Forthcoming publications include *Gertrude Stein* for the Writers and their Work series (Northcote House, 2005).

Caridad Svich's plays include *Alchemy of Desire/Dead-Man's Blues, Any Place But Here, Fugitive Pieces, Prodigal Kiss, But there are Fires, Gleaning/Rebusca* and

Brazo Gitano, among others. She has co-edited *Conducting a Life: Reflections on the Theatre of Maria Irene Fornes* (Smith & Kraus, 1999) and *Theatre in Crisis?* (Manchester University Press, 2002), both with Maria Delgado, and is editor of *Trans-Global Readings: Crossing Theatrical Boundaries* (Manchester University Press, 2004). Her plays have been produced by numerous companies including The Women's Project, Intar, HERE, T.W.E.E.D., Theater for the New City in New York and the Hackney Empire Studio Theatre, London. Caridad is a member of New Dramatists (US) and a founder of the performance/media collective NoPassport.

INTRODUCTION

WOMEN, THEATRE AND PERFORMANCE: AUTO/BIOGRAPHY AND PERFORMANCE

Maggie B. Gale and Viv Gardner

> The experience which I got from this adventure into autobiography was invaluable. It showed me that if I were to succeed in reliving my life in print I must not only dig into the records of my career and into my memory, but I must try also to find out what sort of person I was and am, and how I had gone on year by year performing the automatic miracle of growing up – changing constantly and yet retaining my identity ... I must select and re-select from that wealth of material fact which had been assembled those things which I believe to have both some value in themselves and also as links which bind together past and present. Once I had grasped this idea I realized that no one could bring it to fruition for me. (Lillah McCarthy)[1]

This is the second volume in the series *Women, Theatre and Performance*. The aim of the series, like that of the journal *Women and Theatre Occasional Papers* which preceded it, is to reflect current historical research in the field of women and theatre. Unlike the journal, however, each initial volume in the series consists of themed essays that consider gender, theatre and performance as part of a wider nexus of social and cultural practices. This volume has a broad remit and offers essays which directly address issues in autobiography and autobiographic writing, and others which look at the wider problematics of identity and the female performer.

The field of women and autobiography is substantial and it is telling that in both historical and literary studies the notion of performance and performativity is often used as a framing device in the process of foregrounding the mechanisms of autobiography, autobiographical analysis and identity formation. It is, however, only in recent years that the analysis of autobiography and the autobiographical self, especially in the context of performance, has produced publications which deal more specifically with theatre and the boundaries between gender, theatre and autobiographical form. Recent publications include Sidonie Smith and

Julia Watson's *Interfaces: Women/Autobiography/Image/Performance* (2002)[2] which ranges across performance, performativity and the self 'at visual/textual interfaces'[3] that involve the 'visual, textual, voiced and material modes of embodied self-representation'.[4] A number of live art performers are represented in the book, including Laurie Anderson and Bobbie Baker, and Baker is the subject of Clare MacDonald's 1995 exploratory essay on feminism, autobiography and performance art in Julia Swindells' *The Uses of Autobiography*.[5] 'Staging the Self', which explored several original autobiographical performances, formed part of the 1997 Nottingham Trent University conference 'Representing Lives', and the papers were published in a book of the same name.[6] Lynn C. Miller, Jacqueline Taylor and M. Heather Carver's *Voices Made Flesh: Performing Women's Autobiography* (2003)[7] engages with the performance of historical women's autobiographies (amongst them those of Gertrude Stein, Anaïs Nin and Georgia O'Keefe), and self-representation in contemporary live art. However, very few publications have looked at autobiographical writing in relation to women actors' or other female theatre workers' lives, the analysis or representation of self in a professional or national context, and the relationship between autobiography as evidence and historiographic practice. Nor have actresses' autobiographies been used in more general investigations of gender and autobiography which, considering the relative volume of performers' autobiographies to non-performers' works, is perhaps surprising and may reflect the perceived particularity of the actresses' public/private self. A notable exception is Mary Jean Corbett's *Representing Femininity: Middle Class Subjectivity in Victorian and Edwardian Women's Autobiographies* (1994), in which Corbett records how it was the 'sheer volume' of 'published autobiographies by "leading ladies"' which drew her to them. She had anticipated that these autobiographies would in some ways be different from those of other women authors, as 'professional performers, actresses were [already] fully licensed to represent themselves textually', through their bodies, their performances. She is surprised to find that 'there are as many (if not more) resemblances as differences between actresses' and writers' [autobiographical] texts'[8] and devotes two chapters on actresses' autobiographical representation to exploring issues of gender and class in the late nineteenth and early twentieth centuries.

If critics of auto/biography have been shy of the performers 'reliving [their] life in print', so too has the theatre historian. Thomas Postlewait has contributed two important essays[9] to the debate on the 'use' to the theatre historian. In the first, 'Autobiography and Theatre History', he identifies theatre autobiographies' 'defining character, and often their charm', as depending 'upon the self-serving performance of the autobiographer, a masquerade moving from stage to page'.[10] And he argues that

> the theatre historian, in search of the performer 'in Nobody's Shape but his Own'[11] may well find not only no separation can be established between face and mask, presence and absence, private and public personality, life and art, but also that even these dualisms are too neat because they split identity, documents, and historical conditions in ways that are reductive.[12]

These febrile and unstable dualisms underpin most of the autobiographies *and* autobiographical performances under scrutiny in this volume. Actresses, as one of the first groups of professional women, have used, and use, autobiography and performance as both a means of expression and 'control' of their public selves, of both the 'face and the mask'. These public selves, as constructed through autobiographical negotiations, with considered reading and spectatorship, can reveal a great deal about women theatre workers' professional lives, sometimes their personal lives, sometimes their sense of a 'place in the world'. The notion of 'presence and absence' is a recurring trope amongst all 'performed autobiographies', in a number of permutations. Lillah McCarthy writes, in 1933, of 'the work that ... dies with the worker',[13] and Peggy Phelan, in 1993, of the 'particular cultural moment [which] exerts an urgent pressure to account for what cannot be reproduced'. She goes on: 'As those artists who have dedicated themselves to performance continually disappear and leave "not a rack behind" it becomes increasingly imperative to find a way to remember the undocumentable, irreproducible art they made.'

That 'urgent pressure to account for what cannot be reproduced' informs both the actresses' attempts to reproduce their 'lives in art', and our attempts, as spectators and academics, to 'remember the undocumentable, irreproducible art they made'.[14] The act of reading, as reproducing, will always be partial and interpretive. The particular cultural moment that produced the autobiography or autobiographical performance will be governed by a matrix of factors, of which time and gender are key. The ways in which women approach the autobiographic form, as writers, performers or readers, whether in the eighteenth or twenty-first century, are as influenced by their social, economic and historical positions, of which the theatre event and theatre history are a part, as they are influenced by any general tendencies in autobiographical writing.

The level of social emancipation and education experienced by these theatre women has influenced not only the content of their autobiographical creation but the ways in which they make considered use of autobiographical and narrative forms.

Of gender and autobiography, Jacky Bratton has written that:

> The masculinist assumption is that men choose to publish their life stories when and because they have a sense of their own autonomy and difference, and their unique importance to the public life of their day. The most pervasive characteristic of *female* autobiography, on the other hand, is argued to be self-definition in relation to significant others; so that, rather than a sense of individual autonomy, a sense of identification, interdependence and community is key in the development of women's identity and therefore also central in the stories of themselves.[15]

She goes on to argue that the characteristics of 'female autobiography' are common to 'theatre people' of both sexes, and that 'their own biographies are not an assertion of their own particular importance in the world, so much as an attempt to construct a group identity, in which their individuality is seated'.[16] It is possible to see, however, much autobiographical work by theatre women as an attempt to re-insert themselves, not as individuals, but as part of a constructed 'group identity' or community, into a theatre history, a cultural moment or a performance space, from which they – as women – have been rendered 'absent' or 'disappeared'.

Postlewait rightly urges that, as theatre historians, we should question the reliability and quality of evidence as expressed in autobiography and take more cognisance of 'their formal features, cultural meanings and purposes, and relations to social values and taste'.[17] And Bratton that, 'the medium of print is subject to all sorts of interventions and mediations; its witness to its own times and its transmission of the history of the stage must be read as part of the hegemonic process even where autobiography might seem to offer direct revelation of actions and contemporary opinion'.[18] Taking this into account, where women's voices have been historically denied or undervalued it is important to recognise patterns of self-representation in autobiographic writing by theatre women; as theatre historians we are particularly interested in work carried out by women, and an assessment of the autobiographical can provide a refreshing means of validating experience with the understanding that concepts such as the 'real' and 'inner truth' cannot be applied in isolation from subject formation and the social and historical context. What is true of the written text is also true of the performed text.

Mindful that the 'paradox is that in writing testimony to the power of the undocumentable and nonreproductive [we] engage the document of the written reproducible text itself',[19] and the reductive dangers of the overly 'neat', this volume sets out to explore the 'abundance' of autobiographical forms that have been produced by women in written and performed texts. Like McCarthy, we have had to 'select and re-select from that wealth of material fact which had been assembled, those things which [we] believe to have both some value in themselves and also as links which bind together past and present'. By juxtaposition, we hope to facilitate connections – connections between texts and performances, past and present practitioners, professional and private selves, individuals and communities, all of which have in some way renegotiated identity through autobiography.

The book is divided into three sections: Part I: Telling tales: autobiographic strategies; Part II: The professional/confessional self; and Part III: Auto/biography, identity and performance. The first section includes chapters which investigate the interrelatedness of the creative self, creative output and subject formation. Viv Gardner's 'The three nobodies' takes autobiographical works by three relatively unknown provincial performers who sustained careers through the late nineteenth and early twentieth centuries without ever moving onto West End London stages. Gardner examines the writing for their original context and intent, and places the readings of this evidence in the light of the authors' writing strategies and the ways in which these women use autobiography to identify the difference between their performing selves and their everyday selves, and seek to reposition their professional selves as part of a community of female performers of their time. Nicola Shaughnessy turns to Susan Glaspell, as 'The disappearing subject', in order to examine the interface between our biographical understanding of Glaspell's theatre writing and the characters which she created and often performed. Shaughnessy plays with notions of absence and presence and the ways in which Glaspell can be seen to have integrated the creative act with an autobiographic negotiation of self in her plays. Staying geographically in North America, Elaine Aston's 'Imag(in)ing a life: Adrienne Kennedy's *People Who Led to My Plays* and *Deadly Triplets*' examines the means by which Kennedy's autobiographical works offer a way of 'visualising' her 'uncomfortable world' and locating the cultural and social experiences that shaped her plays.

Part II: The professional/confessional self, explores the interrelatedness of, and the tension between, the professional and public dimension of women's work in theatre and the confessional interior self. Susan Croft's investigation of Emma Robinson, 'The Way to the World: Emma Robinson and the dilemmas of identity', looks at ways in which Robinson worked pseudonymously, at times forced to do so but in others embracing this as a strategy for self promotion and furtherance of her career. Whilst Maggie B. Gale's re-assessment of Lena Ashwell looks at the ways in which Ashwell uses her autobiographic writings to position herself not as a celebrity figure but as someone integral to the development of British Theatre during the early years of the twentieth century. In some ways her autobiographic writings are resistant as she, unlike many of her contemporaries actually talks about her practice and her ideas on the social function of theatre as well as charting and assessing, in various forms, the development of her career. Bella Merlin's 'Tilly and Lulu: the role of her life or the role in her life?' examines Tilly Wedekind's own positioning, later in life, of her performance of Frank Wedekind's Lulu in relation both to her subsequent career and her emotional and psychological development. That her performances of, and with, Wedekind constituted the most significant of her theatre work is not contested, but Merlin considers these with the ways in which her personality and technique influenced the creation of the roles by Wedekind himself. She is both muse and actor/author, just as in her autobiography she writes her history simultaneously recognising and analysing the relationship between that history and her present self. If Tilly Wedekind 'troubled' the identity of her past self, Gabrielle Griffin shows, in 'Troubling identities: Clare Dowie's *Why is John Lennon Wearing a Skirt?*', how Dowie articulates the present gender identity dialogues of the 1990s in her theatre work.

Part III: Auto/biography, identity and performance, deals with contemporary performance. Caridad Svich's 'Latina theatre and performance: acts of exposure' makes an overdue intervention in the debates around performance of gender and ethnicity in which she foregrounds the autobiographical nature of the work of Latina theatre women. She looks at the performance strategies whereby Latina performers have used the autobiographical, confessional model of performance – in stand-up and other comedic forms – and storytelling traditions to explore memory, cultural nostalgia and women's roles in society and destabilise assumptions about women's place. Jen Harvie's 'Being her: presence, absence and performance in the art of Janet Cardiff and Tracey Emin' returns again to the trope of 'presence and absence' in women's autobiographical work. Deidre Heddon's 'Performing lesbians: constructing the self' seeks to locate the construction of self, and the construction of a community identity through performance in the recent work of lesbian performers. And the volume ends with Catharine McLean-Hopkins' interview with performance artist Bobby Baker, 'Re(ci)pertoires of the self: autobiographical strands in Bobby Baker's performance work', in which Baker reflects on the significance of the autobiographical nature of her work, and the conscious deployment of theatre to explore the self.

We start with Lillah McCarthy, 'OBE (Lady Keeble)'[20] and end with Bobby Baker, 'I am a woman, I am middle aged. I am fifty years old.' No neat connections.

Notes

1 Lillah McCarthy, *Myself and My Friends* (London: Thornton Butterworth, 1933), pp. 9–10.
2 Sidonie Smith and Julia Watson (eds), *Interfaces: Women/Autobiography/Image/Performance* (Ann Arbor: University of Michigan Press, 2002).
3 Ibid., p. 4.
4 Ibid., p. 5.
5 Claire MacDonald, 'Assumed Identities: feminism, autobiography and performance art', in Julia Swindells (ed.), *The Uses of Autobiography* (London: Taylor and Francis, 1995), pp. 187–95.
6 Alison Donnell and Pauline Polkey (eds), *Representing Lives: Women and Auto/biography* (Houndmills: Macmillan Press, 2000).
7 Lynn C. Miller, Jacqueline Taylor and M. Heather Carver (eds), *Voices Made Flesh: Performing Women's Autobiography* (Madison: University of Wisconsin Press, 2003).
8 Mary Jean Corbett, *Representing Femininity: Middle Class Subjectivity in Victorian and Edwardian Women's Autobiography* (New York and Oxford: Oxford University Press, 1992), p. 13. See also 'Actresses and Autobiography' in the final chapter of Gail Marshall, *Actresses on the Victorian* Stage (Cambridge: Cambridge University Press, pp. 171–86; and a rare exploration of a historical figure's deployment of autobiographical performance and performativity in Helen Nicholson's work on Georgina Weldon. Helen Nicholson, 'Promoting Herself: The Representational Strategies of Georgina Weldon', in Pauline Polkey and Alison Donnell (eds), *Representing Lives*, pp. 208–17; and Helen Nicholson, 'Not Alone: Georgina Weldon's Dramatic Protest Against The Lunacy Laws', *Women and Theatre Occasional Papers* 3, 1996, 70–94.
9 Thomas Postlewait, 'Autobiography and Theatre History', in Thomas Postlewait and Bruce A. McConachie (eds), *Interpreting the Theatrical Past: Essays in the Historiography of Performance* (Iowa City: University of Iowa

Press, 1989), pp. 248–72; Thomas Postlewait, 'Theatre Autobiographies: Some Preliminary Concerns for the Theatre Historian', *Assaph C* 16, 2000, 157–72.

10 Ibid., p. 252.

11 Colley Cibber, cited in Thomas Postlewait, 'Autobiography and Theatre', p. 250.

12 Ibid., p. 259.

13 Lillah McCarthy, *Myself and My Friends*, p. 13.

14 Peggy Phelan, *Unmarked: The Politics of Performance* (London: Routledge, 1993), p. 31.

15 Jacky Bratton, *New Readings in Theatre History* (Cambridge: Cambridge University Press, 2003), pp. 101–2.

16 Ibid., p. 102.

17 Thomas Postlewait, 'Theatre Autobiographies: Some Preliminary Concerns', p. 159.

18 Jacky Bratton, *New Readings in Theatre History*, p. 99.

19 Peggy Phelan, *Unmarked*, p. 31.

20 Lillah McCarthy, *Myself and My Friends*, title page.

PART I

TELLING TALES: AUTOBIOGRAPHIC STRATEGIES

1

THE THREE NOBODIES: AUTOBIOGRAPHICAL STRATEGIES IN THE WORK OF ALMA ELLERSLIE, KITTY MARION AND INA ROZANT

Viv Gardner

In the preface to *Diary of an Actress*, published in 1885, an anonymous actress writes:

> I have been looking over the pages of an old diary kept during the early years of a very toilsome provincial experience. It has struck me that just now, when there is so much curiosity as to the private lives of those who are before the public, a glimpse of the real life of a provincial actress might be of some interest, perhaps of some use.[1]

This chapter explores three little-known autobiographical works by late nineteenth- and early twentieth-century provincial women performers – one a published diary, one an unpublished autobiography and the third a fictional work that it is fairly safe to assume is based on the author's own experience.[2] The relative 'ordinariness' of the subjects makes them especially interesting in a period in which 'celebrity' auto/biography had become a commonplace. Each document offers a detailed account of the performer's experiences in the British provincial theatre. Each raises questions of 'motive' in writing, of 'use' – for the contemporary theatre historian as well as intended reader – and of gender. But, above all, these accounts offer an opportunity to consider the ways in which the performer/writers employ self-representation, 'autobiographical strategies', to reposition themselves in the hierarchies and histories of the theatre.

The volume of biographical and autobiographical material published about or by late nineteenth- and early twentieth-century performers, whether in newspapers, journals or books, attests to the public's appetite for 'knowledge' of the private stories of actors' lives. These publications had burgeoned in the eighteenth century, and as Thomas Postlewait has argued, 'most significantly, the popular "memoir" (either an autobiography or a biography) was soon not only a commonplace but a necessary adjunct to the role of theatre in society'.[3] As a theatre historian reading this material I am mindful of the need – 'though understandably fascinated by a good story, [to] question this evidence most carefully'.[4] Ephemeral as the theatre is, our 'need to know', to verify, can make disproportionate demands on the records that exist, of which autobiography is a particularly potent one. The *Diary of an Actress* warns against '[t]hose who only see the stage through the glamour of the footlights, who picture the inner life of an actress through the medium of sensational novels or newspaper paragraphs' and 'have very little idea of the real difficulties' that women in mid-Victorian theatre encountered.[5] Equally, for the feminist theatre historian the danger of over-reliance on ostensibly authentic accounts is compounded by personal and political investments in women's stories, particularly those 'hidden from history' by their apparent *lack* of glamour. Unpicking the 'inner life' – or even the 'real life' – from the complex matrix that informs and defines the performer's autobiography is no simple task.

'Nobodies'

In *To Tell My Story* Irene Vanburgh writes insightfully about the ontological relationship between the two selves that she finds in herself as an actress. She asks first:

> Who and what is the person who spends most of his or her life impersonating other people, impersonating them strongly enough not only to convince themselves, but to convince thousands of others? ... What then is the reality; how far has this constant re-creation of yourself obliterated the original? ... [To be an actress] a sort of double life must be led. You are nobody, yet inside you there is a second self who has a way of suddenly appearing and obliterates you completely, a second self that you look at and criticise with a detachment that is almost physical.[6]

This concept of the 'double' or 'dual consciousness' of the actor is a common articulation of the boundaries between the actor and role, and the private self and the performed, public self.[7] For Vanburgh the self behind the performer is the 'nobody'. The second self, 'her inward demon', 'is vividly brought alive by a letter from a manager' and is sustained 'all through the run of the play'. Vanburgh recounts how 'the depressed You [the nobody] who is so different yet so allied to her basks in the same sunshine ... [and how this] insistent second self dictates all her movements and reorganizes her life'. But the ordinary 'nobody' self makes her reappearance when the production ends and the second self 'sinks into insignificance ... the sparkle has gone out'.[8]

The autobiographical narrative of the performer, whilst reflecting these two selves in greater or lesser proportions, and with more or less consciousness, is determined by another voice – the 'character' which 'even though a version of the writer, is a created identity, a representative figure of the author's idea of self'.[9] As Mary Jean Corbett argues, the 'self-representation of a public woman in autobiography is no less a performance than anything she undertakes on stage, and no less a product of the "double process" that operates in any rhetorical act'.[10]

Shaping all is the cultural frame within which the performance of self is created. Corbett, in her discussion of the autobiographies of six Victorian and Edwardian actresses, argues that during this era the 'larger cultural and economic hegemony' had a very particular effect on women's place in theatre. 'The professionalization movement of the Victorian Theater – helps produce [a] paradoxical effect, for the professionalizing theater takes bourgeois values as its standard at every level of theatrical life.' Thus, how actresses, traditionally positioned in a liminal space in society – an object of both fear and fantasy for men and women – 'defin[ing] themselves on stage and in autobiography ... becomes contingent less on the "facts" of their private lives, and more on how well they can publicly imitate and reproduce the signs and attitudes that mark individuals as belonging to a certain class and gender'.[11] By the late nineteenth century these women increasingly replicate the middle-class aspirations of the Victorian theatre on and off stage.

The subjects of the present study all reflect in their autobiographical accounts Vanburgh's 'nobody self'. Occasionally circumstances allow the 'second self' to emerge, and that 'insistent demon' is always present in the aspirations of the women to a more fulfilling performance life. Their writing itself can be seen as an attempt to foreground the 'author's idea of self', in contradistinction to their invisibility as provincial performers, and the submergence of their individuality in the hegemonic norms of the actress. They are also 'nobodies' in a more traditionally pejorative sense. None of these women 'made it' to the West End stage, nor to the celebrity of Irene Vanburgh. Two had a modicum of success, though their names are known to only a few nowadays, one through notoriety in the suffragette movement, one through authorship. The third remains unnamed and unknown, though her diary account is often used as testimony to the suffering, 'victimhood' even, of women performers in the Victorian theatre.[12] Their very ordinariness is what makes them so interesting to the theatre historian. Their accounts of provincial theatre life, though manifestly mediated by the same factors that affect all autobiographical accounts, are not subject to the retrospective 'belittling' of their successful sisters' recollections of their early lives in the provinces. Few actors record their provincial experiences at any length, eclipsed as it has been by West End success; when they do it is often with tolerant condescension towards the theatres, their fellow actors and their audiences and an inability to resist a 'good' – for which read 'amusing' – story.[13] This is not true of these accounts.

There are some interesting congruences between the three 'nobodies'. They all obscured their original selves and wrote – and one lived – under pseudonyms. The *Diary of an Actress* was published anonymously. In the final paragraphs the author invites, then repudiates, speculation as to her identity:

> Does anyone identify the writer with a favourite London actress, with the heroine of some East End melodrama, or with some provincial 'star' of greater or lesser magnitude? I will leave my destiny to the imagination of my readers, content if what I wrote in the sad hours of a lonely, anxious and yet not unhappy life, may help to remove an unjust prejudice from the minds of those who think only of an actress as an almost irresponsible being, without conscience, principle or self-respect, and incapable of understanding the serious duties and responsibilities of life.[14]

The British Library catalogue tentatively attributes the diary to Alma[15] Ellerslie – and I shall use this name from now on – but to date I have uncovered nothing to 'flesh out' this identity or even corroborate it. The second 'nobody', Kitty Marion, wrote her autobiography in the early 1930s after a lengthy career in musical comedy and music hall, a period as an active member of the Women's Social and Political Union and in the American Birth Control movement. She failed to find a publisher.[16] Born Katherina Marie Schäfer in Reidtberg, Germany in 1871, she came to England in 1886 to live with her paternal aunt. She first changed her name on the advice of the song-writer friend of the family who introduced her to the music hall. 'Mlle Kitty' presumably satisfied the curiosity of the Star Music Hall's audience as to the exotic origins of the newcomer.[17] She assumed the name Kitty Marion a year later when the breach with her family, who disapproved of her stage ambitions, was final. Ironically her first engagement as the English sounding 'Kitty Marion' was in the *Germania* spectacular at the German Exhibition in London.[18] Her assumption of British identity was eventually total, as the wartime correspondence between Scotland Yard and the Home Office confirms: 'Miss Marion is to all intents and purposes an Englishwoman ...[she] does not maintain any connection with Germany ... Her sentiments appear to be pro-British, and she has recently been singing patriotic songs at recruiting meetings.'[19]

And the former fellow actress who denounced her to the Home Office in 1915 wrote: 'She is a German – born and bred – she always used to say "Hail, the Kaiser – ages ago. ... She could, and *would* easily pass as an Englishwoman ... she would be a fine person to "spy" for ... her English is perfect – no accent.'[20]

1 Kitty Marion (studio portrait).

After the cessation of suffragette activities, Marion used another pseudonym, Kathleen Meredith, to get work, before leaving for America to avoid the Aliens Restriction Orders. Like Kitty Marion, Ina Rozant trained as a singer and dancer, and 'was for several years on the concert platform'. She first appeared on stage in 1899 at Aberystwyth. Her origins too were German, though her father became a British citizen in 1853 and she herself was born in New York in 1862. Ina Rozant appears to have been a stage name. Her baptismal name was Georgiana Theodora Jacobina Zorn. Whilst not disguising her identity – her Green Room entry gives her birth name as Theodora Zorn[21] – perhaps tellingly, her brothers, John and Fritz, as men and following more reputable professions, did not find it necessary to change their surname.

None of these women came from theatre families, and all were single during the time that they were touring in the provinces,[22] both of which factors increased the women's vulnerability in a number of respects as is clear from Ellerslie and Marion's accounts. Both Alma Ellerslie and Kitty Marion encountered opposition from their middle-class families over their choice of profession. Ellerslie recalls her sister Mary having tried 'her hardest to persuade me not to go [on the stage] … For a long time she would not write to me, and I never thought she would come and see me.'[23] Kitty Marion's engineer father told her that he 'would rather see [her] dead than on the stage. [She] had disgraced him enough without that. "*Sie sind alle schlecht auf der Bühne*" he said.' His favourite insult to her was 'damned actress' (*verfluchte Schauspielerin*).[24] Rozant's position is different, as there is little record of opposition to the stage in her novels and there is some evidence that she was supported emotionally, and possibly financially, by her family.[25]

The diary

> I write about those days at a great distance – not only in terms of time. I cannot feel close to that young woman who went about in my name so long ago … She is often strange to me, sometimes antipathetic, now and then incredible, but for the self-conviction that stares me in the face from the scribbled page [of my diary]. There too I am at odds with her. She records scenes and feelings I have clean forgotten; she leaves out some that in my memory stand fast for ever.[26]

Ironically, the women's single status may have facilitated their writing. Having none of the distractions of family commitments, but with the constraints on their movements and social lives that being women in a strange town brings, may have left them with free time to be used profitably. Their very isolation may also have encouraged the introspection that is one of the prerequisites for the keeping of a diary. Alma Ellerslie kept one, and though one has not survived there are indications that Kitty Marion's autobiography was drawn from some kind of journal or personal record.[27]

The diary is, as many theorists have argued, an ambiguous document. The author is both writer and reader, both the private and the public self. Though traditionally seen as an 'expressive' document – Alice James saw her diary as a means to 'bring relief as an outlet to that geyser of emotions, sensations, speculations, and reflections which ferments perpetually within my poor carcase for its sins'[28] – it is also one that is shaped, consciously or unconsciously, for reading. The publication of a diary within the lifetime of the writer compounds the ambiguity.

The *Diary of an Actress* was published in 1885 with the stated aim of bringing 'the realities of stage life' to the knowledge of the public. To a mid-Victorian readership its anonymity and very title may have promised something else. The independence of the actress in mid-century, and their public lives, made them readily available objects of erotic fantasy and fiction. Well-known actresses were often the subject of semi-pornographic 'biography' and the actress was a frequent protagonist in the erotic novel that masqueraded as 'memoir' or 'confessions'.[29] At the same time, their questionable standing also made the actress an obvious subject of the exemplary or redemptive novel. That the *Diary* was published by a press which also printed hymnals, and its editor was the Reverend H. C. Shuttleworth, a Minor Canon of St Paul's,[30] may too have promised some form of 'confessional' text. It is possible, though, to see the *Diary* as both a Jamesian outlet for a 'geyser of emotions, sensations, speculations, and reflections' – as the *Diary* embodies all those things – and, in its published and edited form, a rebuttal of both types of confessional text. Both author and editor explicitly see their agenda as the re-education of the public in their perception of the actress and the world of the theatre. The material may at times be the stuff of sensation – unchaperoned encounters in the park with military gentlemen – but it defies titillation; and the *Diary* makes no apology for the profession of actress. In addition, if we take the *Diary* to be 'real', which its lack of consistent artifice and plentiful detail encourage us to do, then it also provides a valuable insight into the outer and inner experiences of a provincial actress.

The *Diary* covers a period of some two years,[31] during which Ellerslie travels from Southsea[32] to Linlithgow and Lanark. Though she is in fairly regular employment, much of it is in 'third rate' companies and she experiences many of the vagaries, inequities and poverty of the small, nineteenth-century touring company. The account is replete with detail of touring conditions, rehearsals and performances, financial problems and social experiences. She herself apologises in her preface for this, writing that 'I have shown so much of the practical side of my profession ... only as I was forced to realise it from day to day.'[33]

Like other entrants to the profession from a non-theatrical family, Ellerslie finds herself in a paradoxical position. As an 'incomer' to the world of theatre, she is both observer and critic, yet it is a world to which she fervently wishes to belong. 'I am an "outsider", a stranger. It is different for those who have introductions and friends on the stage', she writes.[34] She 'had dreamed of a life of poetry and romance, of a world peopled with heroes and heroines like those of whom I had read! ... I wanted an art – high, ennobling, a life above the crowd; intercourse with people of intellect, whom I could reverence and look up to.'[35]

She regularly distinguishes between the old theatrical families and the people with whom she has to work more frequently: '[The company] are old stagers, or belong to old theatrical families. Respectable, pleasant-looking people, and they have not the unwashed, unkempt appearance one too often sees in third rate professionals'.[36]

Elsewhere she observes that 'the real theatrical families are as respectable and as exclusive as any other set', and regrets her 'separateness' – 'They know nothing of me.'[37]

In doing so she creates a mythical hierarchy and genealogy of theatre which replicates the mores of the bourgeois world into which she was born – hard-working, businesslike and above all respectable and responsible. Of the 'third rate professionals' she writes: 'It frets me sadly to be mixed up with such a class. I fancied I should meet with such different people. It's not their social standing I care about, but their utter absence of refinement or culture, their vulgarity, their way of looking at things.'[38]

And it is not just her fellow actors from whom she feels alienated. Audiences are sometimes 'rough, but appreciative'[39] but at other times she experiences 'wretched audiences, never a civilized being in the house'.[40] It is not a simple matter of class, she avers, but of education. She travels with her box of books and a desk, and during the course of the diary she reads Swinburne, Thackeray, Mrs Browning, George Sand, Balzac and above all George Eliot, specifically *Romola* and *Daniel*

Deronda. She also speaks and reads French and German. She writes: 'I would rather live in solitude all my life than be fretted and irritated by the constant jarring of incongruous ideas and thoughts. An intellectual life among intellectual people: that was my ideal of the stage. It seems a long way from being realised.'[41] And later asks:

> Why do the papers always write as if there were such a demand for actresses, and especially of the educated class? As far as my experience goes, education is a very doubtful advantage, and any refinement of feeling quite fatal. Loud, vulgar women, who like to make friends with anybody, are far more likely to make their way.[42]

Travelling as she does from one engagement to another, Ellerslie never seems to form any significant relationships with other company members. Her 'fatal refinement of feeling' means that she prefers to read in the dressing room than gossip with the rest of the female members of the company. At the same time she has lost 'caste' with her own kind, her family in particular. Her sister, Mary, did eventually risk her husband's disapproval and visited her on a number of occasions, but, as Ellerslie records, her second sister, Jane, found association impossible. 'She does not wish to be brought down to my level, or to hold any communication except by letter. She has even told me that men might not like to marry her girls when they grow up, if they thought they had an aunt who was an actress.'[43]

Isolated within her profession, alienated from her family, Ellerslie falls prey to melancholy, and with echoes of the melodramas in which she is forced by circumstance to play, writes, 'My fate seems to be to struggle alone. Whether as an artist or as a woman, equally desolate'.[44]

As the diary progresses she sometimes finds herself playing in more congenial conditions and company, and almost despite herself she occasionally finds herself escaping from her 'nobody' self in the pleasures of performance. In Lanark she plays 'a most sensational piece. A lovely dog and a fearful amount of shooting. I am carried off by Indians, in white muslin, of course ... I like my part better now I have played it, and the fights are a source of constant excitement. I always expect to be shot ... The "stars" are American and very pleasant.'[45]

At another time she 'basks in the sunshine' of celebrity that comes with being the professional playing amongst amateurs: 'I have been down to an amateur performance at Yarmouth. They gave me £10. I enjoyed myself very much, and everything went off very well. I felt rather frightened at first. Such huge bills! And I was advertised "of the principal London theatres!!". The papers were very kind.'[46]

By the December of her second year she finds that: 'Once I should have thought it dreadful to have to play in pantomime. I never dreamed of anything less than Shakespeare and black velvet, and now I am very thankful and think myself fortunate to go for a fairy queen in gauze and spangles.'[47] This modest and pragmatic shift in tone seems to reflect the beginning of a reconciliation with her 'nobody self' and is in marked contrast to earlier, more emotive, writing. In his editor's preface, H. C. Shuttleworth claims to have 'left the writer to tell her own story, adding nothing, and curtailing little. Even blemishes, literary and other, have not always been removed from the text. They would sometimes seem to serve as hints to the better interpretation of the author's meaning, or character, or drift of mind.'[48] As a result, the writing in the diary is inconsistent, lacking continuity but not a certain generic self-consciousness. Much of the writing about her personal state of mind is marked by a theatrical phrasing; thus an entry for April 23 reads: 'Unutterably wretched last night ... A tiny room, and a tiny window that could not be seen through or opened. Too tired to eat anything; went to bed unhappy, dreary and desolate; then a terrible fit of crying ...'[49]

Her descriptions are often vivid, novelistic, as in this of one of the theatres she found herself in: 'The front of the house looks infinitely dreary, draped in dirty Holland covers; a few straggling sunbeams just make the darkness visible; sometimes the silence is broken by the cleaner's broom, or by the distant voice inquiring if "he" is wanted.'[50]

However, perhaps the most immediate writing comes in her responses to her encounters with men. These run throughout the diary and it is, perhaps, the honesty of these accounts which Shuttleworth refers to as the 'blemishes, literary and other' that he has left in. And it is here that the text as a whole confronts the 'sex question' that bedevilled the image of the actress in the period and informed both the pornographic and exemplary literature of the time. Ellerslie encounters a predicable number of dubious offers inside the theatre, some from managers and some from fellow actors who after 'an unusual amount of amiability and small attentions' – offer to help find lodgings, look after luggage and escort her home – but 'when they find they are dismissed with a "good night" and not invited to enter, the attentions suddenly drop off!'[51] Sometimes the attentions are from unwanted 'stage-door johnnies'.

> Last night I found a note at the theatre from one who had 'fallen deeply and truly in love with me,' &c., &c., 'a true and devoted love,' 'my kind amiable nature,' &c. A perfect stranger. However he finished four pages of perfect nonsense by saying he would explain it all if permitted an interview, and would wait for me coming out of church. So I thought it would be better to go to another.[52]

But her greatest problem arose when she herself was 'tempted' into one of her 'adventures'. The *Diary* opens with one such encounter:

> On Tuesday afternoon I had one of my usual stupid adventures. How foolish I am! But he was such a handsome fellow, all scarlet and gold, on his way to a court martial. He had seen me play, and of course the usual compliments followed. He wanted to call, but I firmly refused, and came back feeling very good, but *regretting my decision a little bit!*[53]

And later, 'Another stupid adventure. 'Une tasse de café.' How frightened I get! Thank God I am not so vile. What can be worse than a woman who will encourage men, and lead them on, and take all she can get, and stop short just in time. I think an openly bad woman infinitely better.'[54]

Sometimes she is able to stand back and record her own vacillations.

> I have seen someone several times in the park. He is quite a relief from the usual class of people here; very gentlemanly, and he does not seem at all fast. Perhaps I am wrong, but I know I am tired of my own society, and I will give him the benefit of the doubt. He has a very good position – military ... Saturday – Very much disgusted. Is everyone the same? Well, I shall try no more. It is best to keep out of danger ... But he was really very nice and talked quite sensibly. I let him call, and he wanted me to go and dine with him, but of course I would not. Lately I began to feel uncomfortable, but whenever he attempted to make love, I managed to turn the conversation, and he was very pleasant company, till one day he began saying I did nothing but chaff, and that I could not see when a man loved me. I have seen nothing of him since! It really seems as if men were incapable of the slightest interest in a woman, unless it be an improper one.[55]

And sometimes her self-recriminations manifest an almost biblical rhetoric:

> Sometimes I think that I shall one day find myself utterly destitute, and that then a great temptation will come to me as punishment, because I have had small pity for women who could be tempted in such a case; because I have said they must be vile and contemptible, or they would

> have starved and died sooner than fail; because I have held myself as far above the possibility of such degradation as heaven is from hell; so, perhaps one day I too shall be tried, as hundreds of poor wretches are tried every day. But thank God honour and virtue are not empty names.[56]

It is, however, in the prologue and epilogue, that Ellerslie is most clearly in control of her writing. Here she positions the outsider self of the diary, as history. She talks of her 'old self' as one who 'lived in the clouds' and hopes that 'anyone else so foolish ... may learn wisdom and contentment from the life of an actress'.[57] In her epilogue, though leaving 'her destiny to the imagination of her readers', she represents her present self as both a 'victor' and an 'insider'. She states that the 'temptations that surround *our* profession are in no way connected to it' [my italics]. They are, she goes on, 'incidental to any profession or business where a woman has to fight against the world, the flesh and the devil ... But that such battles are fought, and, thank God, won [as this implies she has done], is the experience of everyone *inside the theatrical profession*' [my italics]. 'Outsiders', she says, can have 'no possible opportunity of forming an opinion of [...] women, unknown beyond their immediate circle, their identity merged in the characters they assume behind the footlights'.[58] In dedicating the *Diary* to her mentor, Mrs Kendall, 'who has shown so conspicuously by consistent personal conduct, that her profession does not necessarily involve any sacrifice of the higher qualities of her sex'[59] Ellerslie repositions herself as part of a newly respectable female elite in the theatre. With them she is able now to successfully and 'publicly imitate and reproduce the signs and attitudes that mark ... a certain class and gender'. Ironically it is her 'birth' class. Her bourgeois private self, once in conflict with the representation and expectation of her public self, the actress, is now able to efface her troublesome, unfeminine, public identity 'behind the footlights'.

The autobiography

Effacement does not seem to have formed part of Kitty Marion's agenda in writing her autobiography. One of her motives may have been financial – in 1930 she had lost her income from selling the *Birth Control Review* in New York and struggled thereafter – but the other was almost certainly personal. If the theatre memoir was by now 'not only a commonplace but a necessary adjunct to the role of theatre in society', so too was the suffrage memoir part of a continuing strategy to insert women into the historical record. Many of the key players had already published their stories – Emmeline Pankhurst and Constance Lytton as early as 1914, Annie Kenney in 1924, Sylvia Pankhurst in 1931, and Ray Strachey's history of the women's movement, *The Cause*, had appeared in 1928. Kitty Marion may have wanted to reclaim her place 'basking in the same sunshine' as her theatrical and suffrage sisters.

In 1936 the *New Yorker* ran a series entitled 'Where Are They Now?'. The subject of 'The Crusader' was Kitty Marion. At the time she was working as part of the Works Progress Administration[60] Speech Improvement Project, teaching youngsters in 'the Heart of Hell's Kitchen ... to say "thirty-three" instead of "tirty-tree" or "toity-dree"'.[61] Having been highly visible in the militant movement in England and then the Birth Control Movement in the United States, and having been imprisoned – and in England force-fed – for her causes, her situation, 'living alone in a single furnished room on the second floor of an old brownstone'[62] in the Flat Iron district of Manhattan, must at times have seemed unjust. She appears to have started the autobiography on her return to the States from a visit to England for the unveiling of the memorial to Mrs Pankhurst. She is described as, 'Lonesome for a cause to fight for ... [and having] worn out her shoes looking for a job to no avail, she paid rent for a week and set about writing down her stormy and [word missing] memoirs. She hopes to raise enough money to continue.'[63]

All the accounts of Marion testify to her gregariousness and how 'Kitty would often regale [her friends] with yarns of her experience in England.'[64] She seems to have 'carried her life with her'. She was an indefatigable letter writer, both personal – in some cases maintaining contacts throughout her life – and public; a collector of cuttings, correspondence and memorabilia. One surmises that these formed the basic resource for her autobiography – either that or she had a prodigious recall of names, dates and events. Chapter One opens:

> 'Why don't you write your experiences?' – 'Why don't you write the story of your life?' ... Such and similar are the suggestive questions put to me whenever I reminisce on my stage, suffrage, birth control and ordinary life experiences. Though writing ... is a great effort to me, to justify the faith my numerous friends in England and America have expressed in my ability to do it, I will do my best.[65]

Without further preamble she plunges into a detailed chronological account of her life. The *Autobiography* falls into roughly four parts, her childhood, stage career, suffrage activities and involvement in the birth control movement. It is only appropriate here to concentrate on the 150 (out of 354) odd pages on the stage, but it is important to see this as part of a whole. Following Postlewait's categorisation of 'narrative traits and types' in theatre autobiography, Kitty Marion's *Autobiography* crosses genres. It is part 'adventure story and travelogue ... where the writer tells stories of life on the road', part a narrative of 'behind the scenes', and part campaigning attack on the treatment of women in the theatre. Above all it is a 'measured history of a whole career', what Roy Pascal calls 'the story of a calling', and represents 'the development of [Marion's] career as a coherent, unified and teleological process'.[66] 'The calling' in Marion's autobiography is not the stage, but the women's movement. Though, like Ellerslie, she was drawn to the stage, and had aspirations beyond the provincial success she achieved, the calling *that frames the memoir*, is the fight against the sexual, economic and legal abuse of women. The section on the stage, whilst offering many invaluable and varied anecdotes on the experiences of a provincial performer, is threaded through with stories of the sexual exploitation of women in the theatre. After some ten years on the stage, her autobiography documents the moment her observation of these things was transformed into 'action': 'I gritted my teeth and determined that somehow I would fight this vile, economic and sexual domination over women which had no right to be, and which no man or woman worthy of the name would tolerate.'[67] Her subsequent involvement in the WSPU, as one of Christabel Pankhurst's 'hot bloods',[68] and Margaret Sanger's lieutenants, is constructed as a logical development from this moment.

Kitty Marion started her stage career as a dancer in the pantomime at Glasgow's Theatre Royal in 1889. Writing with retrospective intoxication she recalls her initial feelings: 'Although lost in the crowd, I was *on* the stage, in paradise'; and how, '[a]s fast as they turned me out of one entrance I was in another or up in the "flies" drinking in every word, sound and action. I was going to be a "principal" next year or know the reason why.'[69] For the first three years of her stage life she 'had a run of luck', alternated periods in London in one of the popular spectaculars, including Imre Kiralfi's *Venice* at Olympia, and provincial pantomime. In 1892 she had found herself in the chorus of H. Cecil Beryl's production, *The Lady Slavey*, from Nottingham Theatre Royal. 'Ten weeks certain, thirty shillings per week, half salaries for matinees and two weeks rehearsal'[70] before going on tour. This was to prove an important engagement for Marion. Not only was *The Lady Slavey* 'one of the

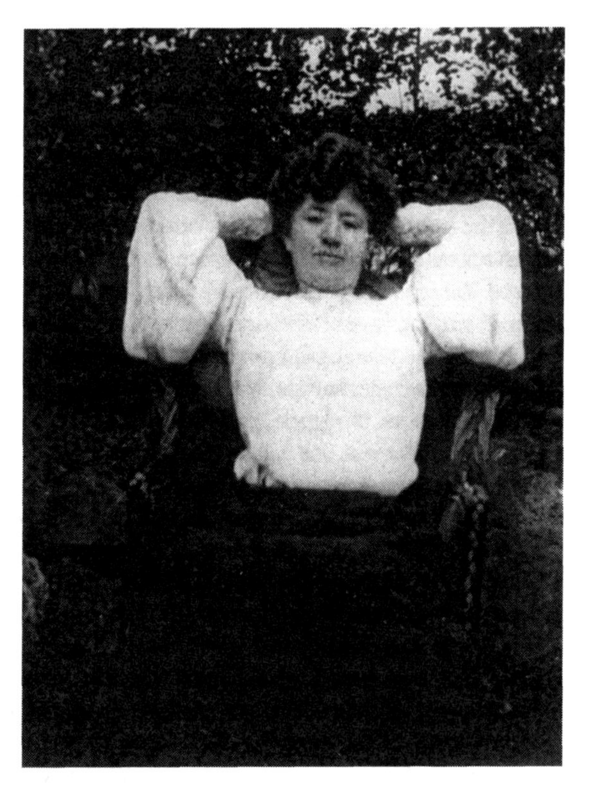

2 Kitty Marion (informal portrait).

greatest successes, financial and otherwise, ever achieved on the stage', but '[w]e developed into quite a happy family with Mr Beryl', who 'had the advantage of being a gentleman as well as a theatrical manager, which put him head and shoulders above many others ... We were a "first class" company visiting all the principal towns and theatres.'[71] Marion toured in *The Lady Slavey* Number One company every year until 1901, understudying the lead 'villainess', Flo Honeydew. Each winter she played pantomime in one of the Number One provincial theatres – in Liverpool in 1896–97 she even 'had quite a nice little speaking part too',[72] in *Dick Whittington* with Vesta Tilley. The 'outsider' had found herself established as part of a reputable company, in regular employment. The 'Slaveyites' would often rejoin the company from year to year, or meet up in pantomime, and thereby the sense of 'family' was reinforced.

However, there were cumulative disappointments. Despite successfully playing Flo in Hull when Mrs Beryl was ill, Marion was never more than 'chorus and understudy'. The touring company itself suffered disappointment when *The Lady Slavey* was taken into the West End with another, 'star', cast. Her sense that she was being overlooked unfairly was increased by the success of her occasional solo performances '"on the halls" which also strengthened [her] self-confidence in [her] ability'. By 1901 the show was 'getting on [her] nerves' and, at her own request, she was engaged by George Dance (author and 'director' of *The Lady Slavey*) for another show, *Kitty Grey*. In the two years that she was with the company as 'chorus, small part and understudy' to Kitty Grey, she again had several chances to go on when the star fell ill, and in each case Marion records that she 'went' as well as the star had done. At the end of the run, she approached Dance and asked for further work. 'My interview with him was very short', she recalls. 'He could offer me nothing but chorus and understudy. When I told him it wasn't fair, he gave parts to people who couldn't sing and act as well as I ... he said petulantly, "Well, if you don't like it you know what you can do." I replied, "Very well, good-bye Mr Dance," and flounced out of the theatre.'[73] Following a period out of work she then found herself in the production that was to be both the zenith and nadir of her career. She was engaged to understudy Emily Soldene in a tour of *La Toledad*, but a short way into the tour Soldene retired and Augustus Moore asked Marion to take over the lead for the rest of the tour. 'I felt that my chorus days were over and I was at last on the high road to success ... to see my name "starred" instead of Emily Soldene.'[74] She completed the tour and then was engaged to play a shortened version, intended for the music halls, at the Palace Theatre, London. 'My spirits soared tremendously ... "topping the bill" ... the applause for my song ... was music to my soul', she writes. But then 'another devastating hurricane struck' when the sketch was withdrawn following an action brought by the London Theatrical Managers Association against the Palace Theatre for 'producing a stage play without a licence'. Marion had, it transpired, been caught up in an internecine fight between Augustus Moore and George Edwardes, 'one of the most powerful men in the theatrical profession'.[75]

There followed four years of struggle as Marion tried, like many other artists, to make a living 'on the halls'. She was by many standards reasonably successful, appearing all over the provinces, even on the premier Stoll and de Frece circuits, all of which is recorded in meticulous detail in the *Autobiography*. Inevitably Marion was drawn into the struggle with the Variety Artists Federation against the Music Hall management whom she saw as inflicting 'unnecessary hardships, nerveracking worries entailed by unjust and inconsiderate treatment, and the misuse of power by those short sighted interests who could only see their own immediate gain'.[76] Increasingly politicised by her experiences, she joined the Women's Social and Political Union in 1907, and became one of its most active and militant members.

Marion never blames her fellow actors for her 'failure to advance'. Indeed she shows great generosity towards the 'nice likeable girl' who took over 'her' part, Flo Honeydew, in the 1897 *Lady Slavey* season, attributing her favour to the fact that 'her fiancé and the agent who booked the engagement for her were friends'.[77] And it is this gendered power nexus that Marion returns to again and again in the theatre chapters of the autobiography. Marion's narrative distinguishes between her development from sexual innocence – 'sex, except as a distinction between boys and girls, was a closed book to me'[78] she writes early in the autobiography – to worldly knowledge, and its significance in her relationships with male friends and those with power over her, and other women, in the theatre. Marion writes with a frankness and lack of 'drama' and self-recrimination – possible retrospective – about her relationships with men. The men in her companies are, for the most part, like brothers, 'chums' and 'pals' with whom she occasionally exchanges a kiss. So too are many of the men that she meets and makes friends with on tour.[79] She finds little harm in the 'stage door johnnies' that she meets, and is open-minded about women's 'irregular' relationships. Of the 'kept' girls in Mr Beryl's company, she writes that they were all 'quite charming, good-hearted and lovable'.[80] She is indignant about the assumptions that the world makes about actresses. When in Bristol she and the other 'Chorus and Ballet Ladies' were invited to tea by what turns out to be a Protestant Rescue Organisation, 'who seemed to take it for granted that in us they had a fertile field'. She found their 'unctuous "rubbing in" of sin and repentance was so nauseous, I could have thrown their tea back at them'.[81] Later she refutes Mrs Kendall's public claim that 'she was the only virtuous woman on the stage'. '"St Madge"', she asserts, 'had plenty of good, virtuous company on the stage.'[82]

However, she chronicles with frequency her encounters with the predatory male members of the profession, from agents to managers. Her first such encounter happened shortly after the end of her Glasgow engagement when she sought work on the halls through an agent she calls Mr Dreck.[83] When Marion called at his office to sign a contract, Dreck to Marion's 'horror and disgust ... threw his arms around [her] and insisted [she] must give him a kiss.' After 'struggling frantically until [her] head struck the edge of the desk', Marion records that she 'lost consciousness'. Dreck's response to this is reported to be that 'he had never met such a fighter, all over a harmless little kiss too. Most girls liked to be made love to and kissed and I would never succeed on the halls if I didn't.'[84]

This scene is repeated in different ways throughout her stage career. Another similar incident in 1907 raises questions, however, as to the way Marion may be using anecdote in the development of her 'campaign' against abuses in the theatre. The story relates to an agent who 'reverted to form' when escorting Marion home in a four-wheeler. His name, it is revealed the following day, is Arthur Hample (sic), the 'man who was prosecuted in the Brixton assault case'. 'Looking up the case' Marion discovers that he had been accused of enticing a woman from Birmingham with a promise of work. 'The case [which was actually of rape] was dismissed as the woman was of age and married and "ought to have known better." But since women don't know better [asks Marion] *must* they be at the mercy of moral vultures?'[85] It seems possible that she may have interpolated this real case into her story in order to reflect both the extent and seriousness of the abuse, and the powerlessness of women in the face of prevailing attitudes.

Only while she is regularly employed by the Beryl/Dance management, when she was 'protected' from the need to use an agent, does she avoid the 'vile tribe' who 'take such brutal advantage of their economic power over women'.[86] In fairness, she also records the agents and managers who don't abuse their position, but her experience with *La Toledad* and the cavalier way in which George Dance had dismissed her request for advancement, though no sexual misconduct is involved, is clearly seen as gendered. It confirmed for her the 'dressing room' discussions 'regarding the difficulties of women advancing in the theatrical profession without influence, money or both', and the view that 'it was impossible to procure an engagement in some London theatres and touring companies unless you were "kept" by some rich man', or were willing to 'exchange' sex for favour.[87] Marion carried on her campaign against these abuses through the letters pages of the *Era* and through her membership of the Actors' Association and Variety Artists Federation,[88] before taking it on as part of the suffrage campaign.

In many respects Marion reverses the process that Ellerslie underwent. Her early success locates her in the 'bosom' of the theatrical family, and it is a model 'Victorian' family, presided over by Mr Beryl, 'a gentleman as well as a theatrical manager'. His wife, and then his daughter, form part of the company and Marion is even asked to act as 'older sister' to the young Nellie. The company play at reputable theatres, and live in decent accommodation. The autobiography is full of details of the 'domestic' business of the company both inside and outside the theatre – rehearsals, costumes, accidents, shopping for food, inviting friends for tea, being invited, developing friendships with fellow actors and non-actors. But, as she tells it, like an increasingly dissatisfied and transgressive child, she challenges the *pater familias* and eventually finds herself on the outside of 'the family' and seeking redress in very publicly 'disreputable' behaviour. Unlike Ellerslie's implicit narrative of reintegration, Marion's meta-narrative is explicitly one of loss and 'expulsion from paradise'. Her increasing sense of self as a performer – not an invisible, 'nobody', chorus member – and as a woman in a 'family' not just dominated by men, but corrupted by men, is central to the trajectory of the autobiography. Thus her reconstruction of the 'model family', her realisation of the flaws within it, and her rejection by, and of, them, is the spine of her 'story of a calling.' The discredited family model is replaced by another within the women's movement. Importantly, the *Autobiography* also casts her as 'actor', as active, even before she joins the WSPU. Though many of the anecdotes might position her as 'victim', she almost always represents herself as 'fighting back' either physically or verbally, and she continually places herself in the narrative at the centre of the action, as the agent or initiator.[89] Her autobiographical account repositions 'femininity' as active, and herself as 'protagonist' within the women's struggle both inside and outside the theatre.

The autobiographical fiction

Postlewait's third category of theatrical autobiography is a 'fictional work about the theatre written by someone whose career has been in theatre ... which often displaces personal experiences and values into narrative'. All the examples that he discusses are by writers already well known as dramatists or actors where it is possible to read the fiction alongside the autobiography or known aspects of their life. He cites the example of Elizabeth Robins' novels which can, he suggests, 'offer some symbolic parallels to events in her acting career and life'.[90] Ina Rozant's *An Actress's Pilgrimage* (1906) is an engaging account of four months in a fit-up tour of *The Days of Nero*, very obviously a thin disguise for Wilson Barrett's hugely popular *The Sign of the Cross*.[91] However, finding any 'symbolic' or other parallel to Rozant's life in the novel is made problematic by her 'nobody' status and by the fictional frame. If, however, we regard the fiction as an extended 'theatrical anecdote' which, in Jacky Bratton's view, 'tend to be both self-exposing and self-protecting, in that while they may reveal weaknesses or personal faults, they simultaneously ward off criticism by making that weakness into an amusing story to disarm the listener [or reader], and fulfil the contract between the entertainer and the audience',[92] then it may offer us another way of unpicking the autobiographical strategies involved. If autobiography can be seen as an attempt to foreground the 'author's idea of self', the autobiographical fiction on the other hand deliberately deflects identification, at least in part.

It may have been known to the reader that the author spent 'a year and a half with Ben Greet in "The Sign of the Cross" and "The Great Ruby"', as this information was in the public domain in *The Green Room*

3 Ina Rozant (studio portrait).

4 Front cover of *An Actress's Pilgrimage*.

Book[93] and the reader may therefore have identified the writer with the 'I' of the novel, Rosie Roupell. *An Actress's Pilgrimage* could, and can, then be read as 'both self-exposing and self-protecting'. What the reader also has, as much as in performance, is 'an amusing story', and a contract between entertainer/writer and themselves as audience/reader. Thus Ina Rozant, the performance/entertainer, diverts her performance self into Ina Rozant the writer/entertainer.

An Actress's Pilgrimage covers a seventeen-week tour of *The Days of Nero*, playing seventy-three towns with '*over fifty one-night stands*' (italics in original) – an itinerary at which 'the really "old pros" [in the company] were simply aghast!'[94] Its narrator identifies herself as an amateur, who, 'as [she] steamed out of Euston ... felt that [she] was fairly on the way to become a Sarah Siddons or Bernhardt'. Like Marion, she says that, 'Almost from babyhood I had hankered for the footlights, and I had had so many disappointments in my struggles to get on the stage, that when at last I really got the offer of a tiny part (and chorus) in that popular classical play, *The Days of Nero*, sent out by a well-known manager, I was ready to jump for joy.'[95]

Again, as in the Ellerslie and Marion narratives, there is a wealth of detail about both the mechanics of touring, the company, rehearsals and performance conditions. The 'Dan Drake Company' is identified as a middle-rank fit-up. They pride themselves on having an advance agent to erect their stage when needed unlike the 'common class of "Fit-up" tour, [where] the actors often have to help with the baggage and scenery'.[96] Nonetheless, they rank below the A and B companies – whose costumes they inherit.

Comedy is often drawn from the absurdity of everyday events in the company – slaughtered Christians crawling back upstage when left stranded in front of the curtain, actors imitating lions in the wings for want of the real thing, bacchanalian orgies where actors' and actresses' costumes become inextricably entwined, and off-key buglers who learnt their trade as post-horn on the Richmond coach.

Social detail is plentiful, the characters 'drawn from life' and with respect. Though some of the women are 'vulgar' – Roupell's partner in 'diggings', Belle Sylvester, is described as 'a big, bold-looking girl ... [with manners and bearing] anything but what our maiden aunt used to call "ladylike"', who 'dangerously' has 'a perfect mania for pickles'[97] – Roupell does not cast judgement on them. While some of the company had taken to the stage 'in strong opposition to relatives' and friends' advice',[98] and there are more than a few tales of landladies refusing accommodation to the actresses on account of their occupation, there is, however, none of the angst or sense of 'sex antagonism' that runs through the Ellerslie and Marion accounts. Overall the picture is one, like Marion's of *The Lady Slavey* company, of a genial 'family' that survives its trials together. Rossiter, the actor-manager, at the end of the tour declares that he has 'never known a nicer company or better staff.' They bid each other farewell as they join hands, 'swallow lumps in [their] throats and ... with shaky voices' sing 'Auld Lang Syne'.[99]

Of Rosie Roupell we do learn some facts: that she is very small – she is nicknamed 'midget' – that her background is educated, that she trained with Dan Drake's, is 'old enough to be the juvenile's grandmother' and that she used to sing before she came into the company. All, bar the first, fits with what we know of Ina Rozant; she came from an educated family, she was 37 when she first went on the stage at Aberystwyth (the first tour date in the novel is a Welsh watering place with a pier), she trained with Ben Greet and she had a career 'on the concert platform' before the stage. This apparent 'displacement of personal experiences and values into narrative' is interesting. In the novel Roupell is very much an observer, she does not 'drive' the narrative, she is not positioned as 'heroine'. She 'fits' into the company but is effectively invisible as, after that opening expression of being 'fairly on the way to become a Sarah Siddons or Bernhardt', she neither foregrounds her own ambition nor makes claims to exceptional talent.

Perhaps one has to look elsewhere to see more of Ina Rozant – to another kind of 'autobiographical' representation, in a source that is rarely explored – *The Green Room Book*. Entries in *The Green Room Book* appear to have been in part solicited. An advertisement in the back of *An Actress's Pilgrimage* requests that

> Artists and other ladies and gentlemen associated with the dramatic, musical and variety professions whose names are not included in the first issue [of *The Green Room Book*] will oblige the Publisher by writing to him for forms, filling in the necessary particulars, and returning the same. ... No charge is made for insertion of any biographical notice, but its inclusion in the book is at the discretion of the Editor.[100]

It is perhaps here that one sees Rozant try and create 'the author's idea of self' or even 'ideal self'. For it is in the interstices between how Rozant represents herself in the directory and what we learn from the novel and other sources, that we can see the aspirational self that seeks to efface the 'nobody' self. Rozant presents herself as a successful actress and author. Her novel certainly received positive reviews, and the permission she received to dedicate it to Ellen Terry was deemed 'a sufficient guarantee that silly and lurid details are altogether lacking'.[101] But her 'year and a half with Ben Greet' may only represent a year and a half with one of Ben Greet's 'ten to fifteen companies "on the road" in this country and in America'.[102] If Roupell is Rozant, she may never have played more than the 'Fit-up Company North' tour of *The Sign of the Cross*. The rest of her career was in modest touring companies, both comic opera and 'répertoire'. *The Green Room Book* tells us that she 'took out her own company in 1905 creating the part of Rachel Huggins in "The Designers"'[103] – a farcical comedy written by her own brother, Fritz Zorn.[104] It is tempting to speculate on who financed this venture. The description of her novel is laudatory, 'an extremely well written story of an actress's experiences on tour', just as her brother's play is 'a singularly bright and ingenious one' which 'like Shaw and Barrie [is distinguished by] strong characterisation'.[105] These are unusual entries in that they offer judgements on work, rather than just listing them.

This insertion of self, and *assertion* of self, in *The Green Room Book* must be seen as an act of 'publicly imitating and reproducing the signs and attitudes that mark individuals as belonging to a certain class and gender'. For *The Green Room Book* itself – as a serious 'guide to the contemporary stage' containing the biographies of 'eminent actors, dramatists and critics'[106] – represents the theatre 'reproducing the signs and attitudes of the professional middle classes'. Rozant's photograph is reproduced with that of Ellen Terry and Mrs Kendall, both now representing not only the 'aristocracy' of theatre families, but also the acme of theatrical and artistic success and respectability. Through this, if only for a brief period, Rozant achieves public recognition alongside her eminent 'sisters'.[107]

Life's understudies

Perhaps I might more accurately have borrowed Rozant's title for her second novel for this chapter. For all three of these women, through their autobiographies, repudiate the notion of themselves as 'nobodies'. Understudies and chorus maybe. Each woman, in her own way, successfully projects an image of the world in which they are *actors*,[108] and in doing so effectively insert themselves as 'somebodies' into the 'hierarchies and histories of the theatre'.

Notes

1 [Alma Ellerslie?] *Diary of an Actress or the Realities of Stage Life*, ed. H. C. Shuttleworth (London: Griffin, Farran & Co., 1885), p. 11.
2 Thomas Postlewait lists 'twelve modes or types' of autobiographical works in theatre. See his 'Theatre Autobiographies: Some Preliminary Concerns for the Theatre Historian', *Assaph C* 16, 2000, pp. 157–72.
3 Thomas Postlewait, 'Autobiography and Theatre History', in Thomas Postlewait and Bruce A. McConachie (eds), *Interpreting the Theatrical Past: Essays in the Historiography of Performance* (Iowa City: University of Iowa Press, 1989), p. 249.
4 Ibid., p. 252.
5 Alma Ellerslie, *Diary of an Actress*, p. 11.
6 Irene Vanburgh, *To Tell My Story* (London: Hutchinson & Co., 1948), pp. 101–2.
7 From this period see William Archer, *Masks or Faces?* (New York: Hill and Wang, 1957). See also Mary Jean Corbett, *Representing Femininity: Middle Class Subjectivity in Victorian and Edwardian Women's Autobiography* (New York and Oxford: Oxford University Press, 1992), pp. 113–14.
8 Irene Vanburgh, *To Tell My Story*, p. 102. There is a third self which is negotiated by the celebrity performer, exemplified by Irene Vanburgh, that of the commodified identity generated by the interstices between the 'nobody' self, the performance and the public self. The 'constant re-creation' of this celebrity self may equally have a way of 'obliterating the original'.
9 Thomas Postlewait, 'Autobiography and Theatre History', p. 255.
10 Mary Jean Corbett, *Representing Femininity*, p. 114.
11 Ibid., p. 108.
12 See Sandra Richards, *The Rise of the English Actress* (Basingstoke: Macmillan, 1993), pp. 90, 105. Tracy C. Davis, whilst using Ellerslie and her trials in her analysis, does at least reflect much of the tenor of diary when she writes that 'this woman asserts that an artistic life gives sufficient compensation for the hardship, isolation, and sexual skirmishes'. Tracy C. Davis, *Actresses as Working Women: Their Social Identity in Victorian Culture* (London: Routledge, 1991), p. 74.
13 There are noble exceptions, for example Cicely Hamilton's serious account of the lives of women that provincial touring brought her into contact with. Cicely Hamilton, *Life Errant* (London: J. M. Dent & Sons Ltd., 1935), Chapter IV 'On Tour', pp. 34–50 and 51–7.
14 Alma Ellerslie, *Diary of an Actress*, p. 159.
15 Sandra Richards refers to her as Anne Ellerslie, but I assume this is a misattribution.
16 Several copies of the typescript are in existence. References are taken from that in the Museum of London.
17 Kitty Marion, *Autobiography*. Unpublished manuscript. Museum of London, p. 44.

18 Ibid., p. 57.
19 Public Record Office (now part of The National Archives) papers, 221.784/32.
20 February 1915. Incomplete letter from Mrs E. R. Browne, née Alice Thorburn, to her brother [?] Thorburn, forwarded by Charles Thorburn to the Home Office. Charles Thorburn was manager of the Vaudeville Theatre. Public Record Office papers, 221.874/22.
21 *The Green Room Book 1907* (London: T. Sealey Clark & Co. Ltd., 1907) pp. 306–7. I am indebted to Shirley Askins for details of Ina Rozant's family background. Rozant was Ms Askins' husband's great aunt.
22 Rozant's father was an Indian merchant, her maternal uncle 'the eminent Anglo-Indian journalist' Robert Knight. However, her late professor uncle was the author of a 'Grammar of Dance' in German. *The Green Room Book 1907*, p. 306. We don't know if Ellerslie ever married as the published diary covers only one year; Marion did not and Rozant married a fellow actor, George Goodwin, in December 1914, aged 52.
23 Alma Ellerslie, *Diary of an Actress*, p. 53.
24 Kitty Marion, *Autobiography*, pp. 15, 22.
25 Her stockbroker brother, Fritz, wrote at least one play and styled himself at one time as a dramatist and novelist. She shared addresses with both her brothers and her mother during the time she was on the stage.
26 Elizabeth Robins, *Both Sides of the Curtain* (London: William Heinemann Ltd., 1940), p. 18.
27 In the account of Kitty Marion's memorial gathering there is a reference to how her 'friends from all walks of life and from all parts of the globe … drank tea or sherry – with Kitty – as if she had been there in the flesh – saw her many books, photographs and papers … [and how] "Kitty spoke" from her interesting Diary kept over a period of years'. Though this may of course refer to her autobiography manuscript. New York Public Library, Schwimmer-Lloyd Collection, Kitty Marion Item 48.
28 Cited in Janet Bottoms, 'Writing Herself: The Diary of Alice James' in Julia Swindells (ed.), *The Uses of Autobiography* (London: Taylor and Francis, 1995), p. 110.
29 See Tracy C. Davis, *Actresses as Working Women*, pp. 134–5 *inter alia*.
30 In fact Henry Cary Shuttleworth (1850–1900), far from being an enemy of the theatre, was a staunch advocate and an active supporter of the Church and Stage Guild that met in the crypt of St Paul's. See: *Henry Cary Shuttleworth: A Memoir*, ed. George W. E. Russell (London: Chapman and Hall, Ltd., 1903).
31 Internal evidence suggests a date of 1880–81 based on the perpetual calendar and references to the work of contemporary novelists, William Black (probably to his novel about the stage, *In Silk Attire* (1872)) and George Eliot (especially *Daniel Deronda*, published in 1876).
32 Ellerslie states in her Preface that 'the names given are, in the majority of instances, purely fictitious, while the names of towns have been entirely changed'. Alma Ellerslie, *Diary of an Actress*, p. 12.

33 Ibid., p. 11.
34 Ibid., p. 100.
35 Ibid., pp. 11–12, 82.
36 Ibid., p. 92.
37 Ibid., p. 100.
38 Ibid., p. 32.
39 At Dudley; ibid., p. 33.
40 Ibid., p. 42.
41 Ibid., p. 32.
42 Ibid., p. 133.
43 Ibid., p. 50–1.
44 Ibid., p. 34.
45 Ibid., p. 131.
46 Ibid., p. 35.
47 Ibid., p. 155, 159.
48 Ibid., p. 10.
49 Ibid., p. 38.
50 Ibid., p. 23.
51 Ibid., pp. 99–100.
52 Ibid., p. 140.
53 Ibid., p. 17.
54 Ibid., p. 83.
55 Ibid., pp. 137–8.
56 Ibid., pp. 165–6.
57 Ibid., p. 12.
58 Ibid., pp. 159–60.
59 Ibid., p. 16. Ina Rozant does not appear to have shared this view of Mrs Kendall. In her theatre novel, *Life's Understudies*, Mrs Tyndall (Mrs Kendall) is spotted in a train, knitting. 'I can't bear that woman!' says the chorine, Lulu Lane, 'Don't she look prim? For all the world as if she looked down on the whole profession and was ashamed she belonged to it. She's made all her money out of it, though …' Ina Rozant, *Life's Understudies* (London: T. Sealey Clark & Co., Ltd., 1907), p. 26. And Kitty Marion makes some tart observations on 'St Madge'. Kitty Marion, *Autobiography*, p. 100.
60 Set up in 1935 as a unified relief project to address the problems of unemployment and poverty, as part of the New Deal.
61 *New Yorker*, 4 July 1936, pp. 22–4.
62 Ibid., p. 24.
63 *New York World Telegram*, 8 July 1932.
64 Annie E. Gray, Schwimmer-Lloyd Collection, Kitty Marion Item 48.
65 Kitty Marion, *Autobiography*, p. 1.
66 Postlewait, 'Theatre Autobiographies: Some Preliminary Concerns', pp. 167–70; and idem, 'Autobiography and Theatre History', p. 254.
67 Marion, *Autobiography*, p. 144.

68 She was responsible for a number of arson attacks (5 according to the autobiography), amongst other militant activities, but was only imprisoned for 1 – the destruction of Hurst Park Racecourse grandstand in June 1913, with Clara Giveen. She was imprisoned 6 times and force-fed 232 times in the UK, and imprisoned 3 times in the United States.
69 Marion, *Autobiography*, p. 41.
70 Ibid., p. 71.
71 Ibid., pp. 75–6.
72 Ibid., p. 102.
73 Ibid., p. 130.
74 Ibid., p. 138–9.
75 Ibid., p. 142.
76 Ibid., p. 163.
77 Ibid., p. 108.
78 Ibid., p. 46.
79 Marion has a long, platonic relationship with an older man, Robert Halford, who becomes a father figure to her. Fascinating and central to Marion's life at this time, it is too complex to unpick here.
80 Kitty Marion, *Autobiography*, p. 80.
81 Ibid., p. 55.
82 Ibid., p. 100.
83 Dreck is 'dirt' in German.
84 Ibid., p. 45.
85 Ibid., p. 166–7. For the case, see *The Times*, 27 May 1907. His name was Hampel, not Hample.
86 Ibid., p. 147.
87 Ibid., pp. 97, 80 *inter alia*.
88 Ibid., pp. 159–160, 177; *Era*, 17 February 1906, ff.
89 Although there are elisions in her narrative, and these are clearer in the suffrage section, there is substantial corroborating evidence for her activities. In an unpublished conference paper, 'Reading between the lines: Kitty Marion's prison experience', I explored the shifting narratives found in Marion's autobiography, the Home Office prison records in the PRO, and letters written on toilet paper between Marion and other suffragettes in Holloway Prison. The events were the same in each, but the versions told very different stories.
90 Thomas Postlewait, 'Theatre Autobiographies', p. 167.
91 For the text of *The Sign of the Cross* and a critical-historical commentary see David Mayer, *Playing Out the Empire: Ben-Hur and Other Toga Plays and Films* (Oxford: Clarendon Press, 1994), pp. 104–88.
92 Jacky Bratton, *New Readings in Theatre History* (Cambridge: Cambridge University Press, 2003), p. 103.
93 *The Green Room Book 1907*, p. 306.
94 Ina Rozant, *An Actress's Pilgrimage*, pp. 14–15.
95 Ibid., p. 1.

96 Ibid., p. 2.
97 Ibid., pp. 7, 114.
98 Ibid., p. 14.
99 Ibid., pp. 158–9.
100 Ibid., p. 165.
101 The reviews are reprinted in an advertisement in *The Green Room Book*. T. Sealey Clark published both the novel and directory. The implicit comparison with other actress fictions takes us back to Ellerslie.
102 *The Green Room Book 1907*, pp. 158–9.
103 Ibid., pp. 306, 385.
104 Fritz Zorn may also have 'inflated' his literary roles. He describes himself as a 'dramatist and novelist'. *The Green Room Book 1907*, p. 385. As far as one can ascertain he only ever published one novel and a report on the rubber industry, and had one play produced. The promised West End production of *The Designers* never materialised, nor did a second play – or at least they are not listed in Allardyce Nicoll's hand list. He was, however, a successful stockbroker.
105 Ibid..
106 *The Green Room Book 1907*, p. xl.
107 Perhaps it is important to note here that Ina Rozant as well as Kitty Marion is listed as a member of the Actresses' Franchise League. 'Membership List' [1910?] The Women's Library, AFL Papers, 22146. This may indicate another side of Rozant's life and worldview we can know nothing of.
108 Bratton writes that we should, 'read this auto/biographical material as far as it is possible in its own terms, accepting the picture it paints as the intended activity of its authors … They are intent on projecting an image of the world in which they are actors, those who do, not objects.' Jacky Bratton, *New Readings in Theatre History*, p. 101.

2

THE DISAPPEARING SUBJECT IN SUSAN GLASPELL'S AUTO/BIOGRAPHICAL THEATRE

Nicola Shaughnessy

We need a Dead (wo)man to Begin. (Hélène Cixous)[1]

The absent (often dead) female protagonist has been a prevalent concern of recent feminist Glaspell criticism.[2] However, as J. Ellen Gainor observes, the feminist interest in such women in Glaspell's plays has proved to be somewhat myopic: 'While the most obvious instances of this device are indeed the missing female characters at the heart of these plays, critics who extrapolate from this a message about the marginalisation of women, for example, miss a larger implication of this stylistic trait because they ignore her absent men.'[3] In this chapter I want to explore the concept of the absent subject in the context of auto/biography, considering how Glaspell uses the medium of theatre to destabilise notions of authorship and character. The plays discussed in this chapter feature the death or absence of an offstage character as the impetus for the action: *Trifles* (1916), *The Outside* (1917), *Bernice* (1919) and *Alison's House* (1930).

The autobiographical mode is usually identified with prose and, less frequently, with poetry: it is often a confessional discourse which, in the former medium especially, reveals the unity and 'truth' of the writing self through a linear, semi-novelistic narrative of self-becoming. But as poststructuralist and feminist work on autobiography has demonstrated, the apparent coherence and facticity of the autobiographical text's mediation of the space between the 'self' and the 'life' is misleading. As Linda Anderson summarises, 'the pre-existing subject of autobiographical theory and its stabilisation within a genre that could, like the self, be identified and recognised, was presented as an illusion, unmasked. Were we also then witnessing the death of autobiography?' Anderson continues: 'The problem with death when it is invoked rhetorically, as it frequently is within poststructuralist theory, is that it is never quite the end, and leaves space for all kinds of ghostly returns.'[4] Paul John Eakin similarly contests the death of the subject: 'Even the most cursory survey of books on the self and the subject in a broad range of fields confirms not only that these concepts aren't "dead" but that they are essential terms required by, yet resisting, analysis.'[5]

My use of the term autobiographical in relation to Glaspell's theatre, involves reading her plays and performances in these ambivalent and uncertain terms; their subject is not the 'self' of realist autobiography. These are not autobiographical dramas in the conventionally realist sense, where the play self-consciously stages events in the author's personal history and generally includes a central, authoritative character who can be identified as the author. The dramatic medium is one which fractures and disperses the subject. The authorial voice is redistributed among a chorus of performers and *dramatis personae*; consequently, the impression of an originating self that is conventionally supposed to stand behind, mediate and control the text's generation of meaning is also subject to dispersal and dissolution. Clearly then, dramatic writing calls into question the author's proprietary claims to the text. Yet Glaspell's theatre, like that of many modernist women playwrights, remains directly and intimately, albeit complexly, concerned with issues of identity, subjectivity and authorship. The staging of these issues involves precisely the kinds of 'ghostly returns' Anderson refers to; they are played out through the device of the absent character as well as through Glaspell's role on stage in the first productions of *Trifles*, *The Outside* and *Bernice*. In each of the plays discussed, the absent protagonist controls the action as well as providing a focus for concerns about identity, loss and desire, which are articulated in terms of the transience of the theatre event itself. Although only *Alison's House* is explicitly concerned with a (dead) writer, all four plays explore the relationship between the disappearance of the author and the scenes of writing, performance and death.

Trifles was Glaspell's first sole-authored play. This one-acter, set in a farmhouse kitchen, follows the investigation conducted by a Sheriff, a County Attorney and a neighbouring farmer, Hale, into the murder of the significantly-named Mr Wright by, as it turns, out, his wife. The irony is that as the men disappear offstage to hunt for clues, two of the wives, Mrs Hale and Mrs Peters, remain in the kitchen and engage in some intuitive amateur sleuthing which leads directly to the discovery of the crucial evidence pointing towards Mrs Wright's guilt. But it also confronts them with a moral dilemma, as their investigations reveal that

Mrs Wright was herself a victim of a brutal patriarch, trapped in domestic servitude, childless and isolated. The piece ends with Mrs Peters and Mrs Hale, in a gesture of empathy towards the absent figure of Mrs Wright, concealing the evidence from their law-enforcing husbands; we are left with the strong sense that this is a morally appropriate action.

Catherine Belsey emphasises that one of the key tactics of the classic realist mode in the theatre is its insistence upon the erasure of the author, and of the textuality of the theatrical fiction: 'direct intrusion by the author comes to seem an impropriety ... the author is apparently absent from the self-contained fictional world on the stage'.[6] On the face of it this is true of *Trifles*, which makes its case through the naturalistic authenticity and coherence of setting and actions – which were based upon real-life events – rather than through blatant authorial steering or commentary. Like the characters in the play, the spectator is to engage in a process of detection and deduction, reading both the scene and narrative as texts to be deciphered. In a quiet way, as a number of critics have noted, *Trifles* interrogates the realist mode in which it ostensibly operates and, in particular, the male narrative of the detective story, or whodunnit, which is, as Catherine Belsey points out, the classic realist genre par excellence. Of the Sherlock Holmes stories, Belsey observes that they 'begin in enigma, mystery, the impossible, and conclude with an explanation which makes all clear and amenable to reason'. These qualities of enigma and mystery are frequently gendered, in stories 'haunted by shadowy, mysterious and silent women'.[7] *Trifles* pulls off the trick of enabling its enigmatic female protagonist to evade the seemingly inevitable exposure and arrest that the practice of masculine reason seeks strenuously, and rather comically, to secure.

Mrs Wright could be seen as occupying the position of the absent author of the classic realist text, in that she is ascribed intentionality as the author of the crime which sets the play in motion. An important factor here, in the almost salon-theatre atmosphere of the Provincetown, is the presence of Glaspell herself in the cast, significantly in the role of Mrs Hale who acts as a mediator between the absent protagonist, Mrs Wright, and the audience. While Mrs Peters uncovers the evidence, it is Mrs Hale/Glaspell who interprets it, and it is she who speaks in Mrs Wright's defence. Glaspell was not, as a realist author ought to be, absent from the self-contained fictional world of the play but a living part of it, guiding the audience's responses.

Mrs Hale is, moreover, a surrogate for Glaspell, as Linda Ben Zvi has demonstrated. In her biography of Glaspell, Ben Zvi identifies the historical source for *Trifles* (and *The Jury of her Peers*): 'the murder of a sixty year old farmer named John Hossack on December 2, 1900 … Glaspell covered the case and the subsequent trial when she was a reporter for the *Des Moines Daily News*.'[8] Glaspell was, as Ben Zvi observes, an 'active participant' in the situation she subsequently dramatised: 'Glaspell was actually a primary contributor to the shaping of public opinion about the woman being tried'[9] and this is acted through her presence on stage. Glaspell's role as a journalist influencing public perceptions of and responses to the case, are mirrored in her stage persona. While Mrs Wright is author of the crime, Glaspell is on stage as the fictional detective/journalist, interpreting the evidence and guiding the spectators' responses to sympathise with Mrs Wright's plight as an abused wife and mother. There are, moreover other ways in which Glaspell foregrounds her role as author/playwright. Ellen Gainor has discussed the ways in which Glaspell explores 'the interplay of acting and staging within a dialogic text'[10] considering how spectatorship and dramaturgy are a major theme of *Trifles*:

> We should consider the idea that Glaspell's connection of spectatorship with her creative process makes her acutely conscious of both the audience and the concept that the spectator is the force somehow allowing or driving the action, the unfolding of character, the revelation of meaning. When Glaspell remarks, 'sometimes things written in my room would not form on the stage, and I must go home and cross them out,' she is suggesting that writing without spectating may not work theatrically. She implies that seeing things onstage first facilitates the creation- as well as the criticism- of that which is to be scripted. She must then transcribe what she sees so that it can be seen again as she has seen it, she writes her play in order to allow her audience to experience as closely as possible her perception of what she has witnessed.[11]

Seen in the context of the play's original conditions of production, moreover, there is another level of authorial involvement. *Trifles* is a text which is strongly implicated within its first performance context. In *The Road to the Temple*, Glaspell records how the writing of the play was tied to the physical conditions of the Provincetown Players' Wharf Theatre:

> So I went out on the wharf, sat alone on one of our wooden benches without a back, and looked a long time at that bare little stage. After a time the stage became a kitchen – a kitchen there all by itself. I saw just where the stove was, the table, and the steps going upstairs. Then the door at the back opened, and people all bundled came in … Whenever I got stuck, I would run across the street to the old wharf, sit in that leaning little theatre under

> which the sea sounded, until the play was ready to continue. Sometimes things written in my room would not form on the stage, and I must go home and cross them out.[12]

Glaspell's construction of space here is gendered. The stage is initially 'bare' but is then transformed into an enclosed domestic space: the kitchen with the stove and the table. This is an example of the space of the imagination and memory merging with theatrical space in the manner observed by Julie Holledge and Joanne Tompkins:

> The enclosed maternal body thus overlaps with the enclosed material theatre space which is also frequently depicted as a container. Our analysis combines these two notions of enclosure: spaces identified with women merge with theatrical space (the space that is generated by the imagination of the playwright, the concepts of the designers and directors, and the spatial associations of the audience) and with theatre space (the theatre building and its location in a social context).[13]

What Holledge and Tompkins have in mind is Gaston Bachelard's notion of 'memory space' whereby 'most people's lives are spent, at one level, attempting to recover the shape, smell, or feel of rooms that they first knew as a child, or even the comfort of the womb ... one may not find a house or space that that actually does resemble the space of home, but one may eventually be able to re-create that safe, protected, secret shell for oneself'.[14] In all the plays considered, Glaspell foregrounds the importance of space in terms of rooms, houses and female identity. However, as Gainor reminds us, it is important not to ignore the 'absent setting' in *Trifles*: the bedroom. The men are offstage for most of the play, in the bedroom, the room 'on top of' the kitchen which is 'through opposition with the kitchen ... a place of male interest and dominance'.[15] A number of critics have read *Trifles* as a play which critiques conventional gender roles and resists and subverts the classic generic forms of murder mysteries. However, Glaspell's appearance on stage in her role as Mrs Hale is also an interventionist theatrical strategy. As Gainor has argued: 'details of the production environment in community theater further work against blanket concepts of the realist form propounded by such theorists as Catherine Belsey ... in the production context [of community theatre] the authors' identities and proclivities, known equally well to the audience as the actors, would preclude the suspension of authorial consciousness even within a realist production'.[16] Thus Glaspell's onstage surrogate persona enables her to resist and to question a series of legal, literary and theatrical conventions.

Glaspell's next play, *The Outside* (1917), also challenges theatrical conventions and continues to explore connections between gender identity and space. In terms of auto/biography *The Outside* refers self-reflexively to the gendered presence of the author. Glaspell played the pivotal role of Allie Mayo in the first production of the play; this enabled her to further explore issues of authorship and identity through performance and, I will argue, provides further evidence of an intersection between her biography – her life and work – and her attitudes towards authorship and performance. The setting for this one act play is an abandoned life station which is associated with the two women who inhabit it. It is presented as a bleak, sterile environment: '*an empty house*', '*a buried house*' on the '*outside shore*'.[17] What we may notice about the description of the life station, however, is its resemblance to the Wharf Theatre itself, both in its general aspect, and, perhaps more significantly, in its positioning between land and sea. By now, the Provincetown Players were at the Playwright's Theatre in New York, so the dim echoes of the Wharf Theatre are nostalgic, even ghostly.[18] The strong sense of place, moreover, is shot through with a sense of loss and this is the major preoccupation of the play. When it begins, three men, the Captain, Bradford and Tony, are trying to resuscitate a body they have recovered, to Mrs Patrick's annoyance: 'This isn't the life-saving station anymore', she protests, 'this is my house! – and I want my house to myself'.[19] Here, the corpse, which may be seen in Kristevan terms as the abject, being 'both human and non-human, waste and filth which are neither entirely inside nor outside the socio-economic order'[20] is at the limits of stage visibility, being seen in Glaspell's stage direction through an open door upstage.

The two women, then, are situated in the space between the inside of the life station and the outside of the sea. Allie Mayo is described as '*a bleak woman who at first seems little more than a part of the sand before which she stands*'.[21] Mrs Patrick is reported to spend her time sitting on the sand contemplating death: 'I believe she *likes* to see the sand slippin' down on the woods. Pleases her to see somethin' gettin' buried, I guess.' While the male characters resist, defy and conquer the external elements in the form of the sea, the shifting sand and death, the two women are outside of the society the men inhabit: they live on 'the outer shore, where men can't live ... the edge of life'.[22] Both are separated from their husbands: Allie Mayo's husband is reported to have died at sea and although Mrs Patrick insists that her husband is not dead, his absence is unexplained. Allie Mayo is further divorced from society by her silence: 'she has got a prejudice against words ... women whose men go to sea ain't always talkative'.[23] Her rejection of language and subsequent recovery of speech can be read in the light of Kristeva's linguistic theory where she argues that language, 'as a symbolic system, is at the service of the death drive, diverts it and confines it as if within an isolated pocket of narcissism'.[24] Allie Mayo's existence is a kind of death-in-life, as she situates herself physically and linguistically on the borderland between life and death.

Christopher Bigsby has described *The Outside* as 'an allegory of the battle between the life force and the death force'.[25] It is also as an allegory for writing and the author's relationship to language. 'Writing forms a passageway between two shores', declares Helene Cixous in 'The School of the Dead', where she meditates on the necessity of death as a prerequisite for 'good' writing. 'To begin (writing/living) we must have death', and, she insists, 'I'm only talking about the death of the loved one.'[26] So, Allie Mayo, after the death of her husband, retreats from language, the symbolic, into the space she describes as the outside. It is a semiotic space, beyond signification, 'not with a name'. Allie Mayo empathises with Mrs Patrick's similar retreat in response to the absence of her husband: 'I know where you're going', she says, 'what you're trying to do ... bury it. The life in you. Bury it – watching the sand bury the woods. But I'll tell you something. They fight too. The woods.'[27] Allie Mayo's awakening to life is expressed through her return to language; her words, similarly, refuse to be buried. Bradford and the Captain have left the body and Mrs Patrick, horrified, starts to follow them before she is 'held' by Allie Mayo's utterance, 'Wait.' Breaking her silence she speaks 'in a labored way – slow, monotonous, as if snowed in by silent years': 'That boy in there – his face – uncovered something ... for twenty years, I did what you are doing. And I can tell you – it's not the way.'[28] Having experienced death, Allie Mayo returns to life and to language and then assists Mrs Patrick in her own rite of passage. In this respect, Allie Mayo functions as midwife to Mrs Patrick's rebirth.

Glaspell's treatment of maternity has been discussed by Veronica Makowsky in relation to Sara Ruddick's notion of 'maternal thinking'. In her comment on *The Outside*, Makowsky sees Allie Mayo and Mrs Patrick as maternal pioneers: 'the women want to save what is best in the town, its future, progress in the form of children, but Glaspell presents their unconventional lives and relinquishment of society's comforts as indications of the direction in which the future should go, toward the innovative, the original, the outside'.[29] Allie Mayo's use of maternal metaphors complements her maternal function in the play, as she, too, becomes a life-saver. Her role is also associated with the author/artist; unsurprisingly, Glaspell played Allie Mayo in the first production. According to Kristeva, the artist, 'in order to function must make himself the bearer of death ... in returning through the event of death, towards that which produces its break; in exporting semiotic motility across the border on which the symbolic is established, the artist sketches out a kind of second birth.'[30] Allie Mayo, then, acts out a kind of second birth, conveyed through maternal metaphors and her maternal function. She is a figure through whom Glaspell explores her own relationship to language and her related concern with death. As in *Trifles*, her role as playwright is important in this respect. The theatre event exists at a perpetual threshold, on the point of a 'self-becoming' through performance which immediately evaporates. Each performance is a life and a death. In writing drama, Glaspell accepts her death as author but by participating in the production of her plays she is part of their rebirth through performance.

This brings us to the possibility of a relationship between the stage spaces Glaspell creates and her own biography. Shortly after her marriage to Jig Cook in 1913 Glaspell suffered a miscarriage and this prevented her from having any further children. Glaspell's playwriting career commenced shortly after. Glaspell's account of the beginnings of her career as a playwright in *The Road to the Temple* appears frequently in Glaspell criticism and biography. She suggests that Cook instructed her to write *Trifles* and when she complained that she hadn't 'studied' playwriting he argued that she had a stage of her 'own' which was all she needed. Gainor argues convincingly that Glaspell's 'resistance' to Cook's directive is part of the fabric of *Trifles*: 'with techniques foundational to feminist writing, she inscribes into the play's subject, form and composition the paradox of "resistant compliance" that she herself experienced in its creation'.[31] So what can we make of Glaspell's comments on authorship through Allie Mayo? Certainly there is initial resistance and ambivalence as her silence indicates. But if Allie Mayo's recovery of language is predicated on the 'death of a loved one' then perhaps Glaspell's is too. The rather unconventional and symbolic staging for *The Outside* is suggestive. Unusually, the focus is upstage, on the 'big sliding door' symbolising the threshold between land and sea, male and female, inside and outside. The space is barren and sterile. I would suggest that buried here is a reference to the barren woman's body as 'an empty house, a buried house'. This makes the significance of Allie Mayo's arm gesture, as documented by Gainor, all the more emotive: 'Glaspell literally embodies this image with Allie's arm gesture-holding it up and curving it around "to make the form of the Cape" embracing its port. Glaspell's description of Allie in fact so closely links her with her surroundings that she becomes a virtual mirror of the play's environment herself.'[32] The fact that the playwright is the performer at this juncture speaks volumes.

Glaspell's practice of performing significant roles in her dramas, then, enabled her to nurture her plays in their development from script to performance and to function as a kind of multiple author. The roles she chose to play have related functions as mediators between absent protagonists and the characters on stage and often serve as vehicles for manipulating the audience's responses. In *Bernice*, Glaspell's first full-length play, we find further intersections between characters, settings, performers and Glaspell. This is another play in which the protagonist is absent. The title character is a dominating force who controls the action from the grave. As Gainor argues in one of the few detailed critical discussions of this play, 'Glaspell's repeated use of this device in her realist plays does not make them less realistic; rather, this technique subtly disrupts verisimilitude, creating between the audience and the characters a critical distance distinctive in its realist dramaturgy.'[33] Bernice has asked her servant, Abbie, to tell her husband, Craig Norris, that she killed herself in his absence, predicting that he will assume that he was responsible for her death. Abbie, the character Glaspell played in the first production (21–27 March 1919, Playwrights' theatre, Greenwich Village) is thus pivotal to the play's action, mediating between the dead female subject and the characters who survive her. She struggles between her knowledge of the 'truth' – that Bernice died of natural causes – and her loyalty to Bernice and comes to exercise a form of personal morality which defies the abstract ethical principle of fidelity to truth, remaining loyal to Bernice in telling Craig the lie about his wife's suicide. The play explores the consequences of this falsehood and ultimately supports both Bernice and Abbie by presenting a justification for their conspiracy.

Although the play has received relatively little critical attention, its significance within Glaspell's corpus and the intersection between the play's characters and Glaspell's biography is central to Gainor's discussion where she suggests a connection to Glaspell's experiences of Greenwich village and her membership of the Heterodoxy Club – a feminist network of artists and intellectuals. The exploration of gender roles and difference, the characterisation of the 'new woman', and the critique of patriarchy were central to the ideology and practices of the club; as Gainor argues:

> *Bernice* is unique among Glaspell's plays, however, for acknowledging the importance of emotional bonds external to marriage. The close, compelling ties between Bernice and Margaret correspond to the bonds the Heterodoxy Club fostered among its members. Moreover, the play suggests additional benefits from these associations by recognising the centrality of sisterhood to personal achievement.[34]

Set against this celebration of female roles, however, is the problematic characterisation of Craig – the male writer/egotist, demanding public acclaim, attention and a self-sacrificing wife. Craig, we discover, has played the patriarch throughout his marriage, declaring that 'you want to feel that you *have* the woman you love. Yes – completely. Yes, every bit of her.' The links to Jig Cook have also been noted: Barbara Ozieblo observes that 'Glaspell must have suffered from the stressful ambivalence of her position in marriage – and observed the strains in the marriages of her friends – for her plays and novels frequently portray independent women who will not be mastered.'[35] The irony is that although Craig believes that he exercised power and control over Bernice in that she supposedly surrendered her life to him, it is Bernice who controls Craig through the fiction she has devised of her suicide.

Bernice is a kind of empty space, occupied by the desires and projections of others; her indeterminacy serves as a basis for the other characters to construct their own sense of self. In *Alison's House*, as in *Bernice*, the play's central character is dead, but in the later play she has been dead for some time – eighteen years, in fact. Like Bernice, the dead woman is central to the action; the other characters are defined through their relationships with Alison, and the plot is motivated by the quest to uncover the mystery surrounding her. The formula is a development of the well-made play convention used in *Trifles* and *Bernice*, whereby the audience are given a series of clues which gradually lead to a revelation as Alison's secret is disclosed. The spectator, then, is like that of the biographer, searching for the supposed 'truth' about the central character.

In *Alison's House*, two male characters serve as intermediaries for the audience, in that they are trying to find out about Alison's history. Richard Knowles, a reporter, is an admirer of Alison's poetry and is 'down to get a little story about the house, because it is being broken up'.[36] He wants the house and its contents to be preserved for posterity. The other character in pursuit of Alison's story is Ted Stanhope, her nephew, whose endeavour to avoid flunking English appears to be dependent upon a piece he is writing about his aunt. Despite his credentials, Ted's interest is not a literary one; indeed, he is more journalistic than Richard, asking questions about what pen Alison used, what she ate and whether she was a virgin. He is cast in the role of the popular biographer, scavenging over the body of his subject with the sole intention of finding material that he can profit from; 'I got to make this grade', he insists. Richard, however, wants to celebrate Alison as an icon. There are some parallels here to critics and biographers of Emily Dickinson, who is generally acknowledged as the subject of Glaspell's play. The resemblances between Emily Dickinson and Glaspell's protagonist Alison Stanhope have been well documented in Glaspell criticism: physical resemblances and descriptions; the reclusive poet; unconsummated love and rejection of adultery; writing unpublished in her own lifetime; poems written on scraps of paper sewn together and protected by surviving sister after poet's death; adulterous relationships elsewhere in poet's immediate family.[37] However, as Katharine Rodier has pointed out, the play has a more nuanced understanding of biographical referentiality:

> Receiving the nebulous truths about Dickinson and her family through perhaps several variants, Glaspell may have recognised the fundamental unreliability of any single account of a human life, particularly one the public seems eager to own. She may also have concluded that conjecture is itself the central fact of any thorough study of identity.[38]

We need to look beyond the parallels between Alison and Emily to perceive the ways in which Glaspell stages the debates surrounding Dickinson's work as well as realising some uncanny connections to disputes surrounding Glaspell's biography and *Alison's House.*

Glaspell's play was written in the context of the centenary of Emily Dickinson's birth. The year 1930 marked the climax of the 'confused decades' of Dickinson criticism, according to Klaus Lubbers.[39] For some critics and biographers, Dickinson has been sentimentalised and mythologised as a heartbroken recluse producing confessional poetry. Mabel Loomis Todd, the co-editor of Dickinson's poems, argued against this but the critical preoccupation with Dickinson's biography as a means of reading her writing was problematic and controversial, fuelling public interest in her work and arguments about authorship. Glaspell was party to these disputes and incorporates them into the fabric of *Alison's House.* As Rodier documents, the play was produced in the context of a feud over the Dickinson estate, aspects of which intersect with Glaspell's dramatic biography. The story here is that Austin

Dickinson, the poet's brother and Todd's lover, had left her some land which caused a bitter dispute with Emily's sister, Lavinia Dickinson. This argument about public property became inextricably related to literary disputes about authorship, identity and ownership. Dickinson's niece Martha Dickinson Bianchi (daughter of Emily's brother and his wife Susan) published a volume of poems in 1914 (*The Single Hound*) and in 1924 brought out *The Life and Letters of Emily Dickinson* and co-edited *The Complete Poems* which, however, were not complete and were followed in 1929 by Bianchi's *Further Poems of Emily Dickinson*. Bianchi's work was extremely popular and reinforced the sentimental myth of unfulfilled love and romantic solitude. In 1929 and 1930 there was an explosion of books about the poet's life and work to mark her centenary. Although these accounts take issue with Bianci's 'inaccuracies' they remain, as Rodier documents, largely faithful to the Dickinson myth.

A number of critics have dismissed *Alison's House* somewhat simplistically as a dramatic biography which celebrates and reinforces the tragic drama of the reclusive genius.[40] However, the play is rather more complex than the early criticism suggests. Ted Stanhope, Alison's nephew is clearly linked to Bianchi, Dickinson's niece, although it is the journalist Richard Knowles who wants to mythologise Alison. The disputes about her use of a pseudonym for Dickinson are refuted by Rodier who suggests that Glaspell chose to fictionalise Alison as Emily:

> a playwright as scrupulous and inventive as Susan Glaspell would be unlikely to dedicate herself to a conventional interpretation of a best-selling tale, a connect-the-dots portrait of the Poet of Amherst. Glaspell's intensity may have derived from the demands of sorting a wealth of dramatic material then assimilating and personalising her own preferred texts, both written and oral, to forge an authentic identity for her poet.[41]

However, it is worth pausing to reflect on Glaspell's use of the format of dramatic biography. By using the persona of Alison, Glaspell is able to contest the myths of biography through the fictional framework of dramatic biography. The dramatic form provided Glaspell with a space to rehearse, or to play with, the textual production of subjectivity.

Dramatic biography was much favoured by English and American women playwrights during the 1920s and 1930s, the impetus for numerous plays recovering and celebrating female historical figureheads ranging from Mary Queen of Scots to the Brontës. Throughout this period, women playwrights often asserted ownership of women's history, positioning women centre stage as theatrical subjects. In *Alison's House*, critics have claimed that Emily Dickinson could not appear as 'herself', for Glaspell was denied permission by the Dickinson estate to use the poet's name or to quote from her work. Hence her appearance under a pseudonym, as Alison Stanhope; Glaspell can be seen to have worked the alleged non-cooperation of the estate into the play itself, by having her family debate, at the end of the play, whether to publish the poems they have discovered which may well tarnish Alison's moral reputation. However, Barbara Ozieblo contends that there is no evidence to support a copyright prohibition (although this was the case for other biographers of Dickinson) and argues convincingly that Glaspell was not 'obliged to changes the locale and the name by the Dickinson family'.[42]

In this play Glaspell explores the relations between the biographer and her subject and raises questions concerning the appropriation and representation of writers who are themselves reconstituted as literary artefacts in criticism and biography. The unease that is often generated by such textualisations of lives (or better still, 'literary lives') again seems closely connected to the Kristevan notion of abjection, in that the half-life of the subject of literary biography is marked by what John Lechte summarises as 'the ambiguous, the in-between, what defies boundaries, a composite resistant to unity'.[43] As in *Bernice*, the space of the dead female subject is the scene of various kinds of writing, as the other characters attempt to author Alison into identities which validate their own agendas: saint, maternal icon, writer. For Stanhope, Alison's brother, she is a saintly figure. He insists that her room should not be disturbed: 'it is to keep its – serenity, the one day it has left'.[44] Nevertheless he admits that 'it wasn't in peace Alison rested'.[45] Like his father, Eban, Stanhope's elder son idealises Alison, but as a maternal figure. He admires her career as a writer, and sees it in relation to his own thwarted creativity: 'I used to write things and show them to Alison',[46] he says, and confides to his father that he is searching for something beyond marriage and his family. Eban's sister, Elsa, has been described as a new woman, who represents an alternative version of Alison.[47] Whereas Alison sacrificed her relationship with her lover because he was married, Elsa subscribes to a radically different morality and lives with a man who has left his wife and children. As such, she is stigmatised by her family who speak of her with anger, regret and, in the case of Eban's wife Louise, scorn. Louise plays a similar role to Laura in *Bernice*, as a matriarchal, pragmatic and rather puritanical figure. According to Louise, 'they ... link

[Elsa] up with something queer about Alison';[48] she wants to bury Alison's memory because of its potential slur on the family.

Anyone familiar with Glaspell's biography will recognise the parallels with her own situation in marrying Jig Cook. Glaspell sympathetically explores this moral issue through various characters who confront a similar dilemma. In addition to the obvious correspondences between Glaspell, Alison and Elsa, there is Stanhope's admission that he had been tempted to pursue an extra-marital relationship but had remained faithful out of loyalty to his children; there are also hints that Eban feels similarly trapped by marriage. These various permutations of marital and extra-marital conflict and desire stage alternative versions of Glaspell's own life story, the might-have-beens, the paths not taken, as well as those that were.

The various responses of the characters to Alison's personal history, and the fight for ownership of her, provokes further reflection upon the relations between biography, autobiography and literary identity. Having been married to Cook, Glaspell found herself acting as his executor, responsible for his death and afterlife as an historical and literary figure. She edited a 1925 volume of his poetry, and in 1927 wrote her biography of him, *The Road to the Temple*. Cook, however, was a difficult subject for Glaspell to write about, given his alcoholism and his many infidelities. Makowsky writes of *The Road to the Temple* that 'Glaspell must come to terms with her role in Cook's life and his role in hers ... to achieve an appraisal sufficiently realistic yet sympathetic, to live without him, to live without him without dismissing her years with him as somehow mistaken.'[49] As a text which moves between biography and autobiography, it is also, Makowsky argues, marked by a generic indeterminacy which is, she suggests, characteristic of women's life writings: thus the disjunctive techniques of what she describes as 'composite auto/biography' in the *Road to the Temple* allow for a shifting and ambiguous relation between the biographer and her subject. I want to suggest that *Alison's House* works in much the same way. Glaspell uses Emily Dickinson as she had used Jig Cook, with the fictionalising of Emily as the absent Alison adding a further element of indeterminacy.

What differentiates *Alison's House* from the other three plays I have discussed is that Glaspell herself took no part in the first production, which was at the Civic Repertory Theatre in New York in December 1930. Thus there was no mediating figure onstage to be identified, in the manner previously discussed, with the author. However, Eva La Gallienne, director of the Civic Repertory Theatre and a close friend of

Glaspell, played Alison. In this play then, the director, the author of the performance text becomes the physical protagonist. Glaspell, moreover, is very much in the play, and not only in the various guises already identified. Her presence is inscribed in the specifically literary qualities of the text itself. *Alison's House* differs from its predecessors in the range, quality and extensiveness of its stage directions, and it is through these that Glaspell is able to function as a kind of omniscient, semi-novelistic narrator of the stage action. A number of the stage directions in this play might well be difficult to realise, as, for example, the description of Stanhope: '*one feels that he has a feeling for others that makes him tolerant, though firm*',[50] or when 'AGATHA *gets an idea, shrinks from it; it is terrible to her, but it grows, she faces it, and for a time she is aware of nothing else, does not move*.'[51] It is as if the stage directions have taken on a life of their own, have, as it were acquired a voice, a point of view – even a 'character'. It is this intrusive, judgemental, narrative voice which mediates between the stage world and the audience. For whatever reasons, Glaspell evidently concluded that her subsequent purposes as a writer would be better served by nurturing this voice in the medium of prose fiction rather than of theatre. She continued to work with the Federal Theatre Project but, after *Alison's House*, wrote no further plays.

Glaspell's subject, then, in *Alison's House* is a woman writer; the dead protagonist is herself an artist. In order to write, Virginia Woolf famously maintained, a woman needs a room of her own and Glaspell seems very much concerned with the personal space of her dead female subjects. In *Bernice* the characters are constantly referring to Bernice's room which is offstage and off limits – she lies dead in it. In *Alison's House* we are given access to the dead poet's room which is the setting for the last act. For the first two acts as in *Bernice* the room is defined as a presence in its absence. Alison's room is sacrosanct – a shrine to her memory. It is Alison's room that Richard Knowles has come to the house to see. Alison's niece, Elsa, returns from her long exile and asks to sleep in Alison's room. The room is associated with the secret in Alison's past so much so that Agatha, Alison's sister, sets fire to it in an endeavour to bury the evidence it contains. The room then, is a space which becomes a site of abjection; it is associated with the corpse, the ghost and the icon whose memory renders it untouchable.

Glaspell's absent female subjects are situated within and defined in terms of the concept of 'memory space' as described by Bachelard. In their discussion of this phenomenon in the theatre Holledge and Tompkins observe that 'one of the most important and recurrent personal and social spaces is the re-emergence of an imaginary perception of 'home', a place that may be accessible only by means of memory'.[52] For Glaspell's absent women, the stage space is a site for the acting out of memories, desires and a quest for redefinition; it is the space in which what is remembered is renegotiated. Fundamental to the thesis put forward by Holledge and Tompkins is the concept of the 'chora'. Developing Elizabeth Grosz's redefinition of the Kristevan Chora as 'an imaginary construction ... within the symbolic realm that is accessed by writers in their creation of imaginary worlds'[53] the authors find that the plays in their study

> achieve a type of *chora* for the playwrights who find in writing and producing theatre their elusive creative space. Each play constructs a memory space based on the playwrights' own lives: through these plays, *chora* becomes not just a physical location but also an equally tangible creativity manifest in the play itself ... Because *chora* is spatial but not restricted to the womb, it offers manifold ways of spatialising women and women's desires.[54]

Glaspell's physical presence as a body in the stage space adds a further layer of complexity. As Holledge and Tompkins observe 'while attendance at a theatre production generally involves an audience watching actors, both performers and audience are controlled by spatial sites of power which operate differently, depending on the type of theatre, its conventions, the performers, and the play'.[55] Glaspell's presence creates an unusual dynamic in which the conventional interplay of control and power in theatre is disrupted. The characters we expect to be present are missing, but the playwright is part of the cast and, to some extent, the narrative. Until, that is, *Alison's House*, when Glaspell remains offstage before her disappearance altogether as a playwright. *Alison's House* is the most obviously auto/biographical piece in which the space of writing is evoked physically and metaphorically through the staging.

I conclude by considering briefly the actual stage spaces defined by Glaspell, reflecting on how memory space is manifest on the real stage. Glaspell's sets are domestic interiors which, however, break the constraining naturalistic frame of conventional theatre staging. The illustration on the front of Bigsby's edition of her plays shows a 1917 production of *Trifles* at *The Theatre*. The blocking is odd and cumbersome but faithful to Glaspell's stage directions. An empty rocking chair dominates the set. The three male characters form a trio around it while the two women are huddled together upstage. The men are conversing with each other; they behave as if they are centre-stage but the rocking chair steals their limelight. The eye is also drawn to the shadowy, rather furtive women in the background. The space feels awkward, cluttered and disrupted. The whole stage picture conveys a sense of absence and loss; indeed, without a prior knowledge of the play it could be read as a funeral wake. In *The Outside*, Glaspell creates a set which refuses the closure of the fourth wall. This is a site specific piece: 'through the open door the sea also is seen. (The station is located on the outside shore of Cape Cod, at the point, near the tip of the Cape, where it makes that final curve which forms the Provincetown Harbor).'[56] Part of the memory space here, as I have explained, is a nostalgia for the Wharf theatre. Then we have the elaborate scene-setting for *Bernice*: 'The living-room of Bernice's house in the country. You feel yourself in the house of a woman you would like to know, a woman of sure and beautiful instincts, who lives simply.'[57] Is this Glaspell? She is there in the centre of the stage picture: 'Abbie, a middle-aged servant, is attending to the open fire.' Glaspell defines here a theatre space which is supposed to function as a memory: defining the identity of the woman to be remembered. She is far more specific about the details of atmosphere than she is about the staging itself. And finally there is *Alison's House*, a play about a house, its rooms, its memories. It is a play which self-reflexively explores the concept of memory space in the context of home and its intersection with the real space of the theatre and the metaphoric space of writing. And, as Cixous has it, 'To begin (writing, living) we must have death ... Writing is this effort not to obliterate the picture, not to forget.'[58]

Notes

1 Hélène Cixous, *Three Steps on the Ladder of Writing* (New York: Columbia University Press, 1993), p. 7.

2 See, in particular Jackie Czerepinski's analysis of *Bernice* and *Alison's House*. She argues that 'Glaspell's use of this device foregrounds ways of knowing and knowledge based on gender as it privileges absence and silence.' Czerepinski demonstrates how in *Trifles* 'truth' is revealed through female signifiers 'incomprehensible' to men and explores a similar 'gendered system of meaning' in *Bernice* and *Alison's House*'. In Linda Ben Zvi (ed.) *Susan Glaspell: Essays on her Theater and Fiction* (Ann Arbor: University of Michigan Press, 1995), pp. 145–55.

3 J. Ellen Gainor, *Susan Glaspell in Context* (Ann Arbor: Michigan University Press, 2001), p. 7.

4 Linda Anderson, *Autobiography* (London: Routledge, 2001), p. 14.

5 Paul John Eakin, *How our Lives become Stories* (Cornell: Cornell University Press,1999), p. 9.
6 Catherine Belsey, *Critical Practice* (London: Methuen, 1980), p. 68.
7 Ibid., p. 112.
8 Linda Ben Zvi, 'The Genesis of Susan Glaspell's Trifles', in Ben Zvi (ed.), *Susan Glaspell: Essays on her Theatre and Fiction* (Ann Arbor: University of Michigan Press, 1995), pp. 21–2.
9 Ibid., p. 22.
10 J. Ellen Gainor, *Susan Glaspell in Context*, p. 38.
11 Ibid., p. 40.
12 Susan Glaspell, *The Road to the Temple* (New York: Frederick A. Stopes Company, 1927), pp. 255–66.
13 Julie Holledge and Joanne Tompkins, *Women's Intercultural Performance* (London and New York: Routledge, 2000), p. 90.
14 Ibid., p. 98. See also Gaston Bachelard, *The Poetics of Space: The Classic Look at How We Experience Intimate Places* (Boston, MA: Beacon, 1994).
15 J. Ellen Gainor, *Glaspell in Context*, p. 55.
16 Ibid., p. 58.
17 Susan Glaspell, *The Outside*, in Christopher Bigsby (ed.), *Plays by Susan Glaspell* (Cambridge: Cambridge University Press, 1987), pp. 47–55. All subsequent citations are from this edition.
18 For a discussion of the staging of *The Outside* see J. Ellen Gainor, *Glaspell in Context*, pp. 75–6.
19 Susan Glaspell, *The Outside*, p. 49.
20 Cited in John Lechte, *Julia Kristeva* (London and New York: Routledge, 1990), p. 160.
21 Susan Glaspell, *The Outside*, p. 50.
22 Ibid., p. 53
23 Ibid., p. 51.
24 Julia Kristeva, 'Revolution in Poetic Language', in Toril Moi (ed.), *The Kristeva Reader* (Oxford: Blackwell, 1986), pp. 89–136, p. 121.
25 Christopher Bigsby (ed.), *Plays by Susan Glaspell*, p. 12.
26 Hélène Cixous, *Three Steps on the Ladder of Writing*, p. 10.
27 Susan Glaspell, *The Outside*, pp. 52–3.
28 Ibid., p. 51.
29 Veronica Makowsky, *Susan Glaspell's Century of American Women: A Critical Interpretation of her Work* (New York and Oxford: Oxford University Press, 1993), p. 81.
30 Julia Kristeva, 'Revolution in Poetic Language', in Toril Moi (ed.), *Reader*, p. 120.
31 J. Ellen Gainor, *Glaspell in Context*, p. 38.
32 Ibid., p. 77.
33 Ibid., p. 96.
34 Ibid., p. 102.

35 See Barbara Ozieblo, *Susan Glaspell: A Critical Biography* (Carolina: University of North Carolina Press, 2000).
36 Susan Glaspell, *Alison's House* (London and New York: Samuel French, 1930), p. 5.
37 Ibid., p. 239. Also see Katharine Rodier's excellent and detailed account of the parallels between Emily Dickinson and Alison Stanhope in 'Glaspell and Dickinson: Surveying the Premises of *Alison's House*', in Linda Ben Zvi (ed.), *Susan Glaspell: Essays on Her Theater and Fiction*, pp. 195–218.
38 Ibid., p. 209.
39 Klaus Lubbers, *Emily Dickinson The Critical Revolution* (Ann Arbor: University of Michigan Press, 1968), p. 198.
40 See Katharine Rodier's account of the critical reception, pp. 198–9, and Arthur Waterman, *Susan Glaspell* (Boston: Twayne, 1966).
41 Katherine Rodier, 'Glaspell and Dickinson: Surveying the Premises of *Alison's House*', p. 209.
42 See Barbara Ozieblo, who argues, 'According to the rumours that Glaspell fashioned her play around the life of Dickinson, she had been obliged to change the locale and the name by the Dickinson family. However, Dickinson's niece Martha Dickinson Bianci wrote to her Houghton Mifflin editor on 20 October 1930 saying, very much in passing, "I hear reports of a play built around her [Emily Dickinson] which is to be produced in New York (so I am told)." Bianchi does not appear to be angry or perturbed, and there is no evidence that she took action to stop the play.' (*Susan Glaspell: A Critical Biography*, p. 240).
43 John Lechte, *Julia Kristeva*, p. 160.
44 Susan Glaspell, *Alison's House*, p. 14.
45 Ibid., p. 23.
46 Ibid., p. 76.
47 See Anita Plath Helle, 'Re-presenting Women Writers', in Lynda Hart (ed.), *Making a Spectacle* (Ann Arbor: University of Michigan Press), p. 198.
48 Susan Glaspell, *Alison's House*, p. 13.
49 Veronica Makowsky, *Susan Glaspell*, p. 93.
50 Susan Glaspell, *Alison's House*, p. 11.
51 Ibid., pp. 27–8.
52 Julie Holledge and Joanne Tompkins, *Women's Intercultural Performance*, p. 99.
53 Ibid., p. 102
54 Ibid., pp. 105–6.
55 Ibid., p. 106.
56 Susan Glaspell, *The Outside*, p. 48.
57 Susan Glaspell, *Bernice* (London: Ernest Benn, 1924), p. 10.
58 Cixous, *Three Steps on The Ladder of Writing*, p. 7.

3

IMAG(IN)ING A LIFE: ADRIENNE KENNEDY'S *PEOPLE WHO LED TO MY PLAYS* AND *DEADLY TRIPLETS*

Elaine Aston

In an interview given in 1989, black American playwright Adrienne Kennedy asserts, 'I'm a black writer who is an Off-Broadway playwright. I'm comfortable with that.'[1] Later she confesses that the capacity for her theatre to make audiences 'uncomfortable' probably accounts for her not making it into the mainstream.[2]

What is 'uncomfortable' about Kennedy's theatre, which began with *Funnyhouse of a Negro* in 1964, is its capacity to present nightmarish, grotesquely beautiful images in an eloquent, and therefore all the more violent, visualisation and ritualisation of primarily (although not exclusively) black female survival in a white culture. In response to questions about her style of playwriting and to the question of influence, a questioning which intensified as Kennedy's plays found their way into North American theatre courses and women's studies programmes during the 1980s, Kennedy wrote her autobiography *People Who Led to My Plays.*[3] In the style of a photograph album with words, *People* offers a way of 'visualising' Kennedy's life; of seeing the social and cultural experiences which helped to shape the vision of her plays. It is not so much that the autobiography comes up with an answer to the question of influence but, as Elin Diamond argues, provides a context for the question.[4]

People has a timeline which extends from elementary school years, beginning in 1936, to Kennedy's return to New York in 1961 after a trip to Africa which provided the inspiration for her first plays *Funnyhouse of a Negro* (1964) and *The Owl Answers* (1965). *Deadly Triplets*, published after *People* in 1990, is concerned with a more limited time period: Kennedy's three-year stay in London from 1966 to 1969. Described on the book jacket as 'a surrealistic intertwining of mystery and autobiography' *Deadly Triplets* is no less experimental than *People*. The book, which mixes autobiographical sketches about the playwright in London in the late 1960s with a mystery novel set in the theatre, is a tantalising and complex fictionalising of the real and factualising of the fictional. Like *People*, through imag(in)ing different ways to write about life as a writer, *Deadly Triplets* poses a radical challenge to the conventions of autobiographical writing. Such an imag(in)ing draws primarily on what I shall term a visual style of writing: of working with and writing in images expressive of a subjectivity caught in a complex matrix of social and cultural factors. The personal emerges as a political and, I shall be arguing in this chapter, feminist landscape, intersecting with (and at the same time dissecting) identity, race, culture, gender and class. In brief, Kennedy is every bit as experimental in her autobiographical writing, the subject of this chapter, as she is in her theatre.

Whilst tackling the subject of 'reproduction and representation' in Kennedy's drama, Claudia Barnett notes that Kennedy 'was never embraced by the feminist movement':

> As she [Kennedy] writes about her characters' inabilities to coexist in true unions, she finds herself excluded from the very communities she might logically expect to join – African American writers, feminist writers, and the theatre world in general. Not surprisingly, she continues to draw characters who face the same exclusions she has met throughout her life.[5]

Exclusion is a key to understanding Kennedy's autobiographical writings: *People* recognises the negotiation of dominant social and cultural systems from a position of marginality that is raced, gendered and classed. *Deadly Triplets*, through a theatrical setting that invites a complex play of the 'real', treats the idea of cultural encounters of the alien kind.

To argue a feminist dynamic to Kennedy's autobiographical writing in *People*, I turn to Liz Stanley's theoretical framing of a feminist auto/biography proposed in *The Auto/biographical I*.[6] Stanley argues anti-spotlight, contingent and anti-realist approaches, combined with an attention to 'textually-located ideological practices' as characteristics of feminist autobiography.[7] She explains that this encourages writers to 'mix genres and conventions' and describes how 'fact and fiction, fantasy and reality, biography and autobiography, self and others, individuals and networks, not only co-exist but intermingle in ways that encourage, not merely permit, active readership'.[8] 'Active readership' is vital to Kennedy's writing and is one of the ways in which she opens up the horizon of autobiographical writing, creating, as I shall argue, a 'space' for the stories of her readers within the story/stories she tells.

People Who Led to My Plays

People Who Led to My Plays is perhaps best described as a scrapbook-styled volume of sketches and photographs. The design of the soft-back book cover suggests the appearance of a photograph album, with pretend corners and textured-look spine. On the cover a photograph of the author as a child is positioned above the signature of the adult. The signature suggests the possibility of authenticity: the writer authenticating her life. The photograph of the child, cut out and off from whatever else was in the original photograph, is framed by a rough border and mounted onto a surround of mottled red. The title, all in lower case letters, is set out down the left-hand side. The lettering of the title has the appearance of being unevenly typed: some characters are better defined than others and gaps are left between letters. 'People' fill the space close to the image of the child. But the mock-textured spaces around the child, volume title, and adult signature are also significant. Not everything can be remembered, explained, commented on or made sense of.

In *People* Kennedy writes 'sometimes I think I see life as like my mother's red scrapbook',[9] and explains that her editors very much wanted her book to resemble her mother's photograph album, hence the red cover.[10] A feminist psychoanalytical reading of *People* might argue the album project as a desire to return to the pre-Oedipal, or the pre-symbolic as Cixous describes it. And, in part, the fragmentation, imaging and white 'spaces' on the pages inside the book could be argued to support such an interpretation. But only in part, for *People* also bears the marks or scars of a social, symbolic order, which is raced, gendered and classed. Kennedy cannot, comfortably, 'write her self' into the realm of the 'feminine' Other, as Cixous commands of revolutionary woman,[11] and ultimately complicates or problematises the binarism of pre-symbolic and symbolic, by insisting on an autobiographical subject who constantly and ceaselessly traverses the two, while belonging to neither. I shall take up this point again in the discussion of *Deadly Triplets*. Troubling the Lacanian narrative through an insistence on seeing race as well as gender adds weight to bell hooks' declaration that: 'there could never be enough autobiographical writing by black women: we have so much to tell the world about our experience, about how we *see* [my emphasis] the world'.[12]

The anti-spotlight approach which Stanley argues is the 'baseline of a distinct feminist auto/biography' is one which not only moves away from the idea of a 'single unique subject', but is also one which takes in rather than leaves out the social context of the auto/biographical subject/s.[13] Kennedy's childhood images of family, relatives, friends and teachers present the complexities and contradictions of growing up in a poor immigrant neighbourhood, with the values of a middle-class black American culture.[14] As a title, *People Who Led to My Plays* places the other, or others, in the spotlight, rather than the self as author-subject. Kennedy has explained how her autobiography emerged from two experiences: a failed autobiography which she tried to write in her forties and the realisation that she wanted to recognise the 'people' who had been important in her formative years, in particular her parents and teachers.[15] The failure of an autobiographical methodology that takes the self as a point of departure – Kennedy was going to start with herself at age twenty-two and work backwards – and the need to recognise the centrality of 'others' in the formation of the autobiographical 'I' are both, therefore, important elements in Kennedy's approach to the autobiographical.

There is no realist storytelling structure to *People*. Like her playwriting, Kennedy's style of image-writing is distinctly anti-realist. Although there is a chronological ordering of material, as in conventional autobiographical and biographical writing, in which Kennedy traces her 'self' from childhood through to 1961, within this timeline there is no attempt to establish a continuous thread of 'telling'. She uses none of the conventional meaning-making strategies of autobiography. Events are not commented upon explained, or pulled together. Rather, Kennedy writes in fragmented, discontinuous moments of remembering. The white gaps on the page between the paragraphed, or, sometimes one-line memories, also 'speak' of what is not recalled. Her writing, therefore, points to the way in which remembering is always an incomplete activity, and autobiographical writing is always marked, haunted, by what is not written, or is written out.

Scattered among her word-based sketches are photographs of public famous figures and private snapshots of family and friends. All of these photographs she collected herself. She does not invite us to view these in a particular or hierarchical way. They are collaged into her fragments of writings without labels, captions, or explanations. There is no attempt at a Brechtian style of montage in which an image is used to index a very clear social or political point. And yet, Kennedy's own presentational style, through collaged words and images, is every bit as 'telling', for the way in which it sketches a biographical (individual) and socio-cultural (shared) history of white on black. Rather than divorce the individual from her social-cultural matrixing, Kennedy shows that she is very much a part and product of it, thereby offering, rather than concealing, as Stanley argues is the case in conventional autobiographies, a contingent viewpoint.

The way in which Kennedy image-writes the tension between the experience of marginality and the living within (desiring even) the mainstream has important implications for the spectator-reader. In *People* Kennedy writes, '*the people in my mother's red scrapbook*: I yearned to know them'.[16] The idea of a 'yearning' to know people is an insightful way of describing the activity of auto/biographical reading. A reading of *People*, for example, might be roughly characterised as a yearning to 'know' the writer: her life, plays and influences. Writing in sketches, touching on moments, which are visited and left without making connections, the reader begins to read in the gaps for her/himself. This may involve interpretation, imagining what might have happened next, or 'seeing' connections between a life event and an incident or character in one of Kennedy's plays (occasionally she makes these connections for us).

It is also a way of writing that invites or allows for our own personal, individual memories to come into play, thereby expanding the cultural memory-scape of Kennedy's collage through time, continents, nationalities, races, classes and gender. To give a brief example of how this works I want to return to the cover photograph of Kennedy as a young girl. When I first looked at this, my attention went straight to the eyes: they are so piercing, so direct in their gaze. Afterwards, however, what '*worked* within me' (and here I am referring to the way in which Barthes describes the effect of the *punctum*)[17] was the uneven, cutting-out of the figure. This is clearer when the photograph is reproduced inside the volume in the section on 'Elementary School', where it appears cut and pasted on a card or paper, with the inscription 'Bolton Kindergarten 1937' underneath in what appears to be a child's handwriting.[18] It is the trace or mark of the infant activity of cutting and pasting which touches and 'pricks' childhood memories of my own, and of my children; memories that might collectively be captioned 'scissor practice': memories of my own circulate in and among Kennedy's images and sketches.

The possibility for this kind of interplay arises from Kennedy's presentational style of visual writing, in which the 'real' arguably makes a more truthful appearance than within the representational. Where conventional autobiography might seek to persuade us that 'this is how things were', Kennedy 'authenticates' the past through a flow of images – images that 'just flooded out' and she committed to paper, rather than to explanation.[19] Kennedy's narrative is neither continuous, nor attitudinal: it neither takes us through a narrative without (apparently) leaving gaps, nor does the autobiographer invite us to take up a perspective or position in relation to a person, an event or an action. As spectator-readers we make sense out of what is put before us, and what surfaces from inside of us as the *punctum* of her 'dreamscape' takes effect. In brief, if *People*, as suggested earlier, provides the 'context' for rather than the answer to the question of influence,[20] to this I would add that it also provides a context for asking the same question of ourselves.

Identifying Kennedy's presentational style brings me back to Stanley's theoretical framing. Stanley's fourth element in her model for a feminist biography suggests a 'focus upon *textual* [my emphasis] practice, innovations which will encourage active reading'.[21] However, I would argue that 'textual' is too reductive a term. Kennedy's presentational style of visual writing, for example, invites us to consider a practice of autobiography which is not 'textual', but performative. Kennedy 'performs' her writing: words are not presented in a continuous line of written prose, but take up a (stage) space on the page. She 'speaks' in a language that is visual rather than textual: through images, through the juxtaposition of images and text, or through the white on the page. Such a performance practice is insightful to a modelling of feminist auto/biography for the ways in which it challenges the 'authentication' of a matrix of gender, class and race.

Kennedy's interrogative performance mode is one which is rooted in exclusion, or rather takes up an outsider's position in order to create a productive, critical 'gap', one in which social and cultural constructions of identity may be deconstructed. The way this works is through the juxtaposition of the adult writer and the child, or younger self. There is no attempt on Kennedy's part to 'become' or to take up the position of the child she once was. Rather, the way this works is similar to the adult-child playing to be found in Caryl Churchill's plays such as *Top Girls* or *Fen*. Adult-child playing permits the co-existence of adult and child; the marks of both are made visible. In this way, the child is a part of and apart from the adult world. This point is well illustrated by the moment in which Kennedy as a child sees, but cannot understand why a movie, or song can make an adult cry, and rationalises this by deciding that a movie must have 'a secret locked inside', a secret 'that caused "adults" to cry, to become quiet, to reminisce'.[22] The 'eye'/I, or vision of the child, shown (not told) by the adult (and this is an important distinction, because in the telling, the adult would try to explain what the child was saying or seeing) is a way of asking us to see differently. Hitler, then, is not introduced and discussed as fascist dictator, but as 'the person who caused a tower to be built in the school playground across the street from our house, a frightening orange steel structure ... that was surrounded by a jagged metal fence said to electrocute you if you touched it'.[23] The 'child' who presents us this image explodes the unifying dynamic of patriotism:

> My elementary school class (Italian, Jewish, Negro, Irish, Polish) every morning sang 'My Country 'Tis of Thee' and then we put our hands to our foreheads, stood facing the flag and said, 'I pledge allegiance to the flag of the United States of America and to the republic for which it stands.' Every morning for six years.[24]

The position of the child is also one that challenges the mimetic frame in other ways. The child does not accept the boundaries of the 'real': fictional characters or dead people can be as 'real' as the living. The first 'people' Kennedy introduces, for example, are '*People on Old Maid cards*';[25] the people in her mother's dreams, had often '"been dead for years"', but they appeared as 'real' as the living.[26] The technique of mimicry also questions the 'real'. Kennedy describes watching her young son Joe playing games in his cowboy suit, whereupon she observes that 'it engaged my imagination and provided a constant example of how real the unreal is. It was all a moving example of how people (from early childhood) naturally take on other identities'.[27] A number of the identities which Kennedy tries on are taken from a movie, a magazine or a book; from a childhood fascination with Charlotte Brontë's *Jane Eyre*, to an admiration for Elizabeth Taylor in *A Place in the Sun*: 'I asked the hairdresser to try to cut my hair like Taylor's', writes Kennedy. 'We all wanted a formal dress like the one she wore when she danced with Montgomery Clift. "He loved her so much," I'd think, "he murdered"'.[28] So much of Kennedy's social and cultural fascination with femininity is bound up in images of whiteness and, thinking specifically of Taylor and Brontë, for example, with a notion of Englishness (one more explicitly explored in *Deadly Triplets*). That said, there are exceptions: 'In the MGM movies as a "Negro" woman, [Lena Horne] was magical, romantic, a person of hypnotic glamour'.[29]

As the child becomes a young woman, the style of questioning changes: moves towards a more acute interrogation of the representational from the position of the 'real', but the critical 'gap' is still there. For example, as a young mother, who now finds she cries at the movies,[30]

Kennedy begins to question the contemporary social and cultural representation of young mothers as being 'in "the icebox years"'.[31] Dreams of writing, becoming a writer, becoming someone, collide on the page with the social invisibility she suffered in becoming a mother. Most telling of all is the silence which surrounds the birth, which has no description, is presented in an incomplete sentence, surrounded by white gaps on the page:[32] '*Our son Joe ... his birth:*'[33]

By challenging the mimetic frame of the 'real', performing identities, playing in the 'gap' between the representational and the self, Kennedy simultaneously constructs and deconstructs formations of social and cultural identity, 'fixing' and 'unfixing' the 'subject' which this produces. In this way, her autobiographical contestation of representational systems which 'fix' gender, race and class, connect up with those concerns that, in more recent years, have been 'troubling' gender critics such as Judith Butler.

Deadly Triplets

Kennedy could not find a way of saying what she wanted to say about her experiences during her three-year stay in London from 1966–69, so she put together her sketches of London life in the form of a theatre journal, and wrote a theatre mystery set in London to be published with it. In her preface Kennedy writes 'perhaps fiction in this form would finally capture the complexity of my feelings towards London'.[34] In 'imag(in)ing her three-year stay in an English landscape, writing in a mixed form of fiction and non-fiction, Kennedy questions a number of the assumed 'truths' and conventions of autobiographical writing, and centrally poses the question of whether writing fiction/s can bring us closer to the 'complexity' of the autobiographical 'real'.[35]

One might be tempted to argue that the formal play of *Deadly Triplets*, the crossing of fictional and autobiographical boundaries, constitutes an engagement with postmodernity, that has little if any connection with or relevance to feminism. However, like *People Who Led to my Plays*, *Deadly Triplets* is concerned with marginality; with the experience of exclusion. *Deadly Triplets* is arguably not so much a reflection on a postmodern condition, but, like *People*, explores the tension between the familiar and the alien; an American playwright negotiating English theatre. Kennedy's American writer-heroine, Suzanne Sand, is an Off-Broadway playwright whose play, *The Heart of Alain Delon*, has brought her recognition and, consequently, to England. *The Heart of Alain Delon*, however, treats the theme of an American being killed while abroad,[36] and the idea of another country as exotic but dangerous landscape is a central thematic in *Deadly Triplets*. Or, as Kennedy writes at the close of her journal: 'Despite the enchantment, there was a subplot to England that I couldn't perceive'.[37] Through Suzanne's fascination with Englishness, with English theatre, and the Royal Court specifically, which has held a special place in the history of English writing for the stage and the political landscape of new drama, Kennedy articulates her own 'enchantment' with, but ultimate alienation from a theatre and a cultural milieu which, in real life, she found both welcoming and excluding.[38]

'Suzanne, a lot is happening that I don't understand', says James Eyre (actor/hero) to Suzanne, a statement that might equally apply to Suzanne, who increasingly finds herself overtaken by, rather than in control of, events and people around her, and to the reader who has the vertiginous task of keeping pace with a text that is constantly shape-shifting between murder-mystery, gothic novel and romantic fiction. The writing/reading experience is one that mirrors Suzanne's insider/outsider position: inhabiting familiar structures that at the same time are made unfamiliar, alien. Uncertainty and foreboding are heightened through events and characters: what has or has not really happened; who is to be believed, who is not. Kennedy acknowledges Daphne Du Maurier's novella *Don't Look Now* as one of her favourite mysteries,[39] and her own writing, like that of the novella deals with trying to guess danger correctly – a task made difficult and, as is also the case in *Don't Look Now*, fatally impossible – through the inability to decide on what is real and what is imagined. Or, rather, Kennedy suggests that perhaps it is more truthful to acknowledge that it is impossible to know where one begins and another ends.

Deadly Triplets deals with a number of 'stories' which characters tell about other characters. In the space of three pages, Michael (villain) has told Suzanne that his brother James (hero) has accused his wife, Vicki, of poisoning him, and that James is trying to kill Vicki.[40] These eventually turn out to be complete fictions. Playing across gothic, romance and mystery pushes the writing towards the textual grotesque. *Deadly Triplets* increasingly reads like an out-of-control soap opera, as the reader is told of a stepsister that might have shot Suzanne's mother, or a long-lost sister spotted at the zoo.[41] Soap opera is a useful point of reference, because soaps (and I am thinking here specifically of British soaps such as *Eastenders* or *Brookside*, rather than a US soap like *Dallas*, located in an extra-ordinary social milieu), ask us to accept the most improbable behaviours and experiences of 'ordinary' characters. The difference with Kennedy's 'mystery-soap' is that it leaves out all the character-establishing devices, techniques of exposition and explanation, and time lag (soap characters have many episodes of ordinary life, before they get caught up again in the extraordinary). Instead the reader has to 'hop' rapidly from one unlikely event or story to another, without being sure which one is true. For example, at the close of her journal, Kennedy offers this description of the ending to the mystery:

> In the last part of my mystery story S., still trying to solve the circumstances surrounding J.'s death in Italy, accidentally stumbles upon the murderer, J.'s twin brother, in Yorkshire where he has hidden. She ends up sobbing out on the moors, because, although she visits him, she cannot get him to answer any of her questions. And has to be dragged sobbing back across the moors to the nearby cottage where she is staying with the British playwright, W., her only friend in England.[42]

The increasing use of melodramatic registers links to the inability to negotiate social and cultural environment. The landscapes Suzanne inhabits are often fictions. Out on the moors, for example, she takes on the appearance of a Brontë heroine. Indeed, Suzanne's life in England is arguably played out through fictions – film, literature, theatre. Figures from literature re-circulate in Kennedy's characters: her hero called James Eyre, a performer known as Anna Karenina. The description of Mrs Shirer's (Suzanne's mother) possible incarceration in a house reads like a melodramatic reinscription of a Brontë 'madwoman in the attic'. And the 'real' plays into the fictional: for example, mystery and journal detail the production of John Lennon's stage biography, *The Lennon Play: In His Own Write*; figures from London's theatre world in the late 1960s merge with Kennedy's fictional characters, and for Suzanne's London home, Kennedy used a description of the real house where she lived in Chalcot Crescent (also used for the filming of the *Avengers* television series).[43]

Structurally, the theatre mystery plays with the three-act organisation of classic-realist drama: an exposition, which sets up the mystery of Suzanne's adopted mother's death and her romantic attachment to James Eyre; a complication which involves the quest for knowledge of her mother and the death of Eyre, and a denouement which solves the mystery of James's death and reveals the hoax to convince Suzanne of events surrounding her adopted mother's death. The overall structure of *Deadly Triplets* is also tripartite in composition. The volume is presented in three parts in which the middle section, separating the mystery and the journal, is an inset of photographs entitled 'London'. Entry to the volume is, therefore, trifurcate: there are three possible, potential 'beginnings'. There is no single point of origin that may be said to be the 'true' beginning.[44]

Thematically, this is echoed in the theatre mystery through Suzanne's quest for her 'mother'. Mid-way through the mystery, she confesses to the realisation that the real reason behind her trip to England is to solve the mystery of her mother's death, or indeed, to be sure that she is actually dead. As someone whose sense of identity is bound up in identifying with others, with places, with fictions such as theatre, film or literature, questing the maternal body appears to offer a way out of a sense of exclusion or alienation, and instead offer a way of 'belonging' in the world. Quoting the Freudian line on the 'maternal body', and the idea of the Mother as the familiar, *Heimlich* landscape, Barthes writes in *Camera Lucida* that 'there is no other place of which one can say with so much certainty that one has already been there. Such then would be the essence of the landscape (chosen by desire): *Heimlich*, awakening in me the Mother (and never the disturbing mother)'.[45] For Suzanne, however, as a child adopted twice over, there is no knowing the landscape of the 'maternal body'; no return to a familiar, *Heimlich* landscape. London, the city that Suzanne knew from living there for three years as a child, is not one she 'penetrates', gets to know.

At this point, one can find a useful theoretical modelling for *Deadly Triplets* in Irigaray's notion of mimicry. Put simply: the feminine, displaced by the phallocentric structures of the symbolic, may, according to Irigaray, mime or overplay the position of other, of alien, as a challenge to those structures that constitute its very exclusion. Reading Irigaray through Butler – that is as not seeking to establish the feminine as 'maternal', 'alternative original', as is sometimes argued, but as offering a 'reinscription of the maternal ... through the paternal language itself',[46] is a way of framing Kennedy's displacement of a symbolic maternal in *Deadly Triplets*. This links to the earlier discussion of *People*, in a way that, I hope, elaborates on and makes clearer the narrative of displacement. Kennedy proposes no alternative feminine maternal and subjects the idea of 'origin' or the maternal symbolic 'home' to continual displacement. This is illustrated in the moment when Suzanne, seeking her mother, attends an avant-garde production of Mary Shelley's

Frankenstein in Amsterdam. The theatre is described as a 'disorientating' space. The production flashes up old classic film versions of *Frankenstein* centre stage. Frankenstein, the non-human offspring, in a space that is 'disorientating' and increasingly marked by violence (Mary Shelley has a twin sister who pretends to be her in order to murder her enemies), points towards the uncanny. But where the uncanny, in Freudian terms, contains the idea of a repressed origin, known, but forgotten, Kennedy suggests that the uncanny belongs only to a theatre space, a space of illusions; it is, like Frankenstein, 'birthed', produced through man-made technology. There are two points to pursue here: the question of illusion and the mark of violence – and usually the two appear together, are connected.

The idea of the double as a danger to identity (as staged in the *Frankenstein* production) is played out and over in the mystery on many different levels, though always with a view to highlighting the violence of the selfsame; of seeing the other only as self. For example, James is increasingly at risk, as his brother, Michael, takes over his role in the production of *Deadly Triplets. Deadly Triplets*, the production in which the brothers appear, and from which the mystery-journal, Du Maurier style, treats the idea of what is in the mind, having dangerous and deadly consequences. Haunted by the apparitions of three murdered nephews, the king loses his identity to each of the three triplets. What, in the theatre, begins as a staging of lost identity and violence, ends up, in 'real' life, as fratricide. The 'mastery of characterization',[47] for which Michael is praised in the theatre, has deadly consequences off-stage, where imperial mastery of characterisation requires the murder/death of the subject to be mastered.

For Suzanne, tracing her past can only be done via the representational, and the failure of representation to represent the 'real' is central to Kennedy's mystery story. *Deadly Triplets* is full of illusion-makers: people who mimic the 'real': actors, writers, Vogue models (who know how to 'make up' a face or to change appearance through plastic surgery), and photographers. In *Camera Lucida,* Barthes describes searching for a photograph (the frequently referenced 'Winter Garden' photograph) of his dead mother in which he could '*recognize*' her (his emphasis), and details his 'looking for the truth of the face I had loved'.[48] Photography in *Deadly Triplets* plays on the desire and danger of 'recognition', inventing 'truths' or realities, as Kennedy uses photographs as displacers of the 'real'. Moreover, where Barthes argued that 'the Photograph reproduces to infinity [what] has occurred only once',[49] photographs in *Deadly*

Triplets tend to break this 'rule': they frequently turn out to be photographs of something that never happened. For example, in trying to trace her mother, or what happened to her mother, Suzanne goes to a house in Brompton Road which is where she stayed as a child, but which now belongs to a photographer, John Sharples. Sharples offers Suzanne a photograph supposedly of herself and her mother. Suzanne has no photographs of herself before the time of her second adoption: has never seen a photograph of herself and her mother together.[50] Sharples 'stages' her lost past or identity through objects and photography. He shows her a trunk of objects which include a 'child's white organdy dress' and a photograph of her adopted sister,[51] and later sends her three photographs of 'a steel wheelchair, a very white nightgown, a pale green day bed with faded splotches that appeared to be blood'.[52] He 'writes' her past and her mother's past in photographs of objects that have nothing to do with the 'real'. All of this turns out to be a hoax, achieved through trick photography;[53] a miming of, performance of, desire for the Lacanian Other. But it is a desire that is as compelling as it is dangerous. On her Amsterdam trip, all the while that Suzanne is visiting the house (once private space), now turned museum (public space) of diarist, Anne Frank, she thinks repeatedly of Sharples. She climbs 'the steep stairs behind the cupboard door which led to the hidden annex ... of World War II photographs and scenes of war, starvation, and man's anger and cruelty', all the while thinking of Sharples, and haunted by the 'images of violence and vengefulness' from the *Frankenstein* production.[54]

Photographs repeatedly connect to danger. Allowing a photograph of yourself to be published, as Suzanne does, is a dangerous way of becoming known to others; of being appropriated by others. It is through the publication of her photograph,[55] and through releasing her biographical details to the *Standard* newspaper after she arrives in London that Suzanne gets caught up in the dangerous events that lead to James's death. In the final part of the mystery, Suzanne reflects 'that my desire to work on the Lennon Project and my desire to be interviewed by the press when I arrived in London had left me vulnerable and in some way perfect for some hidden elements behind James's death'.[56]

In *Deadly Triplets* Kennedy offers a photograph inset entitled 'London'. Initially the viewer is struck by the way in which it is presented in two parts. The first is a selection of photographs that are either of Adrienne, her two young sons, or their London home in Chalcot Crescent; the second consists of photographs of theatre memorabilia connected with Kennedy's work as a playwright. One straightforward and entirely appropriate feminist reading is to see the split between the mother/domestic and the playwright/public. More complexly, perhaps, is the way in which these photographs are also indicative of Kennedy's own representation or 'staging' of the 'real'. For example, the first page presents two photographs of her sons, Adam and Joe. In the journal, however, we read: 'unlike in my stories my son Joe was not always in London'.[57] The front book cover to *The Lennon Play* records Kennedy's authorship, alongside that of John Lennon and Victor Spinetti. Yet, both the mystery and the journal write about Kennedy's exclusion from the Lennon project, and Lennon's intervention to get her back on board. These photographs might, therefore, be described as imaging desires, rather than lived realities or actualities (though none the less 'real' for all that).

Of course, the cultural space for imag(in)ing the 'real' is the theatre. A poignant example of this is to be found when Suzanne, still on the trail of Sharples in Amsterdam, goes to Anna Karenina's performance of *Birds of Prey*. Karenina is a locus marked by the symbolic maternal (as her name suggests), while Karenina, performer of birds of prey, suggests the transformational desire of flight from human (maternal) form. However, Karenina is a performer, a maker of images, and outside of the theatre Suzanne cannot find her; she does not 'exist'.[58]

Karenina's metamorphosing body, from human into bird, which is a strong thematic in Kennedy's work,[59] is emblematic of Kennedy's text: the striving towards excess and grotesque that refuses to be contained or explained away. Suzanne notes that 'this evening too had a direct relationship to my life',[60] but the shape of events, as the theatre mystery makes clear, is only something which can be known retrospectively: only through looking back can we begin to make sense. That Suzanne makes a connection between herself 'and this savage experimental piece'[61] is important for the way in which it insists that the 'savagery' be acknowledged; be kept in, rather than left out. This point extends to the autobiographical.[62] Conventionally the 'savage' and the ugly gets written out or made safe. The element of risk for the autobiographer and for the reader is removed. *Deadly Triplets* on the other hand is dangerous and disorienting in its refusal to confirm an 'identity' – of form (mystery and journal), or of writer (the fictional Suzanne, collaged with the 'real' Adrienne Kennedy), or for the reader who has to find a way, or keep shifting between ways of knowing where she/he is in, or in relation to, the 'text'.

Where being black and female in a white culture is such a strong issue in Kennedy's playwriting and in *People*, the final point I wish to address in the space of this essay, is the way in which *Deadly Triplets* connects to race. Kennedy poses the question herself in the preface to *Deadly Triplets*:

> Over the years since 1969 I had often wondered why I had not wanted to write a screenplay about my life 'in London as a Black woman,' as the film producer had put it.
>
> My plays were filled with the intricacies of race in my life. Why had I refused? Was it because at that moment I had not wanted race to separate me from the Brontës, Wordsworth ... Tintern Abbey?[63]

In the course of the mystery-journal the question that is asked about race is not so much asked of Kennedy herself, but of the English setting for her mystery-journal. If Kennedy, via the personae of Suzanne, enters the mystery as exoticised 'other', with her 'auburn hair, dark golden skin' and look of an 'Ethiopian princess',[64] she exits as Kennedy, Black-American playwright, leaving England as a mystery she cannot solve. The decision to leave comes after her encounter with playwright David Mercer, who expresses surprise to see she is still in England, given the, by then, 'tumultuous racial and social scene in the U.S'.[65] Mercer describes England as a 'washout'. The suggestion of a 'washout', a lack of colour, is pertinent to the blindness to colour which typifies the Englishness Suzanne/Kennedy has encountered. 'Go back to India where you belong', screams a crazed old woman on the final page of the journal. 'Perhaps I should go home', writes Kennedy, 'And I did.'[66] This final invocation of home is not one of racialised belonging or non-belonging, but (potentially) heralds the possibility of contestation, and of becoming.

Notes

1 Adrienne Kennedy in Elin Diamond, 'An Interview with Adrienne Kennedy', *Studies in American Drama* 4, 1989, p. 151.
2 Ibid., p. 157.
3 Adrienne Kennedy, *People Who Led to My Plays* (New York: Theatre Communications Group, 1988).
4 Elin Diamond, 'An Interview with Adrienne Kennedy', p. 147.
5 Claudia Barnett, 'This Fundamental Challenge to Identity: Reproduction and Representation in the Drama of Adrienne Kennedy', *Theatre Journal* 48, 1996, pp. 148–9.
6 Liz Stanley, *The Auto/biographical I* (Manchester: Manchester University Press, 1992).
7 Ibid., p. 253.

8 Ibid., p. 247.
9 Adrienne Kennedy, *People Who Led to My Plays*, p. 91.
10 Elin Diamond, 'An Interview with Adrienne Kennedy', p. 148. Red was also the colour of Kennedy's own autograph book as a child. See Adrienne Kennedy, *People Who Led To My Plays*, p. 20.
11 Helene Cixous, 'The Laugh of the Medusa', in E. Marks and I. de Courtivron (eds), *New French Feminisms* (Harvester: Brighton, 1981), p. 245.
12 bell hooks, 'Critical Reflections: Adrienne Kennedy, the Writer, the Work', in P. K. Bryant-Jackson and L. M. Overbeck (eds), *Intersecting Boundaries* (Minneapolis: University of Minnesota Press, 1992), p. 184. hooks also writes: 'many of the critics writing on women's autobiography are white women (with exceptions), and few of them who are doing such work on women of color call attention to Kennedy' (p. 181).
13 Liz Stanley, *The Auto/biographical I*, p. 250.
14 Elin Diamond, 'An Interview with Adrienne Kennedy', p. 157. For further details of Kennedy's childhood background, see Werner Sollors, '*People Who Led to My Plays*: Adrienne Kennedy's Autobiography', in *Intersecting Boundaries*, pp. 13–20. This is a rather curious essay, in so far as it reads *People* back into a more conventional mode of the biographical.
15 Elin Diamond, 'An Interview with Adrienne Kennedy', p. 147.
16 Adrienne Kennedy, *People Who Led to My Plays*, p. 17.
17 Roland Barthes, *Camera Lucida: Reflections on Photography*, trans. Richard Howard (New York: Hill and Wang, 1981), p. 53.
18 Adrienne Kennedy, *People Who Led to My Plays*, p. 9.
19 Elin Diamond, 'An Interview with Adrienne Kennedy', p. 149.
20 Ibid., p. 147.
21 Liz Stanley, *The Auto/biographical I*, p. 255.
22 Adrienne Kennedy, *People Who Led to My Plays*, p. 12.
23 Ibid., pp. 27–8.
24 Ibid., p. 32.
25 Ibid., p. 3.
26 Ibid., p. 30.
27 Ibid., p. 92.
28 Ibid., p. 71.
29 Ibid., p. 61.
30 Ibid., p. 79.
31 Ibid., p. 82.
32 Kennedy's silence around the birth puts me in mind of British performance artist Bobby Baker's autobiographical show *Drawing on a Mother's Experience*, in which Baker's personal memories of becoming a mother are full of gaps and silences, for moments which are too painful to recall.
33 Adrienne Kennedy, *People Who Led to My Plays*, p. 79.
34 Adrienne Kennedy, *Deadly Triplets* (Minneapolis: University of Minnesota Press, 1990), p. vii.

35 In a volume dedicated to an exploration of the interplay of strands in Kennedy's work, *Intersecting Boundaries* rather curiously splits or fragments *Deadly Triplets* in the volume's bibliography where the journal part of *Deadly Triplets* is listed under 'autobiographical writing' and *Deadly Triplets* as a whole is listed under 'fiction' (p. 232).

36 This also puts me in mind of Caryl Churchill's play *Icecream* (1989), which explores the 'gap' between English and American cultures, and in which, for example, an English character gets killed in America because he looks the wrong way when crossing the road.

37 Adrienne Kennedy, *Deadly Triplets*, p. 124.

38 This is epitomised by Kennedy's initiation, inclusion and then exclusion from the creation of a dramatisation of John Lennon's biography.

39 Adrienne Kennedy, *Deadly Triplets*, p. vii.

40 Ibid., pp. 38–40.

41 Ibid., pp. 69–71.

42 Ibid., p. 119.

43 Ibid., p. 124.

44 In his insightful essay 'Locating Adrienne Kennedy: Prefacing the Subject', K. W. Benson prefaces his discussion of *Deadly Triplets* as 'The Double Scene' (*Intersecting Boundaries*, p. 120.). Although I agree with the way in which *Deadly Triplets* is replete with doubling devices, attention also needs to be given to the 'tripling' devices. My argument surrounding Kennedy's visual style of writing supports the 'London' photograph inset as a 'part' to this volume, hence, in contrast to other critics, I am arguing the volume as tri- rather than bi-furcate.

45 Roland Barthes, *Camera Lucida*, p. 40.

46 Judith Butler, *Bodies that Matter* (London: Routledge, 1993), p. 45.

47 Adrienne Kennedy, *Deadly Triplets*, p. 88.

48 Roland Barthes, *Camera Lucida*, pp. 65–7.

49 Ibid., p. 4.

50 Adrienne Kennedy, *Deadly Triplets*, p. 22.

51 Ibid., p. 19.

52 Ibid., p. 52.

53 Ibid., p. 80.

54 Ibid., p. 25. In *People* Kennedy writes about seeing the Broadway play, *Anne Frank*, and describes how she 'cried aloud in the theatre when the Germans came up the stairs to the annex. It was the evil of Hitler again' (p. 99). In a subsequent entry on Anne Frank she writes: 'Her life seemed a study in courage in adversity. I often thought of that attic in Amsterdam' (Adrienne Kennedy, *People Who Led to My Plays*, p. 102).

55 Suzanne is known to people when she arrives in London because her photograph had appeared in *Vogue* magazine, and Michael Eyre, who turns out to be responsible for James's murder, claims he recognised her from her photograph published in the *New York Times* (Adrienne Kennedy, *Deadly Triplets*, p. 37).

56 Adrienne Kennedy, *Deadly Triplets*, p. 76.
57 Ibid., p. 121.
58 In the sleepless nights which follow her trip to Amsterdam, Suzanne reads and re-reads Karenina's biography in the theatre programme: a biography about withholding identity, or rather the birds are said to express her identity (Adrienne Kennedy, *Deadly Triplets*, p. 45).
59 Karenina's interest in birds of prey, owls and vultures is one which Kennedy develops in her play *The Owl Answers*. In *People Who Led to My Plays* she describes being in Ghana and listening to the sounds of owls while confined to bed during a difficult pregnancy (p. 122).
60 Adrienne Kennedy, *Deadly Triplets*, p. 26.
61 Ibid., p. 27.
62 It is also relevant to Kennedy's playwriting. In her journal, Kennedy recollects a conversation with playwright Edward Albee in which she tried to withdraw *Funnyhouse of a Negro* from a workshopped production, arguing that it was 'too revealing', to which Albee replied 'a playwright is someone who lets his guts out on the stage and that's what you've done in this play' (Adrienne Kennedy, *Deadly Triplets*, p. 101).
63 Adrienne Kennedy, *Deadly Triplets*, p. viii.
64 Ibid., p. 7.
65 Ibid., p. 122.
66 Ibid., p. 124.

PART II

THE PROFESSIONAL/ CONFESSIONAL SELF

4

THE WAY TO THE WORLD: EMMA ROBINSON AND THE DILEMMAS OF IDENTITY

Susan Croft

In his *Recollections and Reflections*, published in 1872, the playwright James Robinson Planché writes about Benjamin Webster's production of Congreve's *The Way of the World* at the Haymarket, for which he was dramaturg:

> I shall never forget the astonishment of Macready at the announcement. 'My G-d! – why they're going to do The Way of the World' 'Yes; I have arranged it for them'. 'You! – why, what in heavens name have you done with Mrs Malfort?' 'Made a man of her'. And such was the fact. By simply changing 'Mrs.' into 'Mr.' I converted a most objectionable woman – the character had been a stumbling-block to the revival of the play – into a treacherous male friend, without omitting or altering an important line in the part; as the phrases which would not have been tolerated in these days from the lips of a female, became perfectly inoffensive when uttered by an unprincipled man of the world, and the plot was in no wise interfered with by the transformation.[1]

The problem lies with words written by a man, Congreve, but performed and spoken by a woman. The way the problem of an objectionable character and her offensive speech is resolved is by the 'transformation' of a woman into a man.

This chapter explores the playwriting career of nineteenth-century writer Emma Robinson and the various identities she presented in offering her work for production or publication. As Tracy C. Davis states: 'Paid public authorship might have been a taboo for women, but it was a taboo frequently breached and just as real and important in the subversion of its strictures as in its observances.'[2] Robinson was one of the many breachers of the taboo and the 'performances' through which she subverted its constraints are themselves strikingly theatrical. As the unacceptable, treacherous and unprincipled Mrs Malfort becomes the acceptable (unprincipled and treacherous) Mr Malfort, the unacceptable female author, Emma Robinson takes on a sequence of disguises or roles to speak publicly and be acceptable. These are of two main kinds: first, the published works which are wholly anonymous, thus no author given on the title page, or which refer to each other 'by the author of *Whitefriars*', which was her first novel, 'by the author of *Whitefriars* and *Caesar Borgia*', or, 'by the author of the prohibited comedy, *Richelieu in Love*'. These identities maintain anonymity, but retain marketability: a reader who has enjoyed *Whitefriars* will be encouraged to purchase *The Gold Worshippers* or *Owen Tudor*. The second set of disguises occurs in the Prologues and Prefaces that accompanied several of Robinson's published writings and in letters published elsewhere. Here she takes on and enacts quite developed authorial identities as a 'young Oxonian' and 'a cadet at Woolwich'. These are, in the first half of her career, invariably male and allow her to adopt outspoken rhetorical postures and to speak in a way that would have been unacceptable from a woman. A third set of identities relating to the ways in which she was represented by others, speculating on who the true author might be, such as a 'mathematical instrument maker', a 'bookseller' or 'the bookseller's daughter',[3] are not addressed in detail here, though she is prey to constant misattribution: a notice in the 'Books wanted' column of *Notes and Queries* 4 November 1865,[4] for example, attributes her second play, *The Revolt of Flanders*, to her father, Joseph Robinson. While women's writing generally has often attracted opprobrium, the position of women writing work for public performance by their own sex or by men has long been seen as particularly problematic. Numerous writers from the Restoration onwards, from Aphra Behn to Harriet Lee[5] and beyond, bear witness in the prologues or forewords to their printed plays to the hostility facing women playwrights or apologise for their temerity in writing in such a form, whether they accept or challenge such prejudice – still they write. Some protect themselves through asserting the distinction between the writing of plays and their performance for an audience. One example, Mrs Hoole, though she wrote plays for the young ladies of a Harrogate boarding school, is insistent in her complete resistance to any sort of public performance. In her published volume of 1810 she writes:

> that the young ladies for whom these little Dramas were written did *not* (and were never intended to) perform them in any way but for their own amusement and improvement during play hours and it is [therefore] presumed that they cannot be accused of exciting a spirit of vanity or love of exhibition; charges which certainly apply to entertainments of this kind when conducted in a public manner.[6]

If, she goes on to say, she had any inkling of the plays being performed before an audience and encouraging women to err from that simplicity and 'meek and quiet spirit' which in a woman is 'above all price', she would have suppressed the plays immediately. The anti-theatrical prejudice which runs through Western culture, as explored by Jonas Barish, has many roots: philosophical, psychological, social but, when combined with social strictures on their visibility and public speech, imposes particular strictures on women either as performers of unacceptable acts or as providers of unacceptable scripts for others' enactment. As Gay Gibson Cima writes: 'because women playwrights and critics were at least potentially more publicly exhibited and more closely associated with actresses than their literary counterparts in the novelistic trade, they faced unique challenges'.[7]

The mid-nineteenth century sees a decrease in women writing for the public stage, at least identifiably under their own or another female name, though there is an increase in output of dramatic poems and in writing for amateur theatricals, which are contexts that allow for the use of dramatic form without the exposure of the public stage. Part of the reason for this decrease is the undoubted movement of the stage downmarket with a concomitant increase in its disreputability for those, women in particular, involved in it. Tracy C. Davis, in *Actresses as Working Women*, quotes numerous examples of women's condemnation for their association with the theatre such as the anonymous actress who wrote in *The Era* in 1853: 'My father's aversion to all dramatic entertainments was very violent. Should he discover my connexion with them, his anger I knew would be inexorable.'[8] The movement towards sensationalist, popular fare – commercial melodramas, replete with special effects – was a phenomenon decried by members of the intelligentsia, many playwrights and a number of producers like Macready who tried to continue to support new playwriting or campaigned for the foundation of a national theatre, as did Planché. One initiative, important both as an attempt to sustain the National Drama and in the fact that it failed, was the competition organised by Benjamin Webster, manager of the Haymarket, who in 1843 announced a prize of £500 for the best modern comedy, illustrative in plot and character of British manners and customs. The committee unanimously chose out of 98 entries *'Quid pro Quo'; or the Day of the Dupes* by Mrs Catherine Gore, a satire on contemporary fads and fashions including private theatricals. Despite a strong cast, and the support of aristocratic and literary circles, the critics largely hated it; said Webster, 'None of the judges had ever supposed it could have been so egregious a failure'[9] and the audience, 'received it with uproar and ridicule'.[10] Ellen Donkin explores in detail the critical and public reaction to the piece (more contradictory than later reports like Pascoe's give credit for) but states that: 'The fact of Mrs Gore's being a woman left her open to charges related to vulgarity that would not likely have had any currency had she been male.'[11]

Thus a woman playwright ran the risk of the opprobrium attaching to female public speech and the role of playwright. If she wrote anonymously, her true identity might be discovered and badly received. Like all playwrights, she ran the risk of failure, but arguably public exposure of her work to 'uproar and ridicule' was a more damaging experience for a woman in a society which, increasingly in the nineteenth century, reinforced her confinement to the respectability of the private sphere, especially if the work was deemed to be immoral. There are many examples of a woman's self-exposure as a writer for performance being equated with sexual self-exposure: to cite but one, the mocking reference by Tate Wilkinson circa 1790, quoted at length in *Biographica Dramatica* in 1812, to actress/playwright Hannah Brand, notorious for her fear of her scripts being pirated to the extent that she made special copies for the prompter leaving out her own part. Wilkinson mocks her protectiveness of her scripts and conflates them with her body in an image which threatens the invasion of both: 'her breast works and all her works were well defended against all assailants ... Troy was not more impregnable within her walls'.[12] The anxiety he mocks had genuine grounds: while Brand seems to have been particularly strait-laced and apprehensive, accounts of actresses' careers such as that of Dora Jordan and those recounted by Tracy C. Davis, to cite but two, reinforce the reality of their vulnerability to sexual assault and to the assumption of their sexual availability.[13] Others like Elizabeth Polack are threatened with the consequences of their sexual non-availability: offered either protection by a man or the threat of spinsterhood by the critic identified only as 'Philo Dramaticus', whose words precede her play *St Clair of the Isles* in the Duncombe edition (1838). After a mocking review, which does however praise the play if not the production, he concludes by deciding that he had better mind his literary ps and qs in case 'Miss Polack meditates a change in her condition ... for husbands of literary ladies invariably carry stout walking sticks.' However, if she does not intend to marry she will be sorry and a few years hence will be moaning, 'Ah wretched virgin! – what shall be my fate? / With books in plenty – but without a mate.'[14] Similarly, writing for performance, unprotected by copyright until published, was especially vulnerable to piracy. But if the medium is in itself considered disreputable for a female author to practice, her reputation was also vulnerable. Publication of a novel – or a play – exhibited the author to judgement by the publisher and then by the critics. Production of a play exposed the author to the judgement of play-readers and management of the theatre or theatres, to that of performers and the rehearsal process, to that of the Examiner of Plays, to critics and to a possibly vociferous public; all of these potentially more hostile and threatening to a woman than a man, whether because her subject matter was judged unfeminine or because the act of writing for the public stage was itself judged unfeminine. In order to run this gauntlet successfully a woman playwright might take on a fictional identity as a man. Women writers in the nineteenth century and before, of course, frequently found the expression of their public voice through writing presented problems: they might be mocked, scorned, de-valued, generally condemned as unrespectable, so often they adopted pseudonyms. Famous examples include the Brontës who, as Currer, Ellis and Acton Bell, took on names which were ambiguous and non-gender-specific (though generally read as male by contemporaries) and George Eliot, who took a man's name, though while keeping the name, she did not maintain the disguise for long.[15] There are numerous lesser known examples including many who wrote as 'A Lady' and undoubtedly many others who have yet to be unmasked or who will never be uncovered.[16] For, as Sandra Gilbert and Susan Gubar point out, the issue of female writers impersonating males is in itself a vexed one and metaphorically wearing male costume 'proved to be as problematical if not as debilitating as any ... more modest and ladylike garments ... For a woman artist is, after all, a woman – that is her "problem" – and if she denies her own gender she inevitably confronts an identity crisis as severe as the anxiety of authorship she is trying to surmount.'[17] Writing for the stage, a space where the performance of identity, the imaginative assumption of several roles and dressing up in male – or female – costumes, is the central activity can be seen as at once liberating and potentially more dangerous. Christie Davies, citing social psychologist Erving Goffman's work on stigma, reinforces this:

> The theatre is attractive to the stigmatized and to those of uncertain identity because it offers a tolerant and amorphous refuge from an often hostile and rigidly structured and bounded world: it is tolerant and amorphous because it is the home of disguises ... Those with a stigma can take refuge in the view that they have the freedom to represent themselves as, or indeed to be, whatever they choose.[18]

However Davies does not deal with the consequences for the disguised, of discovery. While the sphere of performance provides a context where anxiety may be transformed into virtuosity, identity crisis into play, the dangers of detection, of being exposed in an unacceptable disguise, in a disreputable context, are enhanced. Emma Robinson expresses an awareness of the potential danger of discovery for female reputation when Anne of Austria in her play *Richelieu In Love* in response to the Duke of Buckingham's 'I fear nothing', replies: 'Very possibly: you are a man and may brave the world. I am unfortunately a woman, and must study looks as a slave his master's. You men can polish up your reputations like rusty swords; but women's, once breathed on, are dimmed forever, like flawed diamonds.'[19]

In 1844, *Richelieu In Love* was published anonymously by Henry Colburn of Great Marlborough St. It was supposed to have been performed in March of that year at the Haymarket Theatre and was dedicated to Benjamin Webster, the theatre manager, but when the piece was already in rehearsal the Lord Chamberlain's office suddenly intervened to stop the production as the play was said to be calculated 'to bring church and state into contempt'.[20] Like a number of other banned playwrights before and since, the author had the play published instead. Like a few others including Lady Eglantine Wallace in 1795, Miss E. M. Smith-Dampier in 1922, Marie Stopes in 1926 and M. C. Underwood in 1935,[21] the author used the opportunity to voice a fierce condemnation of the institution of dramatic censorship. There is a certain irony in the fact that in order to do so the author had, in effect, to censor herself. She could not speak as Emma Robinson and a woman, but, describing her/himself as a student of 'looks' or appearances, took on male identity. However, as has often been observed in more recent times – in South Africa under apartheid and pre-1989 Eastern Europe, for example,[22] and in the careers of women writers forced to 'speak in code' – the strategies and evasions adopted to avoid overt censorship and self-censorship can create particularly creative and striking work. Robinson's polemic against censorship is a bravura performance, full of rhetorical gesture, defending the work and the dramatist's freedom against those who would judge and condemn it, a parliamentary 'maiden' speech, castigating an outdated and iniquitous institution. In her preface Robinson presents herself as a young man, Eton- and Oxford-educated, addressing his fellows. He is eager and inexperienced 'young and daring',[23] an aspiring dramatist who even hopes to be original, to take drama in a new direction, only anxious in his 'paternal heart'[24] about the opinion of the

Pit about his creation. But he is a fledgling, about to be crushed by the heavy foot of the establishment. For in the eyes of the establishment, he is a danger, treasonous, in effect a terrorist. The innocent pleasures promised by his play are a lure to lead the unwary reader into 'those flowery meads in which my deadly weapons couch in ambush'. [25] The proper authorities have given notice, this is dangerous terrain: 'Steel traps and spring guns!'[26] and the unsuspecting reader has no right to believe themselves invulnerable: 'if you have ever so slight an idea of what is due to the powers that be, you must perceive the infinite impropriety of continuing whole and sound in contempt of court'.[27] For the protection of the public the young playwright must be stopped. In the eyes of the Lord Chamberlain, 'so deeply founded were the objections of the officials, that nothing but the total ruin of the drama could remove them'.[28] The young author, however, intends to conduct 'his' own defence, casting himself in the role of advocate (a role, of course, denied by the institution of the Lord Chamberlain's office, against which there was no right of appeal) to inveigh at length against the censorship of the 'literary Star Chamber ... the invisible but oracular bar at which [the play] was condemned and found guilty',[29] both to exonerate the play against wrongful condemnation and to attack the institution of censorship and defend himself against the stigma attached to such a ban and the assumption that it is likely to lead to among that 'numerous class ... too idle or too busy to form opinions of their own'[30] that the author must be guilty. Having taken on the strong male role of advocate herself, Robinson casts the Examiner of Plays as hyper-sensitive and in terms that suggest effeminacy. He is the timid sentinel of a powder magazine, in the unfortunate situation that he is terrified out of his wits by 'the lurid language of the passions, their lightning revealings':

> While others merely admire the splendour and beauty of the celestial flames ... With him, despair raves blasphemy, love murders licentiousness; Cato talks treason, Tiberius brings the government into contempt, Sejanus is an allusion to the minister of the day, the Gracchi mean to raise a tumult against the Corn Laws.[31]

While the role Robinson chooses to play is one of naïveté, the hapless and innocent young playwright, this was no doubt disingenuous. She, to revert to her female identity, maintains that she had approached her subject innocently, interested primarily in the love story of Charles and Henrietta Maria. If this was the case then her experiences gave her a political education fast and she refers to her/himself, the author, as 'hardened like steel in the fire he has been cast into'.[32] However Robinson is unlikely to have been as naïve as she presents her anonymous author as being. The decision to remain anonymous might suggest either an awareness that a public identity as a woman writer, perhaps especially a woman playwright, was controversial, or that her work might be deemed controversial, or both: the double jeopardy of a controversial play by a woman playwright. More pertinent however is the information that Robinson had been forewarned. Three years previously, in 1841, she had originally sent off her play to Covent Garden, then under the management of Madame Vestris. The theatre's reader at the time was J. R. Planché, then devoted to weeding through nearly two hundred plays and farces, 'without finding one I could consciously recommend', though he did enter into correspondence with the authors of three or four 'which had considerable literary merit'.[33] According to his *Recollections and Reflections*, 'One remarkable example occurred in the case of a three-act drama entitled "Richelieu" [*sic*], purporting to be the composition of a cadet at Woolwich, and which I felt convinced, notwithstanding the smartness of much of the dialogue and knowledge of dramatic effect displayed in its composition, could not hold its ground upon the stage, even it escaped the veto of the Licenser'.[34] The play was not, he makes clear, declined, but could not for this reason be accepted. Three years and several chapters later Planché reports receiving a further letter asking if he has forgotten 'a certain cadet of Woolwich who wrote a comedy which you once honoured with your praise'. The letter asks him to reply 'simply to "The Author of *Richelieu*, care of Mr. Colburn", for I am, by necessity, still anonymous, even to my publisher'. The author refers to enclosing a pamphlet, evidently the published version of the play, and asks Planché to confirm his receipt of 'the copy of this unhappy comedy, which I have directed to be forwarded to you'. Planché's anxieties about the Licenser's response to the play had proved true.[35]

So Robinson had, it appears, been warned about the likely response of the authorities. The play itself, which concerns the visit of young Charles I and the Duke of Buckingham to the French court where Charles woos Henrietta Maria, is remarkably outspoken and gives ample evidence of possible offence to the finer sensibilities of the time in a manner sometimes reminiscent of Shakespeare's *Henry IV Part 1*. In act 1 alone, Villiers and Prince Charles discuss the latter's cuckold-making, referring to 'Madam Eastcheap, my fair city conquest', tying on her garters, while Buckingham propositions Queen Anne of Austria, responding to her protest that they will be the object of gossip for being alone together, with 'then may we not as well eat the peach, as be whipped for it uneaten?' and, asked what headdress he likes best on a mistress, replies 'her nightcap'. When Charles, newly in love with Henrietta Maria, protests at his frivolity Buckingham replies ironically, 'Be not angered. I believe your damsel to be the most virtuous of – of court dames, whose virtues are proverbial'.[36] In her Preface Robinson maintains that 'If Shakspere [*sic*] himself had not flourished before "Examiners" were invented, the author is constrained to admit that he could not have flourished after'.[37] 'For which of Shakspere's masterpieces deem you Reader, would have escaped the blasting mildew of the licenser's red ink?', going on to identify where, on the basis of the political objections made to her own play, *Hamlet*, *Macbeth*, *Richard II*, *King John*, *Othello* and *Coriolanus* would have been unacceptable. 'Can any one doubt that Shakspere meant, by delineating those flagitious sovereigns, to bring royalty into hatred, *let alone* contempt',[38] mocking the Examiner's sensitivity – and perhaps also suggesting that the reader reread Shakespeare politically and learn indeed these lessons – the Examiner against whom she is inveighing is a crown appointee. She goes on to deal with *The Merry Wives of Windsor*: 'If you do license it you must at least expunge that old gross sensual satyr, that Falstaff!'[39] and *Twelfth Night* because it violates decorum for a woman to dress as a 'skirted page',[40] the thing that she, metaphorically and unbeknown to her then audience, is doing. The ribaldry and sexual latitude of her own play, especially had it been known to be the work of a young woman, were of the kind that provoked arguments for greater censorship and control of Shakespeare's influence throughout the nineteenth century and led to the publication of numerous bowdlerised texts including the one which gave the practice its name, Henrietta Maria Bowdler's *The Family Shakespeare* (1807), containing 'twenty of the most unexceptionable of Shakespeare's plays'.[41] Originally attributed to her brother Thomas, Bowdler's book was designed 'to be placed in the hands of both sexes' and 'to remove from the text every thing that could give just offence to a religious and virtuous mind'.[42] In his introduction to *The Boudoir Shakespeare* (1876) editor Henry Cundell specifically makes such concerns gendered:

> in printing these plays of Shakespeare, the editor has confined his labour, one of love entirely, to expunging such passages as, after the lapse of three centuries, might grate harshly on the ear, his aim being to strip the text of all that might wound a feminine sense of delicacy. It is hoped

> that the gentle reader will find nothing from which she may not with the safety of a pure blush of honour come off again, so on the other hand that the habitual robuster student of the Bard will miss none of the cakes and ale, so pleasantly insisted on by Sir Toby: in fine, the plays have been produced in the sincere belief that to the pure all things are pure.[43]

In the guise of a young man Robinson is able to defend Shakespeare where in such a cultural context for a young woman[44] even to have read him unexpurgated, much less understand him and use him as a model to write her own plays, was shocking.

Most of the first act of *Richelieu In Love* takes place at a masked ball, allowing flirtations to take place between Anne and Buckingham, while Richelieu looks on and attempts to intervene with barbed comments. The disguise allows sexual byplay, flirting with danger but with its immediate threat removed. Robinson's own disguise as a man might have protected her reputation in publishing such things, but no one could make such comments on stage in case they might be taken as a reflection on the contemporary court in Britain, while the life of Charles I was in any case, an unacceptable subject with its evocations of rebellion and regicide. The play, according to John Russell Stephens in his *The Censorship of English Drama 1824–1901*,[45] infringed a blanket ban on the subject during the first half of the nineteenth century – the same prohibition that Mary Russell Mitford had run foul of in 1825 – despite the fact that Robinson's play, unlike Mitford's *Charles the First* (1834), deals only with his early life, not his decapitation. It was only with the advent of a new Examiner of Plays, William Bodham Donne, who eventually licenced the performance of a much reduced (three acts rather than five) version of *Richelieu in Love* in October 1852 that this changed. So there are plenty of reasons to question the veracity of the pose of naïveté Robinson adopts. However if she pretended innocence falsely, her choice to do so is extremely effective, allowing her perform a role, rhetorically and strategically, which is highly forceful in expressing her condemnation of theatre censorship. Comparing the Examiner's authority to a despotic regime she continues: 'People in irresponsible authority exercise it with a graceful ease, a decision, a brevity, which must excite admiration in all who have not witnessed the administration of justice in Turkey ... Why should the Drama be the only species of literature still marked with the brand of slavery?'[46] and: 'Therefore, all you young Shaksperes who intend to repolish the mirror of humanity – for such the stage once was – take warning from my sad example, and turn Scotts instead'.[47]

A further possible reason to point to Robinson's performance as strategic suggests itself. Very little is known of her life. The brief details in Frederic Boase's *Modern English Biography* (Supplement, 1921) and my own version are pieced together from scattered accounts and from the title-pages of her own works. She does not seem to have left any autobiographical account. She was born in 1814, the daughter of a London bookseller, Joseph Robinson. It has thus far proved impossible to establish at what stage she became known as or made herself known to be Emma Robinson, though evidently this was known by 1862 when she was awarded a Civil List pension. She wrote about ten novels as well as two plays and one further partly dramatic work. She died on 18 December 1890 in Hanwell County Lunatic Asylum. However, Boase gives another piece of information: 'Her father for a long time kept her out of the proud position she had won as an author of historical novels, by not giving her name out as the author of them.'[48] He cites William Tinsley's *Random Recollections of an Old Publisher* (1900), where Tinsley discusses 'the propensity of people to own other people's work', citing as one example:

> A peculiar instance of not denying, if not really claiming, the authorship of a book was that of Mr Robinson, the father of the author of the novel called 'Whitefriars' and many other novels of the same historical kind. Miss Robinson, I think, wrote the novel without the knowledge of her father.
>
> Strange to say, Robinson for some years made a sort of mystery of the authorship and almost, if not quite, led people to believe that he himself was the author. Perhaps it is too much to say he claimed the authorship; but certainly for a long time he kept his child out of the proud position she had won as authoress, by not giving her name out as author in an unbiased way to the world.[49]

So, apart from her encounter with government authority, Emma Robinson was already familiar with the spectre of paternal authority and indeed literary authority, in the form of her father, the bookseller. Perhaps it is his authority too that she is attacking in the person of the Lord Chamberlain. Whether her father's objections to her public recognition stemmed from a desire to protect her from the social censure attaching to female authorship, his own disapproval of women's writing or envy of her abilities or a combination of the above, is also unknown, however the reason why she had to remain anonymous even to her publisher is reinforced. It seems a strong possibility that she first owned her real name after her father's death.[50]

Robinson's reasons for anonymity and her performance as a male may have a basis in subjection to paternal authority. However, while her writing acknowledges an awareness of the dangers of public exposure and the imputation of disreputability for a female, she does not endorse or necessarily accept the ideology of females as vulnerable creatures for whom the imputation of impropriety could be damning, who would therefore disguise their identity in order to protect themselves from direct attack. As Planché delicately states in *Recollections and Reflections*, in acknowledging receipt of the published copy of the play he 'hinted to the writer that I had some suspicions respecting the identity of my correspondent with any "Cadet at Woolwich"'. She lightly acknowledged his discovery: 'Your flattering distinction between my genus [i.e. gender] and my "genius", to use your word, cannot but reconcile me to the fact that you know it exists'.[51] Planché 'finds the lady'; the suggestion being that he guesses her identity because it's obvious that a woman who was going to be publicly outspoken in writing a play would be likely to do so in disguise where a male author could have owned his identity.[52] Apparently it happened quite often: when he first mentions reading *Richelieu In Love* at Covent Garden it is one of three works he finds by halfway stageable authors: 'an exceedingly poetical but utterly unactable play by Mr Atherstone, and a farce or two by a lady writing under the name of 'Bellone'.[53] Anonymous or pseudonymous women writers, it appears, crop up all the time. However Robinson's letter to Planché refuses any interpretation which might suggest that her anonymity is to afford herself protection from attack: 'I am not anxious that anyone who hears I am a lady in private should win a reputation for courage by abusing me as a gentleman in public. Not that the experiment would answer, for I am far more afraid of having too hot a champion than of wanting one. This is one of the reasons for my anonym.'[54]

That is, she is more afraid of her work being defended because it is by a lady and ladies need protection, than she is of its being attacked. She wants a fair hearing, not a patronising one for a lady author. This position is shared by other pseudonymous women playwrights like Katharine Bradley and Edith Cooper who wrote together as 'Michael Field' and explained to Robert Browning in a letter that, 'the report of lady authorship will dwarf and enfeeble our work ... We must be free as dramatists to work out in the open air of nature – exposed to her vicissitudes, witnessing her terrors: we cannot be stifled in drawing room conventionalities.'[55]

Examined more closely even the suggestion in *Richelieu* of the insubstantiality of female reputation, implying women's vulnerability and need for protection in Anne of Austria's statement, is problematic. The image of women's reputations once 'breathed on' as 'dimmed forever, like flawed diamonds'[56] is a complex one: the proximity of the insubstantial 'breath', also suggesting slanderous speech, and the substantial 'diamonds' suggests a value behind the superficiality of reputation that is either flawed or not flawed, but essentially invulnerable to breath. The rest of the letter, which Planché quotes in full, is also very interesting. Robinson maintains that she has no recollection of Planché's telling her that the Examiner would object to her play: 'until the precise moment he put his extinguisher on me, I had no idea that such a dignitary existed'. She also challenges Planché's protective attitude. He had said that he had not accepted the play because 'it could not hold its ground upon the stage, even it escaped the veto of the Licenser', though he had said it was actable. Robinson disputes that the then Licenser would have banned it and maintains that if it was actable it should have been staged: 'You will forgive the vanity of an author if I assure you that I do not think my play would have experienced any fate from which I should thank the "examiner" for a deliverance. When one considers what modern audiences receive with satisfaction – or at least, endure – I own I should not have felt much terror in submitting my Richelieu to their judgement.'[57]

She goes on to cite the positive response to the published play in evidence: 'What pleases me above all is, that women – women of the highest talents and station – are lavish in praise of my Queen, so she cannot be so very unladylike!'... and 'You are mistaken in thinking that I could not have borne the condemnation of the public better than that of the "examiner"'. It is interesting to note that after quoting this letter Planché writes: 'I had kept no copy of my letters, and could not, therefore, disprove the "lady's" (if she was a lady, for there is still some doubt of the fact) decided assertion.' Planché, the man of the theatre who had chivalrously and flatteringly prided himself on unmasking coy lady playwrights, remains rather unsure in this case – perhaps because she is so unladylike, failing to conform to his notions of female vulnerability. Indeed he goes on to try to define quite what was so objectionable about the play. It was not a question of specific lines which could have been cut, but there remained a tone: 'there would have been great difficulty in *disinfecting* the play of the objectionable atmosphere that pervaded it, and evidently impressed the examiner as unfavourably as it did me'.[58] The play is somehow diseased, contagious, its sentences infected, to use the image that Gilbert and Gubar borrow from Emily Dickinson and explore as a key trope in their exploration of dis/ease in the writing of nineteenth century women.[59] The problem is also somehow unnameable: 'It was the general tone of the work which jarred upon the sense, as undefinable as the objection of the schoolboy who did "not like Doctor Fell", although "The reason why he could not tell," and possibly for the same reason the licenser did not favour the public with his opinions'.[60]

When it was eventually performed in 1852, by now known publicly to be by a woman, the reviewer in the *Builder* also has problems in accepting this play as from a woman. Whether his objections to lack of warmth and feeling in playwrights were general, not just gendered, he certainly finds them a problem here, remarking that for a lady the play was, 'rather a bold one, and chiefly remarkable for terse and sparkling writing, but it is for the most part the sparkle of pounded ice – there is a want of warmth and feeling. Still the piece amuses.'[61]

For those women who did imbibe the ideological construct of the disreputability of the stage and of female outspokenness there was a clearly felt danger in being visibly associated with it, however this is also resisted, mocked and critiqued by others. While Robinson may have had personal reasons why she could not be seen to be a writer – a domineering (or an over-protective?) father and, like Anne of Austria, may have seen her best option in a male-dominated world as studying looks and appearing to be what is required, she does not accept the need for protection and indeed sees anonymity as the best way to avoid it. Her vigorous performance as the young Oxonian or the Cadet at Woolwich is also strategic, a way of entering the fray to fight on her own terms, not to be treated as a lady. She is, arguably, one of the would-be 'young Shaksperes who intend to repolish the mirror of humanity – for such the stage once was'[62] and she is indeed forced by the institution of stage censorship 'to turn Scott instead' and largely produces novels after this experience The problem of respectability, while it was a powerful ideological pressure and one which women like Henrietta Bowdler absolutely endorsed, must not be over-read as a concern of all nineteenth-century women. It is Planché who has to transform women into men, Mrs Malfort into Mr. Though Robinson went on to concentrate on novels she, however, continued to negotiate with the idea of public speech and silencing and also with those of what it might mean to be a nineteenth century Shakespeare, even a female Shakespeare. Her attempts at a playwriting career on the public stage were however not happy ones. Her next play, *The Revolt of Flanders*, was not produced, we are informed in the preface, because there had already been a production on the same topic in 1847, which was so unsuccessful that producers would not risk investing in a probable flop. Again Robinson published her play with a preface where she, again anonymously, claims that her piece had been in circulation for more than two years before the 1847 production of Sir Henry Taylor's *Philip van Artefelde* and suggests that her rival, Macready, may have had access to her own manuscript, thereby hinting at possible plagiarism.[63] Her very successful novel *Whitefriars* was adapted to the stage in 1850 by W. T. Townsend[64] with no attribution or permission given, as adaptations of novels were not covered by copyright law. Similarly, in February 1870 her novel *Which Wins, Love or Money?*(1862) provided the 'story, character, incidents and dialogue' of H. T. Craven's Globe Theatre production of *Philomel,* an ironic title in its evocation of another silenced female voice.[65] However, Robinson found indirect means to write drama and in her 1864 novel *Christmas at Old Court* 'by the author of *Richelieu in Love* &c &c' manages to create a hybrid form, imbedding two plays, with accounts of their fictional staging, in the text. The book is described in the *Athenaeum*'s review of 30 January 1864 as 'a collection of stories, poems and dramatic pieces set into a love story, the principal characters of which tell, sing, read, or act the tales, songs, and plays thus brought together', and opens as Georgiana Glanville writes to her 'particular friend' Verte-Verte, inviting the latter to spend her Christmas at Old Court – 'an ancient mansion, standing in the vicinity of Gloucester, and its well-stored cellar, haunted bedroom, hospitable proprietor, many guests, and efficient stud, containing all the appliances for country-house festivity ...' at a point when Georgiana '... is vacillating between 2 sentimental proposals'. The novel presents Robinson the author in a new hybrid identity, which suggests a complex of layered readings. The playwright, author of *Richelieu In Love,* is in effect hidden within the text of the novel. Her heroine, Verte, who significantly takes the authorial voice, narrating the events of the novel in the first person, together with the other characters dresses up in a farthingale to perform in the Christmas mummery. Both plays within the novel evoke themes of pretence and disguise: in the title of one, *Mistaken Identity* and in the presentation of the second one, *A Spanish Tale,* in a chapter headed 'The Shakspere Forgery'. The identification of the narrator Verte-Verte and the author, Emma Robinson, is reinforced by the naming (separately appended to the end of the poem) of the 'Epithalamium on the Marriage of their Royal Highnesses the Prince of Wales and Princess Alexandra of Denmark' which ends the novel as a work 'by the author of Whitefriars' [i.e. Robinson the historical novelist] while within the narrative it is described as being recited 'by its author', that is, by Verte, who appears dressed in 'the Grecian robes of Clio, the Muse of History'.[66] Verte therefore reads as a surrogate for Robinson, allowing the author to perform within the text. Reviews and the text identify this Epithalamium as having been spoken by Miss Avonia Jones at the Adelphi Theatre on the occasion of Princess Alexandra's marriage. The book opens with a dedication to Benjamin Webster, the champion of a national drama worthy of the Shakespearean tradition, praising 'thy life-long toils, though vain perchance,/ To bring back ENGLISH NATURE to the stage' and referring to the author's own youthful efforts in playwriting:

> And still would [I] fain the grateful task engage
> Could I yet deem as in my haughtier years
> Of couraged youth, I had a voice to reach,
> Like the old bards', so high, clear-starred spheres,
> Above the shingly murmours on Time's beach:
> What can I now?[67]

According to the novel, the play itself, *A Spanish Tale*, is supposed to be printed in an old black quarto pamphlet where it is described as 'an excellently new-conceited tragedy by Master William Shakspere' and said to have been enacted at Essex House in 1599.[68] However, rumour has it, we are informed, as being by Robert Greene (of which Verte is of course, a French, feminine version) and Verte herself identifies it is as being based on Cervantes but a forgery, a pointed layering of attribution and misattribution, where one author obscures another. The whole piece is contained within the narration of a woman dressed first in Elizabethan costume, then later as the Muse of History, a telling and highly suggestive metaphor for Robinson's own writerly guises and self-disguises, as would-be young Shakespeare, as historical novelist, as forger of Shakepeare, as Robert Greene, as Verte and all the other alter egos / surrogate authors in this text. Where her textual performance as the young Oxonian / cadet at Woolwich of the *Richelieu* preface was informed by the verve and gusto of a breeches role in Shakespeare, a Viola (whom she mentions) Rosalind or perhaps most pertinently Portia, but was necessarily not visible as a drag performance to the audience of the time, in her performance as the author/forger of the plays within *Christmas at Old Court* in a context in which her identity as a woman is also at play there is a sense of enjoyment of the slippage between gender and authorial identities which suggest the excitement of (textual) masquerade as explored by Lesley Ferris: 'the masquerade invited women to a social event in which their individual identity became submerged in a crowd, an "anonymous collectivity of masks"'.[69] Verte speculates on how the subject of *a Spanish Tale* would have been treated by 'a dramatist of that nobly audacious age, which dared to give the passions their true language, at every risk; but, even in the wildest aberrations of the choice of a subject, was almost always essentially moral and incorrupt', once again asserting the true blamelessness of the Shakespearean and other Elizabethan models against the powerful lobby of those who would condemn them as unladylike and unsuitable for a female readership, much less as models for female playwriting, or as calculated 'to bring church and state into contempt'. While now Robinson, by the enclosure of her identity in a series of Chinese boxes within the text, draws attention to her own distance, as a woman, from this Elizabethan time of freedom, as a writer and performer in the narrative she also experiments in 'forging' or imitating such a dramatic language, reinforcing, as she had done in the references to Shakespeare in the *Richelieu* introduction, her fantasy identification with and desire for these earlier playwrights from a time before overt censorship, a time of daring and freedom where the passions could be spoken without immorality and without self-censorship. This woman playwright, silenced by censorship, piracy, parental and societal disapproval and the need for an unpatronising hearing, prevented from speaking out in her own voice, finds through self-transformation and by enacting within the text a variety of versions of the role of playwright, a liberating possibility, a voice and a way to the world.

This piece is dedicated to Freya Croft Beringer (born 15 January 2004) with thanks for patience during the editing process!

Notes

See also Jonas Barish, *The Anti-Theatrical Prejudice* (Berkeley: University of California Press, 1981).

1 James Robinson Planché, *Recollections and Reflections: New and Revised Edition* [original edition 1872] (London: Sampson, Low, Marston & Co., 1901), p. 282.

2 Tracy C. Davis, 'The Sociable Playwright and Representative Citizen', in Tracy C. Davis and Ellen Donkin (eds), *Women and Playwriting in Nineteenth Century Britain* (Cambridge University Press, 1999), p. 20.

3 James Robinson Planché, *Recollections and Reflections*, p. 310.

4 *Notes and Queries* 4 Nov 1865, p. 382.

5 Behn's Epistle preceding *The Dutch Lover* (1672) is a scathing indictment of male prejudice against women playwrights. See: *Selected Writings of the Ingenious Mrs. Aphra Behn* (New York: Grove Press, 1950), pp. 119–24. By

contrast Lee, in her preface to *The New Peerage* (1787), expresses her apprehensions as a woman in committing her drama to the press when her sex precludes her 'from the Deep Observation, which gives Strength to Character, or Poignancy to Expression' (p. 3). See also Harriet Lee, *The New Peerage Or Our Eyes May Deceive Us* (Dublin: P. Wogan, 1787).

6 Mrs Barbara Hoole, *Little Dramas for Young People on Subjects Taken from English History* (London: Longman, Hurst, Rees and Orme, 1810), p. vi.

7 Gay Gibson Cima, '"To be public as a genius and private as a woman": The Critical Framing of Nineteenth Century British Women Playwrights', in Tracy C. Davis and Ellen Donkin, *Women and Playwriting*, pp. 35–53.

8 'Genuine Gossip by an Old Actress', *Era*, January 1883, pp. 9–10, quoted in Tracy C. Davis, *Actresses as Working Women* (London: Routledge 1991), pp. 72–3.

9 Webster's farewell address for 1843–44 season, quoted in C. E. Pascoe, *The Dramatic List (Our Actors and Actresses)* [second enlarged edition] (London: David Brogue, 1880), pp. 375–6.

10 C. E. Pascoe, *The Dramatic List*, p. 375.

11 Ellen Donkin, 'Mrs Gore gives tit for tat', in Tracy C. Davis and Ellen Donkin, *Women and Playwriting*, pp. 54–74, pp. 62–3.

12 David Baker, Isaac Erskine Reed and Stephen Jones Stephen (eds), *Biographica Dramatica or a Companion to the Playhouse containing Historical and Critical Memoirs and Original Anecdotes of British and Irish Dramatic Writers…*, 4 vols (London: Longman, 1812), p. 61.

13 See Claire Tomalin, *Mrs Jordan's Profession: The Story of a Great Actress and a Future King* (London: Viking, 1994).

14 Elizabeth Polack, *St Clair of the Isles* (London: Duncombe, 1838), p. 6.

15 Indeed by the late nineteenth century so many women writers were using the name George (for example George Fleming, pseudonym of Julia Constance Fletcher, George Paston, pseudonym of Emily Morse Symonds, George Egerton, pseudonym of Mary Chavelita Dunne, George Daring, pseudonym of Madame Raoul Duval, George Villars, pseudonym of Mrs Randolph Clay), frequently in tribute to George Eliot and/or George Sand, that it was often assumed to designate a female. See Max Beerbohm, 'A Georgian Play', a model of patronising misogyny in criticism, where he discusses the misfortune of men baptised George who 'must either shed the name or be forever dimly associated with womanhood', in Max Beerbohm, *Last Theatres* (London: Rupert Hart-Davis, 1970), p. 80.

16 See Susan Croft, 'A Lost Australian Playwright: "A Lady, c1850"', *Australasian Drama Studies*, April 1996, pp. 99–105, p. 100, for discussion of the numbers of women playwrights using 'A Lady' and similar pseudonyms between 1755 and and 1850. See also Alice Kahler Marshall, *Pen Names of Women Writers* (Camp Hill, PA: The Alice Marshall Collection, 1985). My own research identifies at least 46 women in Britain, publishing or producing plays under a pseudonym between 1837 and 1914 (some known at the time, some discovered since). There are sure to be more women undiscovered among the unknown authors

of the many pages of plays listed in Allardyce Nicoll, *A History of Late Nineteenth Century Drama 1850–1900* (Cambridge: Cambridge University Press, 1946), pp. 638–772. See also Gaye Tuchman with Nina E. Fortin, *Edging women out. Victorian novelists, publishers and social change* (London: Routledge, 1989).

17 Sandra Gilbert and Susan Gubar, *The Madwoman in the Attic: The Woman Writer and the Nineteenth Century Literary Imagination* (New Haven: Yale University Press, 1979), pp. 65–6.

18 Christie Davies, 'Stigma, Uncertain Identity, Disguise', in Efrat Tseëlon (ed.), *Masquerade and Identities: Essays on Gender, Sexuality and Marginality* (London and New York: Routledge, 2001), pp. 38–53, p. 44.

19 Emma Robinson, *The Prohibited Comedy: Richelieu in Love or the Youth of Charles I: An Historical Comedy by the Author of Whitefriars* (London: Charles Westerton, 1852), p. 12.

20 Ibid., p. xi.

21 Lady Eglantine Wallace, *The Whim: A Comedy in Three Acts* (Margate: W. Epps, 1795), Miss E. M. Smith-Dampier, *The Queen's Minister: An Historical Play in Four Acts and an Epilogue* (London: Andrew Melrose, 1922), Marie Stopes, *A Banned Play: Vectia, and a Preface on the Censorship* (London: J. Bale & Co., 1926) and M. C. Underwood, *The Girl from Crawley's: A Comedy of Character in Action etc.* (London: Phipps-Walker and Fuller, 1935).

22 See, for example, 'Censorship and Self-censorship', in Anna Kay France (ed.), *First International Women Playwrights Conference Papers* (London and Metuchen, NJ: Scarecrow Press, 1993), pp. 139–46. This panel discussion included speakers from Australia, Brazil, Denmark, Italy, South Africa, Sweden and the US.

23 Emma Robinson, *The Prohibited Comedy*, p. xi.

24 Ibid., p. vi.

25 Ibid., p. xiv.

26 Ibid. p. xiv.

27 Ibid., p. xv.

28 Ibid., p. xxi.

29 Ibid., p. xi.

30 Ibid., p. v.

31 Ibid., p. xxii.

32 Ibid., p. xxiii.

33 James Robinson Planché, *Recollections and Reflections*, pp. 41–2.

34 Ibid., p. 42.

35 Ibid., pp. 96–103 .

36 Emma Robinson, *The Prohibited Comedy*, pp. 1–12.

37 Ibid., p. xxiii.

38 Ibid., p. xxiv.

39 Ibid., p. xxv.

40 Ibid.

41 Ibid.; Thomas Bowdler, *The Family Shakespeare* (Bath: R. Cruttwell for J. Hatchard, 1807), p. vii.
42 Ibid., p. viii.
43 Henry Cundell, *The Boudoir Shakespeare* (London: Sampson, Low and Co., 1876), pp. 3–4.
44 Emma Robinson was thirty in 1844.
45 John Russell Stephens, *The Censorship of English Drama 1824–1901* (Cambridge: Cambridge University Press, 1980), pp. 48–50.
46 Emma Robinson, *The Prohibited Comedy*, p. xxi.
47 Ibid., p. xvi.
48 Frederic Boase, *Modern English Biography* [Vol. VI, L–Z Supplement to Volume III, 1921] (London: Frank Cass & Co., 1965), p. 486.
49 William Tinsley, *Random Recollections of an Old Publisher* (London: Simpkin, Marshall and Co., 1900), pp. 92–3. Boase quotes Tinsley as citing a further source in an essay by Andrew Halliday called 'The Author of Blue Blazes', dealing with 'Mr R's peculiar treatment of his daughter', which Tinsley remembers as having been published in *Household Words*, the magazine edited by Charles Dickens from 1850–59 (pp. 92–3). However, searches through *Household Words* and its successor *All the Year Round* have failed to trace it.
50 Certainly by 1852 she was known to be a woman. *Builder*, 6 November 1852, p. 709, quoted in Tracy C. Davis, 'The Sociable Playwright and Representative Citizen', p. 29.
51 James Robinson Planché, *Recollections and Reflections*, p. 98.
52 Planché is not the only male critic to believe he can find the (hidden) ladies; see Max Beerbohm in *Last Theatres*: 'Two or three pages of a book, two or three scenes of a play, suffice to determine the author's sex', p. 80.
53 Planché instances them as 'some of the other meagre grains of wheat in the bushels of chaff forwarded by untried authors to the new management of Covent Garden' (*Recollections and Reflections*, p. 267). Planché does not specify how he knew that Bellone was a lady and at this earlier point he does not appear to doubt that the cadet at Woolwich is who and what he says. It is interesting to note the military associations of both women playwrights' assumed names underlying the sense that a woman metaphorically entered a battlefield in presenting her play for public judgement. Hannah Brand too is represented by Wilkinson as a city defending itself against a siege.
54 James Robinson Planché, *Recollections and Reflections*, p. 98.
55 Angela Leighton, *Victorian Women Poets: Writing Against the Heart* (Hemel Hempstead: Harvester Wheatsheaf, 1992), quoted in Viv Gardner, 'Women and Writing at the Fin de siecle', in Marion Shaw, *Women and Writing* (London: Prentice Hall, 1998), p. 183.
56 Emma Robinson, *The Prohibited Comedy*, p. 12
57 James Robinson Planché, *Recollections and Reflections*, pp. 97–102.
58 Ibid, pp. 102–4. Emphasis added.

59 Sandra Gilbert and Susan Gubar, *The Madwoman in the Attic*; see chapter 2.
60 James Robinson Planché, *Recollections and Reflections*, p. 104.
61 *Builder*, 6 November 1852, p. 709. Quoted in Tracy C. Davis, 'The Sociable Playwright and Representative Citizen', p. 29.
62 Emma Robinson, *The Prohibited Comedy*, p. xvi.
63 Emma Robinson, *The Revolt of Flanders: An Historical Tragedy in Five Acts and Verse by the Author of the 'prohibited' Comedy Richelieu in Love* (London: Henry Colburn, 1848), pp. iii–v.
64 The dramatisation is published in Lacy's series of plays, vol. 40
65 According to the entry in Frederic Boase, *Modern English Biography*, p. 486.
66 Emma Robinson, *Christmas at Old Court 'by the author of Richelieu in Love'* (London: Richard Bentley, 1864), pp. 462–3.
67 Ibid., p. iii.
68 Ibid., p. 154.
69 Lesley Ferris, *Acting Women: Images of Women in Theatre* (London: Macmillan, 1990), p. 153. Also see Judith Butler, *Gender Trouble: Feminism and the Subversion of Identity* (London: Routledge, 1990). Note Butler's 'gender parody [that] reveals that the original identity … is a production which in effect … postures as an imitation. This perpetual displacement constitutes a fluidity of identities that suggests an openness to resignification and recontextualization' (p. 138).

5

LENA ASHWELL AND AUTO/BIOGRAPHICAL NEGOTIATIONS OF THE PROFESSIONAL SELF

Maggie B. Gale

> One's early experiences are so far away that it is as though the story is about someone whom one has known and liked. But as one comes to the present it is not so simple to be impersonal; trying to lay bare one's present aspirations and thoughts feels too much like wearing one's heart upon one's sleeve for 'daws to peck at. (Lena Ashwell)[1]

In her autobiographical writings Lena Ashwell frequently distinguishes between her past – devoted to making theatre – and her present, in the case of *Myself A Player*, a spiritually driven journey inspired by her own beliefs and her following of a guru figure who also inspired a number of other Fabian women. Whilst her writing about her professional theatre work is dense and detailed, the way in which she inserts her autobiographical 'I' into the present, the moment of writing, is sometimes poetic but more often vague: these were the details she clearly did not wish the ''daws' to peck at'. This chapter examines the ways in which Ashwell autobiographically negotiates her professional self – where she consciously foregrounds the professional over the personal – and places her own negotiations alongside the ways in which others have historicised her career. Although Ashwell did not lay open her later life to interrogation she was cannily aware not to miss the opportunity to insert herself and her career into a history of English theatre, a history largely written and inhabited by men at the point at which she found herself looking autobiographically back on her own contributions: she appeared to be very aware that actual achievements, especially those of a late Victorian/Edwardian woman, did not guarantee her a place in theatre history.

Born in 1872, Ashwell had a long career in theatre stretching from the 1890s through to the late 1920s and beyond. Coming from a non-theatrical background and being educated set her apart from many of the actresses of the day. She rose to the position of leading lady within ten years of her stage

5 Lena Ashwell as Leah in *Leah Kleschna*.

debut in 1891, often playing troubled heroines or fallen women such as Felicia Hindmarsh in *Mrs Dane's Defence* (1900) and the female leads in *Leah Kleschna* (1905), *The Shulamite* (1906) and *Madame X* (1909). She worked with many of the innovative theatre figures of the day such as George Bernard Shaw, as well as those more steeped in the traditions of the late nineteenth century – Irving and Tree. During the Edwardian period she went into theatre management, most famously at the Kingsway Theatre near Drury Lane. During the same period she was involved in the suffrage movement in general and in the work of the Actresses' Franchise League in particular. The outbreak of war saw her founding of the Women's Emergency Corps and her organising of and performing in concerts for the troops, initially in France but eventually as far afield as Egypt. After the war Ashwell turned her experiences to use in the organisation of theatre outside of the West End and the mainstream. The Lena Ashwell Players/Once-a-Week Players worked with the London Boroughs and at the Century Theatre in Notting Hill surviving until the late 1920s. In her later years she was devoted to the teachings of James Porter Mills and to the promotion of the campaign for Moral Re-armament. Having been granted a divorce from her first husband on the grounds of mistreatment, she remarried the Harley Street surgeon, Sir Henry Simson in 1908. Ashwell had one adopted daughter, received the O.B.E. after the 1914–18 war and died in 1957.

Thus runs a narrative of a theatrical life and most of this information is well known to any theatre historian with a general interest in women's theatre work and a particular interest in Edwardian theatre. In reconfigurations of theatre history, Ashwell probably fares better than many of her female contemporaries but as one of a handful of actresses considered by Bernard Shaw to have 'awakeningly truthful minds as well as engaging personalities',[2] she remains a figure of theatrical significance inadequately reevaluated.[3] Ashwell was what we might call today an active 'mover and shaker' – pioneering independently produced theatre in a theatre economy which was fast becoming dominated by commercial managements, promoting new writing and encouraging the use of extended rather than production-based contracts. After a successful

6 Concerts for the troops.

career playing 'troubled' women, she capitalised on her fame to bring legitimate theatre to the London Boroughs on an informally subsidised basis. There are various essays and chapters which attest to her contributions to the Edwardian theatre or the ways in which her work influenced her contemporaries, although, considering what she did, when she did it and why, there remains remarkably little about her work.[4]

A woman with a discernable and long lasting public profile, Ashwell wrote four books: *Modern Troubadours*, *Reflections on Shakespeare*, *The Stage* and *Myself A Player*, each of which contains strongly autobiographical elements.[5] She also wrote newspaper articles, gave speeches, toured lectures and created other forms of written documentation detailing her experiences as a professional theatre worker and her thoughts about the function and purpose of theatre as part of a process of cultural formation. Liz Shafer has suggested that the writing of so many semi-autobiographical books might be construed as 'strenuous self-advocacy',[6] but lists only three of Ashwell's works, missing out *The Stage*, which is important for the way in which it documents Ashwell's ideas about acting, directing, and the relationship between theatre, culture and the community. Perhaps such a quantity of self-authored, self-reflexive material indicates a desire for self-advocacy: many actresses of her generation only wrote one autobiography and many of these contain little about their professional activities. Ashwell was *more* than an actress of her generation however, and her books bear witness to the fact that she was a theorist as well as a practitioner, that she was a manager and business woman as well as an actress and an idealist. Only one of the three books, *Myself a Player,* was marketed as autobiography and includes the standard division of chapters between early life, middle years and the climb to fame and later years of recapitulation and looking back over life. However, all three contain the autobiographical 'I' where the 'shifting boundaries between self and other, present and past, writing and reading, fact and fiction' drive the narrative.[7]

As a woman professional working during a period when womens' social identity generally was in a state of transition, Ashwell's career doesn't fit easily with those of her female contemporaries. Three of her books, *Modern Troubadours*, *The Stage* and *Myself a Player* are predicated upon her autobiographical negotiations of both her experience and her projected identity as a theatre professional and celebrity, but they also tell us as much about the relationship between the individual, in this case middle-class woman, and the social and professional structure in which she worked. During the 1920s and 1930s, the writing of testimonials became part of the conscious effort to re-construct the work and lives of those involved in the suffrage movement,[8] and clearly, Ashwell was conscious of the importance of her own work as a professional woman of the theatre in an age where the assertion of a relationship between professionalism and women's working lives was a fraught one. *Modern Troubadours* is very much a testimonial to her war work but, as with her autobiography and *The Stage*, Ashwell consistently intertwines her private self, her public working self, the 'life of the theatre' and her ideas of progression and change. She is simultaneously retrospective and introspective, conscious of both the specialist and general reader at whom, for example, the series in which *The Stage* was published was aimed, but Ashwell is also aware of the opportunity such writing gives the author, for stating her experience-fuelled ideas about and theories of theatre and its social role.

Thomas Postlewait has pointed out that, although often anecdotal and factually unreliable, theatre autobiographies can be of use to theatre historians as one of the means of understanding the working conditions of any given era. Through an analysis of the method and purpose of 'shaping a life story' and through looking at recurring themes and issues we might better understand the 'cultural practices' and working values of a particular moment of theatre history.[9] Although warning the theatre historian to be cautious around questions of truth, reliability and accuracy, Postlewait suggests theatre autobiographies as a still relatively untapped source and this is, I would suggest, especially the case for the theatre historian interested in womens' contributions to theatre culture, even though many female authored theatre autiobiographies tell us remarkably little about professional activities: Ashwell is unusual in her emphasis on the professional and on her theories of theatre's place in cultural formation.

Written in her late fifties, *The Stage* offers Ashwell's ideas on acting, production and 'tradition' in theatre practice as well as an important assessment of her own career. Here she divides her working life up until the point of authorship into three phases:

> My life has been divided into three periods of actual work: service in the Theatre, service with the Imperial forces during the Great War and service in cooperation with the great London Boroughs ... In the first phase I was a great success, mounting the ladder from supernumerary to the position of actor-manager and star; and what may appear more important than anything in our modern world, my work brought me in a considerable amount of money.
>
> In the second phase of success the service was honorary, but I was overwhelmed with gratitude, appreciation, love, letters of congratulation from the smallest and the greatest.

> In the third phase I lost all the money I had made in the Theatre, my position was honorary, and at the present moment I am doubtful whether the last ten year period of work contains anything but failure. My great hope is that it holds the elements of success for someone more capable to take hold of.[10]

As author Ashwell intentionally states the different roles she played as a theatre worker, with the last being, in her eyes, a 'failure'. This last period of work with the London Boroughs and her running of the Century Theatre in Notting Hill, was an experiment intended to establish a formal and mutually sustainable economic relationship between the theatre and the geographical and social contexts in which it could potentially exist. Acknowledging her own financial independence, in part due to her successful career, in part due to her second husband's professional standing, Ashwell was essentially attempting to formalise a community-based subsidised theatre and as such was unique; that the attempt 'failed' financially over a decade or so should not undermine its historical significance in terms of the development of British theatre. Working against the grain with the London Boroughs who, unlike Ashwell, were unconvinced of theatre's social or educative value within the community, Ashwell states that the work was 'almost a success' as a 'pioneer enterprise' whereby her companies had created eager audiences for the types of plays being put on in non-commercial London theatres and national repertory companies. She was also aware of the need for such venues to be networked and linked thus,

> if a National Theatre is ever to be realised, it should be the final apex of a system of civic co-operation in every borough, town, and city, just as the Universities are at the apex of a system of education begun in the primary schools ... the people's theatres would leave the commercial theatre untouched financially, but give them a larger and more appreciative public.[11]

Her assessment of this work comes at a point where she would have felt the full financial and emotional effects of letting go of a project, the beginnings of which could be traced back to her years of management at the Kingsway in 1907/08. She even suggests a way forward with such work, again, conscious of the need to organise and network and to encourage a younger generation to pick up the gauntlet:

> in abler and younger hands the venture could be carried on to complete success, perhaps to the actual founding of the National Theatre. Owing to the perfection of modern transport it is easy, from a centre to send

> out plays in every direction within a radius of twenty miles. All that is needed is a sufficient number of halls to employ two companies. This could be arranged either in twelve halls worked from one centre, or six each from two centres. In the latter case the companies would be interchangeable.[12]

Although Ashwell was involved in the setting up and organisation of E.N.S.A during the 1939–45 war – for which Basil Dean has always received much of the credit – and continued to fundraise and give public lectures, her full-time theatre career ended with what she later summed up as 'the gruelling experience of failure and defeat'.[13] However, in the presentation of her career and her professional self, Ashwell is always keen to contextualise her work and her projects both socially and theatrically: at the same time as suggesting failure, she places that supposed failure in the light of the impossibility of the task in the first place – she often stresses the consistent state resistance to validating the social and educational benefits of theatre and as such can be placed historically alongside Shaw, Archer and Barker.

Lena Ashwell frequently asserts her professionalism: 'some stupid idea that the [London Borough] companies were composed of amateurs', was overcome by the fact that she 'determined to act in all the boroughs myself as no one could accuse me of being anything but professional'.[14] However an historical re-evaluation of the status and significance of the Lena Ashwell Players is not always helped by disparaging remarks made by the next generation of actors. So for example, Olivier, who was sacked for un-professional behaviour by Ashwell, derides their work not just because of the 'frugality of [her] productions'[15] but because of the impetus behind the work: 'Miss Ashwell obeyed the dictates of social conscience and sent her company ... to unthought of parts of London'.[16] The Player's contracts were low paid and the work seen by Olivier as potential employment amongst the 'elbowing throng of the unemployed':[17] he refers to her company of actors briefly as the 'Lavatory Players' in his book on acting and as the 'scrappiest mixture' in his slightly later autobiography.[18] Actor's autobiographies often play on the creation of a 'rags to riches' or a humble but 'unrecognised talent' narrative, but Olivier's comments are important as they give an indication of the way in which Ashwell, who had 'enjoyed a name of considerable renown' fitted into an overall picture of potential professional development. He tells us that she had 'fallen prey to the inducements of actress management' as if this were a well known but ill-advised career move for women of her generation.[19] But there really weren't that many independent managements by the inter-war period, let alone actress-managers.

In fact, at the point at which Ashwell went into management and as a consequence, became a business-woman, the numbers of professional women in England were relatively small. Census figures for the period 1891–1901 show a rise in women working in the acting profession in England and Wales from 3,696 to 9,171. Figues for men in the profession

1914–1915.
FRANCE.

1915–1916–1917.
FRANCE EGYPT. MALTA.
ADRIATIC FLEET.

1917–1918–1919.
PALESTINE. EGYPT. FRANCE.
BELGIUM. GERMANY.

1920–1923.
LONDON and PROVINCES.

The Lena Ashwell Players, Ltd.,
Season 1923-24.

ESME CHURCH
MERCIA CAMERON
MARGARET MURRAY
OLIVE WALTER
ESTHER WHITEHOUSE

GEORGE BLACKWOOD
STRINGER DAVIS
WESTON FIELDS
GEORGE MORGAN
DAN. F. ROE
PHILLIP REEVES
CYRIL TWYFORD
DUNCAN YARROW

The
Lena Ashwell Players, Ltd.,
Season 1923-24.

will appear at 8 p.m.

Every Monday,
LONGFIELD HALL, Ealing,
and
ST. PAUL'S INSTITUTE,
Winchmore Hill.

Every Tuesday,
TOWN HALL, Battersea,
and
TOWN HALL, Ilford.

Every Wednesday,
LADYWELL BATHS, Lewisham,
and
TOWN HALL, Edmonton.

Every Thursday,
BOROUGH HALL, Deptford,
and
CENTRAL HALL, Northwood.

Every Friday,
BOROUGH HALL, Greenwich,
and
PUBLIC HALL, Sutton.

Every Saturday,
ST. JOHN'S HALL, Watford.

SPECIAL MATINEES
at
ST. GABRIEL'S HALL,
Anson Road, Cricklewood,
Saturday, December 1st,
also
January 19th to March 1st.

7 Publicity/advert material from The Lena Ashwell Players 1923–24 season.

are roughly the same although there are more women in the profession at each point.[20] These figures include only those censured from the total female population aged between 20 and 44 in England and Wales of 5,405,513 in 1891 to 7,307,019 in 1911,[21] and do not differentiate between kinds of performance work undertaken. Jane Lewis suggests that the percentage of married women working during the late nineteenth and early twentieth century was actually lower than during the mid-nineteenth century and that even when census figures showed information on married working women in 1911, the figure up until the early 1930s remained around 10 per cent.[22] The majority of women who worked did so in domestic service or in the textile industry: within the professions – which were usually teaching or nursing – the figure ranges between 6 per cent and 8 per cent from 1891 and 1931.[23] The point here, is that amongst middle-class working women, Ashwell experienced an unusual level of autonomy, and that amongst married middle-class women, an unusual level of geographical and social freedom; this is the context into which an analysis of her autobiographic negotiations of the professional self has to be inserted.

As an actress Ashwell spent only a relatively short time in low-paid touring jobs and worked with leading figures of the day such as George Alexander, very soon after her professional debut. She would have been afforded some professional status from the beginning and as such, was somewhat of an 'exception to' her sex.[24] Within a short time Ashwell had become a professional amongst other acting women, 'occupying widely different locations within the vast territory called the "middle class"'.[25] Despite this seemingly respectable position Ashwell writes of her father who, although he was determined that his daughters should be able to earn a living, was angst ridden that she should move into a profession which he considered to be the 'Mouth of Hell'.[26] She refers to her career choice as taking the road to the 'nether world, that of the artist' and of how she was thus to 'lose caste'.[27] In fact, although Ashwell is making a play of her family's provincial naiveté, she was clearly moving outside of familial expectations in her career choice. Ashwell had a knack for being slightly out of kilter with women of her generation and class, even at a time when the boundaries of the feminine and femininity were in a fairly constant state of flux. Despite the fact that she was working in a profession which at this point often reflected the transitional in terms of social identity for women, Ashwell's professional profile was still unusual and she seems to have been conscious of this fact throughout.

Having married a fellow actor in her twenties only to discover that he was a violent alcoholic, Ashwell separated from him in the late 1890s and was granted a divorce, despite her first husband's family employing a detective to find evidence of her adultery years after their separation, in 1908, just prior to re-marrying.[28] Just as she makes note of her divorce in her autobiography, she later talks without inhibition about her reputation for playing 'fallen women' on stage; there is a conscious effort to play with reader expectation. By the time the autobiography is published in 1936, Ashwell is known for her good deeds and her successful career both as actress, as manager and producer.[29] But when Ashwell remarried in 1908, in her mid-thirties she was also outside the average age range and beyond the conventional status for marriageability.[30] The way in which she layers information about her early life, her unsuccessful marriage and consequent long-awaited divorce, her adoption of the child of a second cousin – whose birth certificate she locates for the reader – sustains an impression of an unusual woman who went against the grain both socially and professionally, but still found success and public recognition.

Managing, marketing and creating an identity for the Kingsway

Although Lena Ashwell had ventured into theatre management for brief periods previously, it was her management of the Kingsway Theatre which launched her into a major long-term commitment to a way of working and to a particular theatre. The possibility of taking the 'lunge into management alone' was opened up by the enthusiasm for such a project which Ashwell managed to create between two aristocratic friends who she names anonymously as Lady Jane and Lady Caroline. She couches the project in terms of its aesthetic and ideological value.

> Filled with admiration for the work done at Antoine's Theatre in Paris, I poured forth plans for producing plays by unknown authors to break down the commercial ring. Full of the ideals of democracy as promulgated by the red-haired, red-bearded Irish enthusiast, George Bernard Shaw, I would sweep the profession clean of all artificial standards of value, all inhibiting control by the aristocracy of the profession. Room must be made for the unknown author, for experiments with new lighting, for new ideas of scenery. Here was all the enthusiasm of the young.[31]

Thus, the project was unquestionably connected to the campaign around creating a sustainable non-commercial or a National theatre so prevalent during the Edwardian period.[32] Ashwell's foray into permanent management was made possible by the donation of start up costs of

£3000: a first instalment for a lease, refurbishment and publicity. 'I was to take a long lease of a theatre, engage a company which would be the nucleus from which to cast any play, engage these actors by the year to do away with the casual labour method and give the sense of security so necessary to sound work … I was to be allowed to create with … money behind me.'[33]

When the personal relationship between Ashwell and her donors faltered the project lost its financial backing: she lost the promised regular wage regardless of ticket income and the trusts which had been drawn up for her sister and for her long-standing dresser were cancelled. Ashwell states that this was because she was not prepared to be a social 'puppet' for her aristocratic female backers. At this point Otho Stuart came on board as a co-producer and at the end of the season Charles Frohmann employed most of the company.[34] Like all such projects, start-up funds alone are insufficient, and although Ashwell had two hits with *Irene Wycherley* and Cicely Hamilton's *Diana of Dobson's*, her solo management of the Kingsway was short lived. She had to continue paying for the lease until she was able to sell it after the First World War. What is interesting however, is the actual setting up and management of the project as well as her choice of theatre building. Her autobiographical writings stress the excitement and organisational activities around this project but leave the historian to find much of the detail in other forms of documentation.

The Kingsway had an important geographical status in Great Queen Street, which, although a 'little hidden theatre',[35] made it within walking distance of other parts of the West End. The venue had opened in 1882 as the Novelty Theatre and housed a range of theatrical entertainments: comic operas and 'serious' drama such as Ibsen's *A Dolls House* in 1889. In June 1907, the Kingway housed the first London production of Synge's *Playboy of The Western World* direct from the riots it had caused amongst the audiences at the Abbey Theatre in Dublin.[36] After the close of season in July 1907, Ashwell set the process of redecoration and refurbishment in motion, and it was this which marked the Kingsway as 'an established fact'.[37] Granville Barker and Lillah McCarthy leased the theatre from Ashwell in 1912 for a transfer of Shaw's long-running *Fanny's First Play* and J. E. Vedrenne and Denis Eadie leased the theatre just before the 1914–18 war. After the war Barry Jackson brought his Birmingham Repertory company to the theatre during the famous 1925–26 *Hamlet* season. It is this potential protocol of innovation which Ashwell built upon and used to set the Kingsway's cultural significance in place. The

English Stage Company bought the lease in the mid-1950s and it was from the Kingsway that they originally planned to launch the work of the company, although a last minute change of heart by the then owner meant that they went to the Royal Court instead.[38] The point here is that Lena Ashwell, on taking on the refurbishment of the theatre also took on its remarketing and the creation of a concrete identity for the Kingsway as a theatre which cultivated innovation and promoted non-commercialism in production.

Despite limited experience of management Ashwell is very clear that she wanted the Kingsway to be perceived culturally in a certain light. Dennis Kennedy states that the re-furbishment made the theatre 'a pleasant home for the management, which clearly intended to stay in business',[39] but in reality, Ashwell's re-launch established the Kingsway's twentieth-century cultural identity. In her publicity materials, contrary to some historians' statement that she, rather femininely, merely 'redecorated',[40] Ashwell points to the fact that the theatre had in fact been gutted inside and greatly altered on the exterior.

> The seating of all parts of the house has been more conveniently and comfortably arranged, every seat … being numbered and reserved, thus avoiding the necessity for tedious waiting …The electric lighting of the Theatre has been entirely re-arranged and brought up-to-date, and I am assured that no theatre in London has a more complete and effective system … The means of access … is now peculiarly accessible. Within a few yards of the Theatre is the Kingsway itself, with L.C.C. trams and a fine service of horse and motor buses … the Theatre can be reached in two minutes from the British Museum Station … or in one minute from the Holborn Station … The cab fare from nearly all the principle hotels and railway stations is 1s … I have also arranged with some of the best known Authors to supply me with Plays, and have secured several pieces of great interest by the younger generation of dramatists …[41]

Ashwell engaged a company for a year in order to build an ensemble and avoid the insecurity, for both actor and manager, of short-term contracts. The publicity for the opening of the theatre lists company members such as Norman McKinnel, Denis Eadie, Gertrude Scott and Muriel Wylford. She also talks in detail about the music she was planning to commission from younger composers, and even details the arrangements for refreshments of the 'best quality' and afternoon teas in the large foyer. Ashwell wanted to establish in the public mind, the geography and accessibility of the theatre, alongside its newness, the style of which – Louis XVI-period – she is also careful to detail. Her detailing of potential travel arrangements indicates a desire to attract different classes and different generations of clientele into the theatre – albeit that the price range would still have been out of the reach of anyone from the lower end of the social scale. The colour-coding of her marketing by means of posters and programmes printed on pink candy-striped paper and card signifies femininity but equally gave the marketing campaign what we might call a corporate identity. She was as concerned to signify comfort as well as innovation. The Kingsway had something different to offer its clientele, and although her autobiographical writings lack the detail on how this was done, Ashwell is keen to state the impetus and intention behind the project.

The documenting of Ashwell's reign at the Kingsway is interesting in part because of much of comes from those working with her on the project or from the press – it is almost as if she wants to leave the importance of the project for others to configure. For Ashwell, management meant running a business, employing and coordinating staff, managing a precarious financial situation without the back-up of permanent investment and so on. The company she employed was cannily chosen and her desire to have innovation in so many areas of production was time consuming. Edward Knoblock, whom Ashwell mentions in *Myself a Player*, as being very good at sourcing second-hand furniture for the re-furbishment job as well as being someone who read plays for the theatre, claims that Ashwell went into management with Norman McKinnel (McKinnel was in fact an actor/producer or director in a modern context). He also claims that his play-reading skills lead to the finding of the first two scripts produced and to his up-grading from a very part-time to a full-time employee, effectively as a literary manager.[42] According to Knoblock it was because of his insistence Ashwell decided to produce *Diana of Dobson's*. In his eyes, the working team running the Kingsway consisted of Ashwell, McKinnel and himself. This misconception ended in Ashwell berating him for interfering in the configuring of the public profile of the theatre (he had complained to a journalist friend that Ashwell wouldn't listen to him as the brains behind the unit). Her response to the ensuing article, 'The Intelligence Department of the Theatre' was that it implied she had no brains of her own; Knoblock resigned and rarely met with Ashwell, a 'woman of "infinite variety"' again.[43] Knoblock's autobiography is rather self-inflatory but the agenda at play in his retelling of his working relationship with Ashwell characterises her in particularly chauvinistic terms – she was an actress and did not know what plays to choose, how to work on them and so on. Her 'infinite variety' implies that she was a dilettante, capitalising on her 'star' status as a performer, that if only she had moved over and let him get on with it, the venture would have worked. In *Myself a Player* Ashwell implies that her concern with negative publicity was that she needed to keep her own profile and that of the theatre in the public eye but in positive terms only – she had taken on a venture with huge financial implications and knew the power of publicity to damage such a project. She had also taken on a venture where public negativity towards something which had a 'strong air of militant woman suffrage ... with its manageress and a woman playwright'[44] had to be well managed: she was perfectly aware of being a woman in a theatre and media world largely controlled by men. It was all very well for her second husband Henry Simson to say 'I don't mind being Lena Ashwell's husband' but some, such as Knoblock, would have found it very difficult to take orders from and be employed by a woman. There are certain parallels here between Ashwell and recent revaluations of Annie Horniman's work in Manchester – her famous fall-out with Lewis Casson may well have been due to his inability to take instruction from a woman, who in turn had made a substantial financial investment in a theatre which was not pulling the crowds. The point here is that both women have been characterised as conservative and as blocking the way to innovation when in fact both had made substantial financial investments from personal reserves. Independent theatre is expensive for those who fund it, and both women had to make management decisions which were unpopular with their experimentalist, often male, colleagues.[45]

Ideological shifts: censorship and political activism

Lena Ashwell regularly figures in discussions of theatre censorship during the Edwardian period. Her dealings with Granville Barker's intended production of his banned play *Waste*, for example, often place her in a poor light. Shaw is also more reticent in his dealings with her around this period. Ashwell clashed twice with Barker over issues around censorship; the first occasion came in the form of her refusal to release Norman McKinnel from his contract so that he could perform in Barker's *Waste*. Kennedy suggests that Ashwell was happy to release McKinnel to play in a Vedrenne-Barker season production but that she did not 'wish to risk association with a prohibited play'.[46] Shaw berated her for having 'deserted' himself and Granville Barker 'in the face of the public' but conceded that he couldn't 'honestly pretend it is in your (*sic*) interest to fight the battles of the authors and of the Stage Society when you have enough to do to take care of yourself. I can only rage hopelessly'.[47] Shaw must have been aware of her financial position with the Kingsway but although subsequent correspondence suggests, contrary to Kennedy's implications, that McKinnel had in fact been temporarily released from his contract, Shaw insisted that Ashwell take on the anti-censorship cause.

> The issue between us and the censor is a very big one; and it is part of the dignity of the position you have won that you should act in it as an artist and a woman of genius without regard to the mere business advice which business people are bound to give you ... Mac by the way will act all the better for having his feelings deeply stirred. He may be feeling deeply about you; but the public will think he is feeling deeply about Barker's play.[48]

Shaw went on to flatter Ashwell by pointing out that he would have liked her to play the female lead in the proposed Stage Society production of *Waste*. Ashwell herself knew that many of the changes which the censor demanded of scripts were often ridiculous but she was very clear that she did not wish to risk the closing of her theatre, she simply could not *afford* for the theatre to be closed. Whereas Shaw wanted her to be 'one of the boys' and fight the fight whatever the cost, Kennedy's implication is that Ashwell was somehow naïve about the power of censorship. Ashwell does not refer to the specifics of the *Waste* fiasco in her autobiographical writings, but rather points out that although much censorship was foolish, she was concerned that, as had happened in America, the actors in a banned play might be professionally scarred by a production of such a play going ahead. Ashwell also later tried to get an injunction to stop Lillah McCarthy and Barker's production of Eden Phillpotts *The Secret Woman* at the Kingsway in 1912.[49] Phillpotts and she had corresponded in the past around possible parts for Ashwell in his plays, and the move for injunction, which was refused as the performances were to be free, was not personal but was to do with her wish to keep the theatre open and unquestionably operating within legal boundaries.[50] Her views on censorship were simple: 'The actor is not responsible for the dialogue he is obliged to learn, and as authors are very reluctant to any change it seemed to me that the actor did need some protection'.[51] A production being closed down was not part of what Ashwell perceived as good quality control, even from the removed position of licencee as opposed to manager. In her autobiographical writings she speaks of issues such as censorship in general terms – thus avoiding mention of particular individuals at the same time as acknowledging her engagement with what was a current debate.

Autobiographies are often created in terms of a framework of cultural reference points; one writes oneself in relation to others in the field, the public knowledge of which helps the author to create a particular slant on their own life. Certainly, Ashwell was part of a network of theatre workers who became known for innovation and experiment and yet to some extent she distances herself from them in creating a narrative of her life. Her professional relationship with Shaw is underplayed whereas her connection to Charlotte Shaw – at the point when she is looking back in time to those things or people who have influenced where she sees herself as being situated in the moment of writing – appears to have been, in autobiographical terms, more emotionally significant. Nor does Ashwell mention Lillah McCarthy with whom she had connections through both Barker and her work with the Actresses Franchise League; Kennedy implies that Ashwell capitalised on Barker's work and actively blocked his projects – but her failure to detail their relationship, in the context of her lack of detailing of other professional relationships is less significant. Others with whom she worked, such as the actress manager Gertrude Kingston and Nancy Price, another pioneer and co-founder with J. T.Grein of the People's National Theatre, do not mention Ashwell in any detail in their autobiographies.[52] Cicely Hamilton, in *Life Errant*, refers to Ashwell in positive terms whilst talking of her work in the army camps in Abbeville, but when referring to the fact that she made little financial gain from the production of *Diana of Dobson's*, Ashwell, unnamed, becomes the 'shrewder person' in a business deal. Ashwell's retort on Hamilton is one of her few active autobiographic engagements with her critics – she writes of what she sees as the 'constant criticism' over the financial dealings with *Diana of Dobson's*, pointing to the fact that when the film rights were sold she split the after-tax profits with Hamilton: for Ashwell it was a business arrangement where she took the initial financial risk on an unknown author.[53]

Ashwell was less interested in theatrical gossip than she was in the social causes through which she channelled her early political activism: from her work with the Actresses' Franchise League through the work with the Women's Emergency Corps, the YMCA and entertainments for the troops during the 1914–18 war, her work with the British Drama League to her work at the Century Theatre and the Lena Ashwell Players/Once A Week Players. Equally, *Modern Troubadours*, constructed as a narrative-driven testimonial to her work during the war, and including diary entries and letters from both those working with her and soldiers who attended performances, reveals Ashwell's own sense of the historical significance of the *work* as well as her *own* historical significance. Is this a form of self-advocacy, or simply something unexpected of a woman of her generation? In autobiographies written by actresses who were her contemporaries there is rarely such a conscious attempt to assert and analyse the trajectory of a professional career in such a systematic way.

All historians have experienced the problems of the archive: a resource which holds such great promise as a means of reconstructing experience but, for various reasons, rarely lives up to expectation, often only serving to remind us of the impossibility of such a reconstruction in the first place. Where the work of theatre women is concerned, records are frequently incomplete or patchy, material often goes uncatalogued or collections are split in order to provide background for other, larger archives, often those of their male contemporaries. Ashwell is again somewhat of an exception in that a great deal of material related to her early work was placed in scrapbooks (now housed at the Theatre Museum and the Imperial War Museum in London), and along with the *Daily Express* cuttings files in the British Library and the extensive range of correspondence materials scattered, mostly, amongst American university collections, these form a substantial archive of materials relating to her work. It was not uncommon for celebrities and public figures to subscribe to cuttings services, but Ashwell's laying out of materials in her scrapbooks, meticulously organised production by production, indicate a conscious desire to be historically framed in a specific light. There is no indication as to who put these scrapbooks together – it is likely to have been one of Ashwell's sisters – but many contain comments in Ashwell's hand, suggesting for example which photographs to have enlarged and printed. One of the scrapbooks in particular pays witness to her early desire to place herself amongst well-known literary and theatrical figures of the day: it is almost entirely made up of letters from well-known figures or simply the signed portion of letters congratulating her on her performances or wishing her luck with her venture at the Kingsway. This desire, to place herself inside the environs of celebrity, appears to have waned by the time of her autobiography in 1936. But in terms of other women working in the theatre at the time, the amount of archive materials scattered amongst academic and public collections is rather extraordinary – Ashwell consciously created an archive of her work, providing biographical material which could easily be placed beside and interrelated with her later autobiographical writings by the theatre historian.

The phases of her work which Ashwell chooses to narratologise are those with which she still has an ideological affiliation by the end of her theatrical career. Again, her writing about her work during the campaign for suffrage is totally driven by her own sense of professional identity and the need to create a better professional environment specifically for women in theatre. Contributions to such publications as Edith J. Morley's Fabian collection *Women Workers in Seven Professions*, show Ashwell's public concern for her fellow female workers in a profession where, 'for the average actress ... there is little security'.[54] Whereas Cicely Hamilton claims to not have been 'wildly interested in votes for anyone' but rather in any possibilities to undermine the 'tradition of normal woman',[55] Ashwell was genuinely concerned at the inequality afforded women as citizens. 'I began to discover that the world of theatre was not the only world and that there were movements going on; for the seeds of revolution were germinating. There was much in the world that needed to be put right ... I became immersed in the suffrage movement.'[56]

Recapitulating in 1936 she appeared to be aware that such a political affiliation might need contextualising for the readers of her official autobiography, thus looking back from her early sixties she stated her position.

> There was much in the world that need to be put right, and I became immersed in the suffrage movement and the position of women ... It is impossible to realise now the scorn which women who thought they should be recognised as citizens drew upon themselves from otherwise quite polite and sensible people. Managers, authors, pressmen became quite passionate in their resentment and, wise in their generation, did not associate themselves with this unpopular organisation.[57]

Ashwell's work with the Actresses' Franchise League has been fairly well documented elsewhere, and there is surprisingly little detail about it in *Myself a Player* as in her other works.[58] She pointedly talks about her affiliation with what Katherine Kelly has identified as an organisation made up of largely middle-class Englishwomen,[59] in the context of a *generalised* increase in her political consciousness, and her activities around changing laws which prejudiced against women such as the Married Women's Tax Law. Ashwell also consistently places emphasis on the power of, and thus subsequent need for, networking. She talks of Fabianism and socialism in loose terms but clearly had a strong sense of a need to accommodate and support those theatre workers whose social status did not afford them the kinds of economic comfort to which she had access by the time of her second marriage to Henry Simson. When she founded the Three Arts Club on the Marylebone Road, such clubs for women were a relatively new feature in London. Her sister had already opened a club for the 'girls who sold programmes in the theatres', and the Three Arts Club was intended to provide cheap but good quality accommodation for women working in arts professions in London, women who Ashwell identified as either wishing to or being 'obliged to make their own living'.[60] Press coverage, scant as it is, indicates that it was an unusual but socially acceptable venture. Membership was a guinea for those living in London and half a guinea for those based outside of London. The bedroom and cubicle accommodation for 'about a hundred women' at a cost of 19s 6d with 'board and upwards' was to do away with 'lonely lodgings, exasperating boarding houses and the inexorable domination of landladies', and provided affordable independence and a safe social space for women working in the arts. Ashwell had set up the club with the intention of extending its remit nationally, she had wanted it to be the 'centre of a group and co-operate with those in the great towns outside London' and to provide a means of overcoming on a national scale, the squalor and domestic insecurity in which actresses were supposed to operate.[61] Her desire to network on a larger scale caused her to fall out with the managing committee and she removed herself from the project sometime after the declaration of the First World War.

Social conscience, war work and after

In founding, alongside Eva and Decima Moore and Eve Haverfield, the Women's Emergency Corps at the beginning of the war Ashwell was not out of line with others from her class who wished to help in the war effort, but once more, she was pushing against the boundaries of the social expectations of a woman of her era. Again looking back from her sixties she proposes:

> It is easy now to see the necessity for the help of women, but before the war there were very few occupations that women were considered fitted for, so when we took the list to the men who, we felt, would help us, they were really horrified. 'Women on the land? Impossible! Women conductors on buses! Women porters! Impossible Impossible! Impossible!' ... women poured down upon us from every quarter of the country. They came in thousands full of enthusiasm, willing to do anything and go anywhere, on to be allowed to serve England.[62]

Ashwell's job was to network, publicise and fundraise and through this work she developed the project with the YMCA which was to take her through the war years and beyond.

L. C. Collins, amongst others, has documented Ashwell's work with the YMCA and Entertainments for the Troops and it is not the detail of this work which I intend to examine here but rather the ethos of and the impetus behind the work and its effect on the development of Ashwell's career after the end of the war.[63] Collins states that Ashwell 'had strict control from the start' and that although conditions of service asserted that there should be 'No advertisement, no making use of the war to aggrandise one's professional popularity', Ashwell 'made certain that she got top-billing and that her name was printed in larger and bolder type'. For Collins, Ashwell's career 'in no way suffered by taking time out to play in productions not usually covered by the critics in the national newspapers'.[64] However, Collins does not accord Ashwell, who appears 'by all accounts to have been a strong willed and dominant character', her professional status and standing in the theatre of the period.[65] Billing and advertising had the purpose of marketing a product, that the product could be associated with high status theatre and entertainment professionals would have enhanced the reputation of the concerts. It has to be remembered that such a state acknowledgement of the needs of soldiers for cultural and educational diversion, was relatively new and that for a woman to be overseeing the organisation and administration of this venture was extraordinary. Ashwell was aware of the 'suspicion of the English people with regard to the theatre' and was glad of her white hair and 'solidity of figure' when she arrived at her first meetings with the YMCA; she was associated with a mature and respectable side of the English theatre.[66] Kelly has attested to other kinds of army based entertainments organised by women previously connected to the Actresses' Franchise League,[67] but the *scale* of Ashwell's operation was phenomenal. For W. MacQueen Pope, in one of his nostalgic assessments of theatre before the second world war, Ashwell's project was the unacknowledged impetus behind Basil Dean's setting up of E.N.S.A. during the 1939–45 war.[68] Dean in turn, acknowledges her work with the setting up and running of E.N.S.A. at which point Ashwell would have been in her late sixties, but does not historically connect E.N.S.A. to the organisation she set up during the First World War.[69] Similar to Dean, Ashwell's work with the 'Concerts at the Front' was driven by a desire to provide professional engagements for performers as much as it was driven by a desire to contribute in general to the war effort.

Ashwell's *Modern Troubadours* is constructed in part around her own reminiscences, sometimes in diary form: throughout there is a sense in which Ashwell is trying to simultaneously provide detail, with overview and assessment as well as a sense of what it was like to be part of the work, to be part of the war on the front line: she also heavily stresses the professional organisation and character of the work. She insisted that actors were paid 'with a view to meeting the out-of-pocket expenses which would go on at home while they were abroad': fees were usually paid on return.[70] Equally, she talks again and again of the importance of bringing quality work to the troops. Certainly her own assumptions about the kinds of entertainment troops would want were quickly undermined, as one testimony stated: 'I am more convinced than ever the men are hungering for good stuff. It's an awful injustice to treat them to slop.'[71] Ashwell, probably for the first time finding herself performing to large audiences of men – the majority of whom would have been drawn from the working classes – frequently refers to the mixing of the sexes: 'Has there ever before been a war where women were able to walk freely amongst men, respected and accepted as fellow workers for a national cause?'[72]

Although her account of the war doesn't give witness to such violence as Susan Kingsley Kent argues was being capitalised upon by media propaganda,[73] Ashwell was clearly shocked by the horror of seeing wounded men and by the degrading conditions of warfare in general. Aware also that she was treated in a privileged way in terms of comfort and transport, Ashwell used her influence and her social status to accrue funds for the work at the front. Her descriptions of the fundraising bazaars and charity collections and sales as well as the numerous lecture tours to raise awareness of and funds for the work with the YMCA are detailed and witty and tell us a great deal about the largely feminised culture of charity work during the period. She was ruthless in her determination to find the money to carry out the work on a hitherto unimaginably large scale. Again, what comes across in reading these sections of *Modern Troubadours*, is Ashwell's own sense of how to administrate and run business activities and how to capitalise on her own reputation and marketability as a performer: she knew how to take advantage of the experiences she had gained in management and felt that she had a 'capacity for dealing with people and measuring their capabilities'.[74]

The auto/biographical negotiation of the professional self: an 'active striving of will'

In the various autobiographies written by those who worked with Ashwell there is often a reticence to acknowledge her significance or to talk about her influence in any detailed way. She clearly had some power within the industry and may have been a difficult employer: her projects were driven by a determination and ambition seen at the time as unusual in a woman and it may be that some did not want to be associated with, or publicly shaped by, impressions of *her* achievements. In her autobiographical writings she places great emphasis on the 'ordinary people' around her and on her determination to ensure the survival and success of her projects. Ashwell states on a number of different occasions that her war work made her realise that 'theatre matters' and that the work during the war forced her to 'change [her] attitude towards Theatre, and transformed me from being very ambitious for myself into being still more ambitious for a cause'.[75] As an actress Ashwell had created an achieved celebrity and a public persona which she could both develop and capitalise upon in her work off stage as well as on: other women of her generation, once finding that age placed them outside of the market for substantial and well paying stage roles, often moved out of the limelight. Her religious background and her interest in spiritualism were born out in her work with James Porter Mills, who, although described by Michael Holroyd as 'a bad tempered old man who had travelled the world perfecting what he called the 'Teaching',[76] greatly influenced the way in which Ashwell both perceived the world and placed herself within it . Equally, just as Samuel Smiles's popular and influential work, *Self Help* first published in the mid-1850s had proposed, Ashwell was clearly amongst those of her generation who believed that 'celebrity carried with it public responsibilities and duties'.[77] Certainly, Smiles's promotion of an 'active striving of the will'[78] is something which drove Ashwell's work from what she saw as her humble beginnings, and more consciously so after her initial encounters, through her friendship with Charlotte Shaw, with Porter Mills and meditation.

Lena Ashwell was essentially an Edwardian woman but she was also very modern: she lived through phenomenal changes in both the theatre and in the society in which that theatre happened. Her rise to fame during the late Vitorian and Edwardian periods linked her with tradition as well as radical political movements and with innovation in theatre: and although the 'Edwardian attitude to working middle-class women had greatly changed',[79] one Scottish journalist's assessment of her as a 'theatrical damsel of a very aggressive type' must have been coloured by the fact that she was a woman displaying and capitalising upon her celebrity status and professional power within a public arena.[80] Her autobiographical writings suggest a complex figure, out of the ordinary but driven to bringing theatre to ordinary people's lives and the historical evidence bears this out. Ashwell was always concerned about the economic and working conditions of professional actors, both male and female, and was equally concerned with the 'art' of acting. Very much part of the movement to establish a National theatre in England, her writings do not necessarily or overtly connect her to those more remembered for the campaign. But she was clearly an innovator who tried to open out the social function of theatre: she talks for example, of how her actors were used to working with a few army blankets, planks and soap boxes as props and scenery and of how they managed to build regular audiences for live plays in the London boroughs ignored by the central London acting fraternity; Ashwell saw poverty as the 'mother of invention', and saw the work of her company as being, 'in the nature of a pioneer movement'.[81] She also encouraged young actors and worked with many, especially during her war activities, who had established theatre careers, such as Gertrude Jennings, John Drinkwater and Cicely Hamilton as well as those who later went on to establish their own careers, such as Athene Seyler, Esme Church, Basil Dean, Ivor Novello and Nancy Price.

Lena Ashwell acknowledges that she had the financial stability afforded a woman who had had a successful career and then married well: her husband's professional circle included royalty. Yet she does not shy away from the detailing of how her projects were run, both administratively and financially: a business woman applying her abilities to charity work, she allows the reader to understand the workings of a business and the complexities of fundraising for and organising theatre. In assessing her autobiographic identity there is a strong sense of her own awareness of the trajectory of her career both as an artist (from youth to maturity) and as an enabler and innovator (from theatre manager to a producer of community touring theatre). Her keen awareness of the cultural shifts and professional developments which were changing the ways in which the art of acting and theatre was configured culturally are often autobiographically interwoven with details of what she actually *did* in terms of her various projects. In her autobiographical writings she deliberately constructs her identity as one of a woman with a strong social conscience, a networker, a political activist, an organiser, a fundraiser and a business woman. This was clearly an autobiographic strategy aimed at creating and controlling her own projected identity as a professional, socially conscientious, spiritually driven and multi-dimensional woman of the theatre. Such a strategy forces the reader to go beyond a fascination with celebrity towards an understanding of a complex woman theatre practitioner who was genuinely concerned that theatre have a proper role in the cultural formation of England during the first half of the twentieth century.

Notes

1 Lena Ashwell, *Myself a Player* (London: Michael Joseph Ltd., 1936), p. 274.

2 Quoted in Claire Hirshfield, 'The Actress as Social Activist: The Case of Lena Ashwell', in Ronald Dotterer and Susan Bowers (eds), *Politics, Gender and the Arts: Women, the Arts and Society* (London and Toronto: Susquehanna University Press, 1992), p. 75. See also Margot Peters, *Bernard Shaw and the Actresses* (New York: Doubleday, 1980); Barbara Bellow Watson, *A Shavian Guide to the Intelligent Woman* (London: Chatto and Windus, 1964); and Stanley Weintraub, *Bernard Shaw 1914–1918: Journey to Heartbreak* (London: Routledge, 1973).

3 Margaret Leask's meticulously detailed thesis is the only work which takes the trajectory of Ashwell's career chronologically, through her early years touring to her work for Moral Re-armament in the 1950s and some analysis is beginning to emerge on her work with the London Boroughs in the 1920s. See Margaret Leask, *Lena Ashwell 1869–1957: Actress, Patriot and Pioneer*, PhD thesis, University of Sydney, Australia, June 2000. Also see Chris Dymkowski, 'Lena Ashwell and her Players: Popular performers in Extraordinary Stages', in Jane Milling and Martin Banham (eds), *Extraordinary Actors: Essays on Popular Performers* (Exeter: Exeter University Press, 2004), 1 pp. 120–34.

4 For detailed reminiscences of her performances see A. E. Wilson, *Edwardian Theatre* (London: Arthur Barker Ltd., 1951) and W. MacQueen Pope, *Give Me Yesterday: A Backward Glance Down the Years* (London: Hutchinson, 1957). For the general context of Ashwell's work with the A. F. L. see Julie Holledge, *Innocent Flowers: Women in the Edwardian Theatre* (London: Virago, 1981); Claire Hirshfield, 'The Woman's Theatre in England: 1913–1918', *Theatre History Studies* 15 (1995), pp. 123–37; and idem, 'The Suffragist as Playwright in Edwardian England', *Frontiers* 9: 2 (1987), pp. 1–6.

5 Lena Ashwell, *Modern Troubadours* (London and Copenhagen: Gyldendal, 1922); idem, *Myself a Player* (London: Michael Joseph Ltd., 1936); idem, *The Stage* (London: Geoffrey Bles, 1929); and idem, *Reflections on Shakespeare* (London: Hutchinson, 1936).

6 Liz Schafer, *Ms – Directing Shakespeare: Women Direct Shakespeare* (London: The Women's Press, 1998).

7 Liz Stanley, 'Is There Life in the Contact Zone? Auto/Biographical Practices and The Field of Representation in Writing Past Lives', in Alison Donnell and Pauline Polkey (eds), *Representing Lives: Women and Auto/biography* (London: Macmillan, 2000), p. 4; and idem, 'From "Self-made women" to "women's made-selves"', in Tess Cosslett *et al.* (eds), *Feminism and Autobiography: Texts Theories, Methods* (London: Routledge, 2000), pp. 40–60.

8 See Hilda Kean, 'Searching for the Past in Present Defeat: The Construction of Historical and Political Identity in British Feminism in the 1920s and 1930s', *Women's History Review* 3: 1 (1994), pp. 57–80; and Laura Nym Mayhall,

'Creating the "Suffragette Spirit": British Feminism and the Historical Imagination', *Women's History Review* 4: 3 (1995), pp. 319–44.

9 Thomas Postlewait, 'Theatre Autobiographies: Some Preliminary Concerns for the Historian', *Assaph C* 16 (2000), pp. 157–72.

10 Lena Ashwell, *The Stage*, pp. 140–1.

11 Ibid., pp. 176–7.

12 Ibid., pp. 177–8.

13 Lena Ashwell, *Myself a Player*, p. 238.

14 Ibid., p. 248.

15 Donald Spoto, *Laurence Olivier: A Biography* (London: HarperCollins, 1991), p. 31.

16 Laurence Olivier, *Confessions of an Actor* (London: Weidenfeld and Nicholson, 1986), p. 32.

17 Ibid., p. 31.

18 Laurence Olivier, *On Acting* (London: Weidenfeld and Nicholson, 1982), p. 114; and idem, *Confessions of an Actor*, p. 31.

19 Laurence Olivier, *Confessions of an Actor*, p. 31.

20 Tracy C. Davis, *Actresses as Working Women: Their Social Identity in Victorian culture* (London: Routledge, 1991), p. 10.

21 Martha Vicinus, *Independent Women: Work And Community for Single Women 1850–1920* (London: Virago, 1985), p. 293.

22 Jane Lewis, *Women in England 1870–1950* (Brighton: Harvester Wheatsheaf, 1984), p. 149–50.

23 Ibid., p. 156.

24 Tracy C. Davis, *Actresses as Working Women*, p. xi.

25 Katherine E. Kelly, 'The Actresses Franchise League Prepares for War: Feminist Theatre in Camouflage', *Theatre Survey* 35:1 (1994), p. 122.

26 Lena Ashwell, *Myself a Player*, p. 44.

27 Ibid., pp. 44–6.

28 See the *Daily Express* obituary files in The British Library Newspaper Collection, London, for surprisingly scant media coverage of the divorce.

29 Divorce was expensive and the laws were gender-biased: see Jane Lewis, *Women in England*, pp. 4–5 and p. 78.

30 Ibid., p. 4.

31 Lena Ashwell, *Myself a Player*, p. 140.

32 See William Archer and Harley Granville Barker, *A National Theatre: Schemes and Estimates* (London: Duckworth, 1907); and Dennis Kennedy, *Granville Barker and The Dream of Theatre* (Cambridge: Cambridge University Press, 1985).

33 Lena Ashwell, *Myself a Player*, p. 145.

34 See Daniel Frohman, *Memories of A Manager* (London: William Heinemann, 1911).

35 Ray Mander and Joe Mitcheson, *The Lost Theatres of London* (London: Rupert Hart-Davis, 1968), p. 233.

36 Nicholas Grene, *The Politics of Irish Drama: Plays in Context from Boucicault to Friel* (Cambridge: Cambridge University Press, 1999); and Christopher Morash, *A History of the Irish Theatre 1601–2000* (Cambridge: Cambridge University Press, 2002), pp. 103–30.
37 See Ray Mander and Joe Mitchenson, *The Lost Theatres of London.*
38 Philip Roberts, *The Royal Court Theatre and The Modern Stage* (Cambridge: Cambridge University Press, 1999), pp. 22–35.
39 Dennis Kennedy, *Granville Barker and The Dream of Theatre*, p. 118.
40 See Ray Mander and Joe Mitcheson, *The Lost Theatres of London.*
41 Ibid., pp. 222–33.
42 Knoblock claims that he begged Ashwell to do Elizabeth Baker's *Chains* but see Sheila Stowell, *A Stage of Their Own: Feminist Playwrights of the Suffrage Era* (Manchester: Manchester University Press, 1992), pp. 106–8 for a full account of Knoblock's misremembered influence on the genesis of the production.
43 Edward Knoblock, *Round the Room* (London: Chapman and Hall Ltd., 1939), pp. 85–103.
44 Ray Mander and Joe Mitchenson, *The Lost Theatres of London*, p. 234.
45 Lena Ashwell, *Myself a Player*, p. 161. See also Viv Gardner, 'No Flirting with Philistinism: Shakespearean Production at Miss Horniman's Gaiety Theatre', *New Theatre Quarterly* 14: 3 (1998), pp. 220–33.
46 Dennis Kennedy, *Granville Barker and the Dream of Theatre*, p. 87.
47 Dan H. Lawrence, *Bernard Shaw: Collected Letters 1898–1910* (London: Max Reinhardt, 1965), p. 719.
48 Ibid., p. 720.
49 Lena Ashwell, *Myself a Player*, p. 105.
50 See letters dated 19/22 January 1909 and 13 February 1909 in the Lena Ashwell correspondence held at the Harry Ransom Theatre Collection at the University of Texas in Austin.
51 Lena Ashwell, *Myself a Player*, p. 106.
52 Gertrude Kingston, *Curtsey While You're Thinking* (London: Williams and Norgate, 1937); Nancy Price, *Into An Hour Glass* (London: Museum Press Ltd., 1953); and J. P. Wearing, 'Nancy Price and The People's National Theatre', *Theatre History Studies* 16 (1996), pp. 71–89.
53 Cicely Hamilton, *Life Errant* (London: J. M. Dent & Son, 1935), pp. 63–5; and Ashwell, *Myself a Player*, pp. 172–3.
54 Lena Ashwell, 'Acting as a Profession for Women', in Edith J. Morley (ed), *Women Workers in Seven Professions: A Survey of their Economic Conditions and Prospects* (London: George Routledge and Sons, 1914), p. 313.
55 Cicely Hamilton, *Life Errant*, p. 65. Also see Liz Whitelaw, *The Life and Rebellious Times of Cicely Hamilton: Actress, Writer, Suffragist* (London: The Women's Press, 1990).
56 Lena Ashwell, *Myself a Player*, p. 163.
57 Ibid., pp. 163–4.

58 Julie Hollege, *Innocent Flowers*; and Claire Hirshfield, 'The Actress as Social Activist'.
59 See Katherine Kelly, 'The Actresses Franchise League Prepares for War', p. 122.
60 10 June 1908, *Daily Express* Press Cuttings File, British Library at Colindale.
61 Lena Ashwell, *Myself a Player*, p. 181. See also Lena Ashwell, 'Acting as a Profession for Women'.
62 Lena Ashwell, *Myself a Player*, p. 182.
63 L. C. Collins, *Theatre at War 1914–18* (London: Macmillan Press Ltd, 1998). See also Michael Sanderson, *From Irving to Olivier: A Social History of the Acting Profession 1880–1983* (London: The Athlone Press, 1984).
64 Ibid., p. 150.
65 *Ibid.*, p. 175.
66 Lena Ashwell, *Modern Troubadours*, p. 4.
67 See Katherine Kelly, 'The Actresses Franchise League Prepares for War'.
68 W. MacQueen-Pope, *Ghosts and Greasepaint: The Story of the Days that Were* (London: Robert Hale Ltd., 1951), p. 301.
69 Basil Dean, *The Theatre At War* (London: George Harrap and Co. Ltd., 1956), pp. 79–84.
70 Lena Ashwell, *Modern Troubadours*, p. 37.
71 Ibid., p. 16.
72 Lena Ashwell, *Myself a Player*, p. 223. See also Annabelle Melzer, 'Spectacles and Sexualities: the "Mise en Scene" of "Tirailleurs Senegalais" on the Western Front 1914–1920', in Billie Melman (ed), *Borderlines: Genders and Identities in War and Peace, 1870–1930* (New York and London: Routledge, 1998), pp. 203–44, for a detailed account of other, less conventional, forms of entertainments for troops.
73 Susan Kingsley Kent, *Making Peace: The Reconstruction of Gender in Interwar Britain* (Princeton: Princeton University Press, 1994).
74 Lena Ashwell, *Myself a Player*, p. 276.
75 Lena Ashwell, *The Stage*, p. 141.
76 Michael Holroyd, *Bernard Shaw: The One Volume Definitive Edition* (London: Chatto and Windus, 1997), pp. 427–8.
77 Chris Rojek, *Celebrity* (London: Reaktion Books, 2001), p. 117; and Samuel Smiles, *Self Help* (London: IEA, Health and Welfare Unit edition, 1996).
78 Samuel Smiles, *Self Help*, p. 137.
79 Duncan Crow, *The Edwardian Woman* (London: George Allen and Unwin, 1978), p. 147.
80 Lena Ashwell, *Myself a Player*, p. 203; and L. C. Collins, *Theatre At War 1914–1918*, p. 174.
81 Lena Ashwell, *The Stage*, p. 161.

6

TILLY WEDEKIND AND LULU: THE ROLE OF HER LIFE OR THE ROLE IN HER LIFE?

Bella Merlin

Very little material exists concerning the life of Austrian actress, Tilly Wedekind (1886–1970), either in German or in English. On the surface this may not seem particularly surprising: there are many artists whose biographies remain obscure. However, Tilly's role as the wife of the widely acclaimed and pioneering actor-writer, Frank Wedekind (1864–1918), to whose plays she devoted much of her professional career and for whose later creations she was often the 'muse',[1] justifies a more significant place for her in theatre history. There is a substantial amount of material available on Frank Wedekind, not least his own *Diary of an Erotic Life*[2] and Elizabeth Boa's *The Sexual Circus: Wedekind's Theatre of Subversion*.[3] Yet Tilly Wedekind's relative absence in academic studies becomes particularly noticeable when contrasting her working relationship with and marriage to Wedekind with that of Anton Chekhov (1860–1904) and Olga Knipper (1868–1959), for example, or August Strindberg (1849–1912) and Siri von Essen (1850–1912). With these partnerships, the complexities of playwrights writing for their actress-lovers have been well documented.[4] When it comes to Tilly, however, the main resource available to us is her own autobiography, *Lulu: Die Rolle Meines Lebens* (1969) – translated as *Lulu: The Role of My Life*.[5] The title of the autobiography alludes to the protagonist in Wedekind's two 'monster' or 'sex' tragedies: *Earth Spirit* (1898) and *Pandora's Box* (1905). While the premières of both plays shocked the censors, the character of Lulu – the archetypal angel-child/demon-woman – has inspired actors and directors throughout the century since her first incarnation. She achieved her celluloid icon status in Ernst Pabst's 1929 silent movie, *Pandora's Box*,[6] with Louise Brooks. More recently, Lulu was played on the London stage by a string of British stage and film stars: Joanne Whalley Kilmer, Susan Lynch and Anna Friel.[7] The longevity of Lulu's potency is therefore marked, and nowhere is that potency more keenly felt than in Tilly Wedekind's *Lulu: The Role of My Life*.

Tilly Wedekind (née Newes) completed her autobiography while in her early eighties, and in 1969 it was published in Germany, one year before her death at the age of eighty-four. In other words, *Lulu: The Role of My Life* is an account by an elderly woman reflecting back on the events of her life. Structurally the book is divided into three sections: 'Part One: Tilly Newes' (pp. 13–76); 'Part Two: Tilly Wedekind' (pp. 77–200); and 'Part Three: "His Widow Tilly"' (pp. 201–99). Although Wedekind makes his first appearance as early as p. 38, a third of the book is devoted to the fifty years after his death. In this final third, Tilly refers to various theatrical roles that she played beyond the Wedekind canon,[8] as well as a number of other romantic encounters in her life.[9] Frank Wedekind and the character of Lulu however percolate the entire narrative long after Tilly was too old to play the part and Wedekind had long since died. Indeed, the allusion to Lulu in the title of the autobiography provokes questions in itself: does Tilly wish to suggest that Lulu was 'the role of her life' in that she excelled in it professionally? Or was Lulu the role that Tilly found herself playing in the actuality of her married life? This chapter seeks to assess why the fictional character of Lulu exerted such a profound influence over Tilly, and to what extent she colluded in perpetuating that influence. To facilitate this assessment, I begin by examining Tilly's literary 'voice' (how it is structured and where it fits in to autobiographical theory of late twentieth-century Germany). Thereafter the chapter incorporates Wedekind's 'voice' as articulated through his creation of Lulu. As we shall see, the cross-over points between Lulu the stage character and Tilly, actress and autobiographer, become quickly evident.

Tilly Wedekind: autobiographic motivations

One question underpinning any investigation into autobiography is centred around why the subject felt prompted to reconstruct her life experiences through the medium of autobiographical writing in the first place? Sidonie Smith and Julia Watson argue that 'Autobiography has been employed by many women writers to write themselves into history'.[10] Certainly, the reader of *Lulu: The Role of My Life* senses Tilly's underlying desire to emerge from the often oppressive shadow of Wedekind's fame and establish her own autonomous identity. However, a more specific answer is presented by Tilly towards the end of the autobiography. In 1968, while at the Max-Planck-Institute for Psychiatry in Munich,[11] undergoing treatment for the depression which had haunted her for most of her life, Tilly was provoked into identifying the root of her illness by a young Dr Dieter Schwarz.[12] In an attempt to pinpoint the precise moment when Tilly's depression began, Schwarz asked to read some extracts from her unpublished memoirs. In response to what he read therein, he presented her with the book, *Literature and Lies*, by Karl Kraus (1874–1936).[13] Kraus's book contains an account of a speech which he gave on the first night of the 1905 production of *Pandora's Box*, which Tilly did not hear at the time, as she was waiting backstage for the play to begin. In his speech, Kraus suggests that the source of all man's troubles lies in 'Pandora's Box' (as propounded in the myth in which Pandora

8 Tilly and Frank Wedekind in *Earth Spirit*.

unleashes all manner of evils upon mankind, discussed in greater detail later in this chapter). In her autobiography, Tilly implies that the details of Kraus's speech, as she read of it in *Literature and Lies*, suddenly revealed to her that the root of her depression could be traced back to playing Lulu in Wedekind's play. With that realisation, 'The depression was blown away in ten days'.[14]

'What [women's] life stories reveal', proposes Estelle C. Jelinek, 'is a self-consciousness and a need to sift through their lives for explanation and understanding'.[15] This is evidently the case with Tilly, seeking an explanation for and an understanding of her depression. Jelinek continues: 'The autobiographical intention is often powered by the motive to convince readers of their self-worth, to clarify, to affirm, and to authenticate their self-image.'[16] Indeed, the writing of *Lulu: The Role of My Life* can be seen to serve Tilly as a therapeutic, almost cathartic, means of presenting events and structuring a narrative in order that she may publicly 'convince us of her own worth' and personally 'authenticate her own image'. But what is that self-image which Tilly wishes to authenticate? And how does she strive to portray it, in terms of writing style, content and context? If we turn to her account of an event from early in the Wedekinds' relationship, we can begin to see the inherent potential in Tilly to fit the Lulu 'type', and consequently the ease with which her 'authentic self' might be subject to manipulation.

The autobiography: style and content

Tilly met Wedekind (aged forty-three to her nineteen years) in Kraus's 1905 production of *Pandora's Box* at the Trianon-Teater, Vienna, in which she played Lulu to his Jack the Ripper. Their subsequent engagement took place in February 1906, though the events leading up to it were auspicious. Wedekind had been asked to contribute to a theatrical evening at the Small Theatre Under the Lime Trees in Berlin, at which he presented a prologue clearly inspired by Tilly. When she failed to thank him for his flattering tribute at a social supper following the performance, Wedekind began to hurl a stream of insults at her. Tilly's account of her response illustrates several stylistic choices made in the overall writing of the autobiography, as well as revealing a number of personality traits which link her psychology to that underpinning the character of Lulu:

> I was very unhappy, drank more and more champagne, bit into the glass I was drinking from, and spat the bloody fragments into my hand. [...] We

> set off, Frank and I, driving in a carriage. He wanted to drop me off at my boarding house, but I wanted to go to his. I thought we would be able to settle the dispute. When we reached his place, he disappeared – I thought he would come right back. But he didn't. (He had gone straight to a bar for a glass of beer and to calm himself down.) I thought he had deliberately left me alone, and I went to bed. I was seriously sloshed, had the mean blues, and in my despair, I bit into the bolster. The material was rotten and torn, and the feathers fluttered round the whole room. I didn't notice at all.
>
> Then Frank came back. He saw the mess and thought I had done it deliberately. He fell into a fury and began to abuse me dreadfully. He took the photographs of me which were positioned all around his room, tore them into pieces and stamped on them. I leapt from the bed, stuck my arms out to stop him, and in so doing, I knocked over the oil-lamp. It immediately burst into flames and began to burn my pictures. Frank ran to the stove, scooped out some ashes and threw them onto the lamp to extinguish the fire. I seized the moment and ran out of the room and down the stairs. I was wearing only a chemise and knickers. I stood still for a few seconds in the hall – I heard Frank on the stairs and I hoped he would catch up with me. But he didn't. I ran through the gate, over the street, across the parkland – and down to the river Spree. There were some stone steps down to the water, and apple-barges on the bank. I was lucky I didn't leap onto the stone steps or into one of the apple-barges. I could have broken my bones. I leapt into the water.[17]

This extract from early in the book establishes some basic connections between Tilly and Lulu. There is a simplicity and immediacy in Tilly's narrative style, not dissimilar to the 'voice' of Lulu.[18] Furthermore, the combination of volatile emotion and impulsive action is highly reminiscent of Lulu,[19] as indeed is the self-knowledge with which she manipulates others,[20] revealed here by her momentary pause to check whether Wedekind is following her. Other links include her violence (biting the glass),[21] her intoxication (though Lulu's intoxication is metaphoric),[22] and the implicit theatricality of her behaviour.[23] On the surface, therefore, it would seem that Tilly's personality inclined itself towards those traits displayed in the fictive Lulu. However, the issue is not clear-cut. An extract from the penultimate page of the autobiography supports the opposing notion that Wedekind's own masochism precipitated his manipulation of Tilly into the Lulu 'type': 'I seemed to him like a heavenly creature, which, as he described it, 'brought him luck'. But precisely because from the moment of our first meeting his wishes came true, because at last with me he found longed-for success – precisely for that reason he saw me more and more as the Bringer of Disaster.'[24]

The autobiography: a historical context

Tilly's words pinpoint the paradoxical identities projected onto her within her marriage, a conflict of identities which led to the gradual fragmentation of her 'authentic self': she was perceived by her husband as both a 'heavenly creature' and the 'Bringer of Disaster'. In other words, she was heavily implicated in Frank Wedekind's eternal – and tormenting – inner quandary: was Woman ultimately a Redeemer or a Destroyer? This complex negotiation of destruction and redemption impacted significantly on Tilly's perception of herself, both personally and professionally. In fact, when placed in the context of autobiographical trends of the time, Tilly's desire to 'authenticate her self-image' proves remarkably radical. Published in 1969, *Lulu: The Role of My Life* may be considered – as Wedekind's writing was in the theatrical field – to be ahead of its time. The 1970s in Germany marked an explosion in women's autobiography, contributing to the development of *Neue Subjektivität* or 'New Subjectivity'. Along with an investigation of personal experience and self-exploration, New Subjectivity revealed a sense of 'self-criticism, resignation, melancholia and mourning'.[25] These concerns were usually linked to issues of national and cultural mourning following the Second World War and the division of Germany. To a certain extent Tilly shares those collective concerns, although frequently her 'loss' resides in the personal domain, as deaths and suicides saturate her autobiography. Among the more graphically described suicides are those of her sister, Paula (who, in 1906, cut her throat with a razor blade in a manner deemed by the newspapers reminiscent of Schwarz's death at the end of Act Two in *Earth Spirit*),[26] her mother (who, in 1915, swallowed needles, and died when they perforated her kidneys),[27] and her friend, the actress Lila Breda (who, in 1929, telephoned her lover then threw herself out of a fifth-storey window before he could reach her apartment).[28] In addition, there is Tilly's own suicide attempt on 30 November 1917, when, having booked herself into a room in Munich's *Deutscher Kaiser* Hotel, she swallowed poison.[29]

Amid this catalogue of deaths, tragedies and bouts of debilitating depression, we sense a figure in isolation. Here Tilly's autobiography appears as a precursor to another cultural emergence in Germany of the 1970s: *Verständigungsliteratur* (*Verständigen* meaning 'to inform or communicate').[30] Here, amateur writers sought avenues of autobiographic literature to articulate their experiences, difficulties, fantasies and thoughts. In this way, they emerged from their isolation and publicised the process of

9 Tilly and Frank Wedekind on their way to rehearsal at the Berlin Kammerspiel.

national transformation in both social and personal situations.[31] Throughout her autobiography, we feel Tilly's emergence from isolation as she consolidates her new-found sense of *self* by investigating and negotiating her sense of personal and professional *loss*.

While Wedekind's death was unquestionably a major loss and, despite other romantic liaisons, she never remarried, arguably the most profound loss that Tilly mourns in *Lulu: The Role of My Life* is that of an independent career. Much of her desire to find her voice by means of her autobiography, and to emerge from the shadows of Wedekind's success, is related to her need to redefine the public persona with which she was associated. Theatre practitioners and writers of autobiographies share in the same inevitable process, wherein the boundaries between fact and fiction become blurred. The process is further complicated with Tilly's negotiation of her life, since not only are her own boundaries as an autobiographical author inescapably blurred, but also Wedekind's boundaries of fact and fiction became merged in his complex perception of their relationship. In *Lulu: The Role of My Life*, Tilly confronts the uneasy fact that while her public image as Lulu launched her professionally, the private experience of herself as Tilly became infected by Wedekind's jealousy. Because he suffered the same 'persecution mania' with which he endows Dr Schön in *Earth Spirit*,[32] innocent actions executed by Tilly off-stage became distorted in Wedekind's mind as he projected onto her aspects of Lulu.[33] The extent to which Tilly suffered this projection or in fact colluded with it becomes clearer once we start to bring Wedekind directly into the debate by looking at the characteristics which comprise his fictional Lulu, and comparing them with the components that comprise Tilly's personality. Then by means of a 'metaphorical Venn diagram', the similarities and differences will, to some extent, emerge. In this way, we can begin to determine whether Lulu became 'the role of Tilly's life' because she shared personality traits, or whether in fact Tilly 'became' Lulu in her domestic life as an unavoidable reaction to Wedekind's 'persecution mania'.[34]

Frank Wedekind and Lulu: the power of the erotic

As soon as we bring Wedekind's 'voice' into the debate, we return to his inner quandary: his perceived belief in the tension between a revered and a reviled female sexuality. The conflict between Woman as deity (Redeemer) and Woman as devil (Destroyer) is illustrated by his very choice of Earth Spirit and Pandora as the original reference points for the character of Lulu. Both of these figures are incarnations of the legendary first female: Pan-dora ('of all gifts', and maybe 'gift for all'?)[35] was a mortal woman, while the first spirit of the earth was Gaea.[36] Wedekind's ambivalence towards female sexuality and spirituality is highlighted by Tilly towards the end of her autobiography: 'For thousands of years, the various religions of various people have concurred that all evil was brought into the world by women.... And considering that Frank's favourite "subject" was "Religious knowledge", then it is perhaps no wonder that he saw his marriage to me as the beginning of the end.'[37]

Possibly one of the most disturbing manifestations of Wedekind's Redeemer/Destroyer conflict is the murder of his protagonist, Lulu, at the hands of Jack the Ripper in *Pandora's Box*. Although Jack the Ripper remains tantalisingly mysterious in criminal history, his identity here in Wedekind's dramatic fiction is clear: he is the purger of society, the destroyer of female sexuality. Yet Wedekind's inner conflict didn't stop there. In his writing and in his life, he was not only torn between Woman as Redeemer and Destroyer, but also between his experience of the Erotic and the Logical.[38] With his creation of Lulu, it would seem that his rational and logical side regarded Woman as Destroyer because she *represents* the uncontrollable, instinctive, erotic and natural. However, his anti-bourgeois and erotic side regarded Woman as Redeemer because she *rejects* the controllable, rational, logical, and material. In other words, Wedekind simultaneously feared and celebrated Woman for the very same reasons. He manifested this tension both in one encounter – as the 'logical' male, Jack the Ripper destroys the 'erotic' female, Lulu – and in the contrasting fates of Lulu within each of the two 'sex tragedies'. Thus, with the Lulu of *Earth Spirit*, we see the celebration of sexual, erotic, feminine energy, despite the fact that it results in the destruction of her husbands Goll, Schwarz, and Schön. Then in *Pandora's Box*, we see the hunted animal, fleeing from society, having broken the law by murdering Dr Schön. Through this crime, she, like Pandora, has now released all evil and malice upon the world, and therefore upon herself. Consequently, the private/public tension is heightened: although Lulu commits murder behind closed doors, she unleashes the powers of society to haunt her publicly. This public/private tension was also manifested by Tilly. By jumping into the river Spree, she turned private passions into public affairs, risking the exposure of both herself and Wedekind to media attention. Wedekind's insurance tactic was to bribe the boatman who helped to save her and the landlady who gave her dry clothes, thereby preventing the event appearing in the newspapers.[39] On this occasion, he protected his 'private property' from public ownership.

Silencing the erotic: the Pierrot painting

If Wedekind was afraid of the potential chaos reeked by Woman's sexuality, then he needed to contain it or at least control it. Certainly the issue of control or ownership is central to the relationships that men have with Lulu in the 'sex tragedies'. This is due in part to the fact that: 'Each of the men who succumb to her power understands a different part of her and completes her with his own illusions'.[40] Through this 'completion', they believe that they own her, albeit temporarily. In many ways, Wedekind repeated this pattern with Tilly: by encouraging her to appear in his plays, he completed her professional 'role' and thereby 'owned' her theatrical life. This ownership was felt acutely by Tilly, who on at least two occasions turned down opportunities to perform in other theatres without Wedekind, for fear of arousing his unbearable jealousy.[41] At the same time, she struggled with the knowledge that, much as she was indebted to him for the professional exposure provided by his plays, it was to a significant degree *her* acting talents that guaranteed *his* success. Yet, she silenced her own independent career 'voice' to promote his.[42]

In *Earth Spirit*, this tension of silence, power and professional exploitation is at the heart of Lulu's experiences of men. With Schwarz, she is the model and, once he has married her, his paintings become immensely fashionable and saleable.[43] For Schön and Alwa, she is the dancer who must incarnate the latter's choreography and perform for the former's fiancée.[44] She is a possession, a muse who – through the medium of art or dance – is silenced and exposed for general consumption. Nowhere is this more overt than in her portrait (painted by Schwarz in Act One of *Earth Spirit*) as Pierrot, the innocent lover-fool. As an archetype, the Pierrot is loaded with meaning, not least with regard to his silence. In her essay 'On Women and Clothes and Carnival Fools',[45] Efrat Tseëlson refers to the three voices shared by women and fools: the proper voice, the provocative voice and the (paradoxically) mute voice. By presenting Lulu as Pierrot, Wedekind has manifested these three voices. Like the fool, Lulu is truth-speaking (proper),[46] she is subversive and inspirational as well as erotic and sensual (provocative),[47] and she is ambivalent in her beliefs (mute).[48]

As described in *Lulu: The Role of My Life*, the Pierrot painting becomes as powerful a symbol in the Wedekinds' life as it is in the two 'sex tragedies', where it continually reappears as a backdrop to Lulu's social rise and decline.[49] Since every production of *Earth Spirit* required a portrait to be painted of each new actress, one was needed of Tilly for the 1905 Viennese production; the artist employed for the job was Emil Holitzer. The details surrounding the sitting, as recounted by Tilly, are self-consciously Lulu-esque:

> Holitzer invited me, along with Karl Kraus and Wedekind, to dine at his house for the sitting. After dinner, I went up into the studio alone … to put my pierrot costume on. I was almost ready when the door opened

> and in came Wedekind. He evidently wanted to return the kiss I had given him backstage [at the first production of *Earth Spirit*]. But in my pierrot costume I was very nimble, I slipped away from him and ran through the studio, round tables and chairs, and he ran after me. Suddenly he stopped dead in his tracks, clasped his brow and cried: 'But this is *Earth Spirit*, the first act.' To which I replied: 'Why do you write such stupid plays!' ... At that moment, the door opened and, as if on cue, in walked Kraus and Holitzer.[50]

This story reveals the extent to which Tilly colludes in her construction as Lulu. She was unquestionably familiar with Act One, in which the artist Schwarz chases Lulu round his studio, as she and Wedekind had already performed the play together earlier in the season. She must therefore have been fully conscious of the resonances of her actions.

Tilly's awareness of her collusion is demonstrated by the references (which are scattered throughout her autobiography, in a repeating motif that echoes the Pierrot painting in the 'sex tragedies') to a particular photograph that Wedekind owned of her as Lulu wearing men's pyjamas from Act Two of *Earth Spirit*. For their 1916 tour to Berlin, a 'gifted and nice young actor, Fritz D.'[51] played Alwa to Tilly's Lulu and Wedekind's Schön:

> During our final performance of *Earth Spirit*, [Fritz D.] appeared in the last act, in which Alwa presents me with flowers, not with the usual paper ones, but with a wonderful bouquet of fresh golden roses. Frank told me that I must throw the flowers in the river Spree. 'But, Frank,' I said, 'it's quite harmless! It's also so obvious that Fritz D. likes me best in the second act when I wear men's pyjamas! He likes boys ...' A photograph of me in these elegant men's pyjamas hung in Frank's room. After our return journey, Frank suddenly declared that he didn't want to see this photograph any more. He took it off the wall and gave it to me. I didn't know what to do with it, so I stowed it away in my wardrobe.[52]

By removing the photograph from his study, Wedekind essentially 'silenced' Tilly's sexuality, leaving her *metaphorically* to 'shut her Pandora's box' through the *actual* gesture of stowing the provocative picture away.[53]

Exhibiting the erotic: transvestism, masquerade and lace-up boots

Yet the inescapable paradox remains that, for all the 'silencing' and containment of his 'Woman', Wedekind continually placed Tilly on public display by featuring her in his dramas: there he could present her and dress her up according to his taste and fancies. This exhibiting serves as another indication of the displacement of Tilly's 'authentic self', particularly when she appeared *en travestie* where the femaleness of her sexuality was consciously distorted. In fact, three of the four roles written for her in *The Stone of Wisdom* (1909) are breeches parts. It would, therefore, seem to be no coincidence that Tilly's photograph (as discussed above) portrays her in 'men's pyjamas', since the relevance of transvestism in the Lulu Plays, and indeed in Wedekind's psychology, is not to be underestimated. When considering his exploration of eroticism and how it relates to Tilly, it is worth noting that Wedekind insisted on young girls playing the adolescent boys' parts in his plays.[54] Thus, Tilly was originally cast as Bob the Liftboy in *Pandora's Box* before she was 'promoted' to Lulu, and the love-struck schoolboy Hugenberg was performed by young actresses in both Lulu Plays. As Tilly states, 'There were hardly any lads in the theatre who were pretty and gifted enough to reproduce the entire magic and innocent eroticism of this age group.'[55] In other words, by dressing women in male apparel, Wedekind was inviting a particular 'gaze' from his audience. There is an inevitable *frisson* of sexual danger, for both men and women, in transvestism, given its potent allusions to masquerade and permissiveness. Whereas 'male transvestism is an occasion for laughter', female transvestism is 'another occasion for desire',[56] one which often suggests undertones of bisexuality. Such an undertone is evident in *Earth Spirit*, when the lesbian Countess Geschwitz appeals to Lulu to 'dress as a man' at her ball for women artists.[57] How far Tilly herself responded to such bisexual undertones is debatable. It would certainly be erroneous to argue from the contents of her autobiography that she herself explored any bisexual relations; in fact, unlike Wedekind's erotic diaries, her writing is almost devoid of sexual reference).[58] However, her descriptions of other females are frequently loaded with erotic awareness.[59]

In either male or female costume, Tilly was clearly conscious of the allure of her on-stage presence:

> At that time, it caused a sensation when I showed my legs in literary pieces. People were used to it only in operettas, the circus and variety. Frank was aware of this sensation. It was his intention and his preference. He himself enjoyed going to the operetta, and even more to variety shows though his favourite was the circus. He had a poster printed for [*Censorship* (1907)], in which I was pictured in six different costumes and always showing my legs.[60]

As the object of public gaze, the Actress (as a generic identity) inevitably provokes within the audience desire and the illusion of availability, and Wedekind clearly both exploited and feared this provocation. Indeed, Tseëlson's observations on eighteenth-century masquerade would not seem at all out of place here, since 'Much of the fear of the masquerade ... is related to the belief that it encouraged female sexual freedom and female emancipation generally'.[61] Given that the Actress's profession *is* the masquerade, it is not surprising that Tilly aroused such fear in Wedekind. Furthermore, the fragile delineation between the masquerade and the truth – and therefore the extent to which Tilly might be sexually free – became even more blurred for Wedekind as the result of another theatrical tradition of the time. It was customary for actresses to provide their own costumes for their roles, which meant that, while masqueraders may return to moral and social norms once the party is over, Wedekind knew that Tilly's costume trunks were crammed with the accoutrements of her professional masks: these trunks were veritable Pandora's boxes. In fact, Tilly's autobiography details various social events at which she wore her theatrical costumes,[62] once more blurring the boundaries between the sexual availability of her various characters (not least of which was Lulu) and of herself in real-life encounters.

Yet, in a characteristically masochist manner, the fear conjured up by the merge into masquerade arguably fed Wedekind's erotic imagination. His love of female attire is evident in his stage directions to the Lulu Plays,[63] and it was a love that Tilly seemed willing to enflame. Her particular penchant was for lace-up boots, a recognisably 'fetishistic' item of clothing. Referring to a pair of bright red boots, Tilly describes how 'They really were coquettish boots. But Frank loved such effects and in my naiveté, I also found the little boots heavenly.'[64] Although clearly she herself loves the provocative footwear, we also sense Tilly's youthful anxiety to please her older husband, despite the fact that her public fashion statement would surely have conjured up images of the Parisian Pigalle girls with whom Wedekind was all too well acquainted in his promiscuous youth.[65]

A similar boot incident arises out of an encounter on a train in the spring of 1907, as Wedekind and Tilly travel from Germany to Switzerland: 'On the train we met the composer Eugen d'Albert with his beautiful, young, elegant wife. ... Straight away I fell in love with the high-heeled buckskin leather boots that she wore. As soon as we arrived in Zürich, I also bought myself a pair of lace-up boots made from light brown buckskin leather. They were Frank's great rapture.'[66]

The collision of 'self' and 'self-image'

The desire to mimic another 'young, beautiful, elegant wife' reveals Tilly's complex relationship with herself. If we consider Jacques Lacan's 'mirror stage' in which 'the child comes to recognise its image in the looking glass; but as it looks in the glass it sees its image as an other',[67] we can begin to unravel the behaviour patterns into which Tilly falls. She sees another 'desirable' female: in that female, she identifies components that she knows to be attractive to Wedekind: therefore, she replicates the external details, to see herself reflected back to herself in a similar image.

Lacan's 'mirror' concept raises three significant questions which further enable us to determine the extent to which Tilly colludes with Wedekind in the construction of her own identity: firstly, how willingly does Tilly collaborate with the public's view of her as 'Lulu'? In other words, if she were to look in the mirror, or sit in the audience, what image would she wish to see reflected – or presented? Secondly, how does she respond to other actresses who play Lulu? In other words, how does she respond to the process of having reflected back to her, through a female 'other', elements of her 'self', whether that 'self' be of her own or of Wedekind's making? And thirdly, how did Wedekind reflect her personality back to her through his later plays, in which he publicly explored private aspects of their relationship and in which she then had to perform?

The first question deals primarily with 'self' and 'self-image'. This in turn links directly with the actual process of writing autobiography, the very act of which 'gestures towards a desire for the "self" and the "self-image" to coincide'.[68] There is a sense in her autobiography, that Tilly is attempting to understand whether her 'self-image' really is that of her own making or that created by external bodies. As an actress and the wife of a nationally acclaimed writer, she 'belongs' to the public in the image that they have come to expect her to convey. This becomes startlingly apparent when, on reaching her eightieth birthday (an event about which she feels great unease), she is told by her daughter, Anna-Pamela, that she will have to celebrate it, since announcements of her birthday have already appeared in the newspapers. Indeed, one headline reads: 'Lulu turns 80'.[69] 'Lulu' is the identity provided for her by Wedekind and subsequently projected onto her by the public, despite the fact that the part was not written for her, as the Lulu Plays were completed before she and Wedekind met. Tilly's autobiography seems not so much concerned with *coinciding* 'self' with 'self-image', but rather

10 Tilly Wedekind as a young woman and in old age.

with *colliding* them. In this way, she can voice her anxiety at having sacrificed her 'authentic self' to an identity perpetuated by her husband and the public. To some extent, her 'authentic self' has been submerged by Lulu.

The *cri de coeur* is most overt in Tilly's expression of professional frustration, believing that Wedekind 'had forgotten that he had married an actress in her own right', who had only surrendered her own career 'in order to champion his work'.[70] Later she argues: 'Had I not put my youth, my talent completely at his disposal? Had I not helped him to reach success? Had I not brought him luck – as he told me himself – and relinquished classical roles for which I was born to get (perhaps) great acclaim?'[71] Tilly's words are reminiscent of Lulu's to Schön in Act Four of *Earth Spirit*, when she declares, 'You may have sacrificed the evening of your life to me, but you've had my whole youth in exchange. You know ten times better than I do which is of greater value'.[72] Through her autobiography – published fifty one years after her husband's death – Tilly strives to reclaim the career and talent which she clearly felt she had surrendered to Wedekind, and which arguably may have been 'ten times better' had she not worked so extensively with him and for him. This belief is supported in two specific examples, one of which follows her discussion of Wedekind having been labelled by the press as an artistic 'dilettante': 'And I too, who followed his directorial instructions exactly, suddenly became classed among the dilettantes although I had already been acting at various leading theatres for three years and had been very successful in tragic roles.'[73] Again, she is publicly given an 'image' – 'dilettante' – which does not necessarily coincide with that which she would have claimed for her 'authentic self'.

The second example follows Wedekind's death by which Tilly is freed to play other parts. When Klaus Mann (1906–49)[74] and his mother, Katja, saw her play Kirstin in Strindberg's *Miss Julie*, 'they were really surprised how good I was as the cook. Since they had only known me in Wedekind-plays, they had no idea what I was capable of.'[75] Through her autobiography, Tilly is 'convincing readers of her self-worth', letting us know her potential, relinquishing herself from the role of Lulu and releasing herself from the constraints of Wedekind, both as a theatre director and a possessive husband. Yet despite her evident frustration, Tilly's connection with Lulu is not entirely unwilling; indeed, she is proud in claiming her right to the part: 'I was exactly the type that Wedekind envisaged for the role – young, naïve and definitely full of eroticism – a mixture rather lacking in many people. An instinctive nature, with an alert understanding, but led by one's impulse. Not refined, but on all sides fired by good and evil.'[76]

Within her self-description lies a definite narcissism, as she emphasises the attributes that she bears, but others lack. This narcissism links directly with Lacan's 'mirror theory' and also brings us to the second question: 'How does Tilly respond to other actresses who play Lulu?'

'Mirror' images of Lulu

Throughout *Lulu: The Role of My Life*, we sense Tilly's desire to be taken seriously as an actress outside Wedekind's dramatic canon. And yet she too seems to be seduced by the character of Lulu and driven by her narcissistic urge to 'own' the part. Mary Ann Doane suggests that 'the female spectator's desire can be described only in terms of a kind of narcissism – the female look demands a becoming'.[77] If this can be applied to Tilly, then a tension exists between what she sees in other Lulus and what she wishes to retain for herself as the 'archetypal' Lulu. Leonie Taliansky, who played Lulu in Carl Heine's 1898 Leipzig production of *Earth Spirit*, is called by Tilly 'the ideal type, a sweet, innocent, open creature': 'Such a child of the angels ... seemed to Wedekind to be the ideal disposition for Lulu'.[78] As Wedekind's real-life embodiment of Lulu, Tilly must – by implication – possess these qualities too. Maria

Orska, who played Lulu opposite Wedekind in Berlin (1917) receives less favourable comments as recorded by Tilly, primarily from Wedekind, who is more convinced by his wife's interpretation than by Orska's: '[Her] performance was too refined. "Lulu must be a child of nature, like my wife".'[79]

Tilly's success in the role becomes in itself a source of tension between husband and wife. The Zürich Post's review of *Earth Spirit* (which was performed as part of the Wedekinds' tour of Switzerland in 1917) is quoted by Tilly as saying:

> 'She presents the figure with graceful ease, with all the moves and nuances in which that "beautiful little animal" dazzles: she is wary and bewitching, naïve in her depravity and full of indestructible vitality, triumphant and soulless in every word and tone; furthermore, she is glittering and captivating in her appearance. It was a performance, which demands unreserved recognition.' And how did Frank react to this? He said, 'I congratulate you on your success. I no longer have the inclination for us to play together. I can take no competition with me.'... And that's how my success panned out![80]

Thus Tilly's success became her downfall, and yet Wedekind refused to let her play other roles. Just as Lulu must dance for Schön's fiancée, so too was Tilly forced to perform the roles in which she was cast. Which brings us to the third question connected to Lacan's 'mirror theory': 'How did Wedekind reflect Tilly's personality back to her in his later plays?'

'Mirror': the performance of self

In Wedekind's later dramas, Tilly was to incarnate characters using her professional resources of body, imagination, emotions and spirit, and yet the characters that she was incarnating were constructs formed by her husband who took, as his starting point, her own human traits as he perceived them. Thus, *Censorship* (1907) is a play clearly dealing with the problems of their marriage, with Tilly's character Kadidja throwing herself off a balcony (in a manner reminiscent of the Spree incident in the previous year). With *Simson, or Shame and Jealousy* (1914), Wedekind put on the stage 'his own personal feelings of powerlessness, of helplessness, of surrender'.[81] For Tilly (as Delilah), it can only have been professionally and personally excruciating to receive the worst reviews of her life for her performance, even though her very own personality had been the source of the play's subject matter: 'Frank had thought about me when he had written this cold, cruel corruptress. He had even credited me with all those things!'[82] The critics' opinion that, ironically, Tilly was wrong for the part endorsed the view that maybe she was not the cruel, heartless woman into which Wedekind was trying to contort her, either on the stage or behind closed doors. His continuing anxieties about their marriage are taken further in *Herakles* (1917), when Tilly's role as Dejaneira shows marriage to be the bringer of murder, calamity and death. Certainly her account of his one-act play, *Uberfürchtenichts* (1916) – which she 'could not bear'[83] – painfully reveals Wedekind's suppression of his wife:

> ... in it I had to say to him, 'Holy Heaven, how old you have become,' and he replied:
> 'Go away! Some other thin-grown child
> Is now playing the breeches parts,
> Who, thank God, is less deaf and blind
> To my lively and mysterious poetry.'
> So as far as he was concerned, I was deaf and blind![84]

Taming the erotic: the allure of the circus

If Wedekind's intent was to contain, silence and suppress 'Woman', his final step in mastering what was essentially his own conflict between eros and logos was to tame her. Echoing Lulu in the Prologue to *Earth Spirit*, Tilly Wedekind became something of a circus animal, caged in an unhappy marriage. Divorce was out of the question as both she and Wedekind acknowledged the profundity of Schön's words to Lulu: 'Does one divorce when one has grown so together that half of oneself goes too?'[85] Nor could she cease acting in his plays: Wedekind's torturous threats to leave her if she accepted other work hung in the air like a Damacles' sword, rendering her – like a tamed animal – dependent on his employment of her. In fact, it is to the forms and imagery of the circus that we finally turn in assessing the extent to which Tilly colluded with Wedekind in embracing Lulu as the role of her life.

The Prologue to *Earth Spirit* opens to 'disclose the entrance to a tent from which emerges the sound of cymbals and the beating of drums'.[86] In walks an animal-tamer wearing the familiar attire of a ring-master, whip and revolver in his hands. Lulu, the *schöne Tier*, 'the beautiful animal', is paraded before us, silent, tamed, but threatening danger.[87] Instantly we are plunged into territory both familiar and deeply inspirational for Frank

Wedekind: the circus.[88] His particular passion was for tightrope walkers and trapeze artists – who have been described as 'waltzers of the sky', 'flirters with tragedy'.[89] Within such artists lay a symbiosis of life and profession, the art of which was 'maintaining oneself in an always tricky and dangerous medium, surrounded by the incalculable and operating in seeming defiance of physical laws'.[90] Implicit in the trapeze artist's invitation to mortal danger and her subsequent flouting of that danger, we see manifested in physical form Wedekind's own inner conflict between flesh and will, eros and logos. If an individual's moral structure is determined by his or her ability to subjugate the body to the will, nowhere is it more clearly demonstrated than in the trapeze artist's defiance of gravity. As David F. Kuhns describes it, circus becomes the 'purest embodiment and expression of the morality of the flesh'.[91]

At the same time as symbolising morality – or the conquest of the flesh – the trapeze artist paradoxically arouses carnal desire: she becomes, in the words of Jean Starobinski, 'an idol of perversity'.[92] Mary Russo elucidates this point:

> For the artist who both identifies with and desires the female acrobat, several fantasies converge: the fantasy of a controlling spectatorship, the fantasy of artistic transcendence and freedom signified by the flight upwards and the defiance of gravity, and the fantasy of the femininity which defies the limits of the body, especially the female body.[93]

Russo goes on to describe how the female acrobat has served in literature as a muse, one which 'was lifted off the classical pedestal to fly or at least dangle in the heavens. Femininity airborne and in motion figured as the highest expression of the lightness of being'.[94] Indeed, there was something in the quality of Tilly, including her youth and slight build, which invited Wedekind to elevate her to the status of muse. When they moved into their Munich apartment in 1908, Tilly records how he decorated a vast red study with pictures of her in various roles, in the midst of which he set up a two-tiered podium with a carved armchair and a footstool placed on top: 'it was like a proper tall throne, and it was Frank's wish that my place was usually up there'.[95] Thus, he literally and metaphorically placed Tilly on a pedestal.

In sharp contrast to his adulation, Wedekind wrote into his plays circus-like tasks for which Tilly was to be 'trained'. With the role of Lamia the arch-temptress,[96] in his play *The Stone of Wisdom* (1909), she had to learn to walk on an enormous ball, and, from her description, we can sense the mild sadism lurking in the task that Wedekind set her:[97]

> As this devilish being, I wore a white atlas costume with a very short little white skirt, which stuck out like a bell with six or seven bright blue net petticoats. … And I balanced on a ball that rolled across the stage. Of course I seriously had to learn to do this first. It was extremely difficult, especially in my high heels, and I had to speak verse too.[98]

There is, however, a pride implicit in Tilly's account of how she conquered such challenges, a pride which is endorsed by the revelations within *Lulu: The Role of My Life* of her innate attraction to aerial danger. Her penchant for real (and symbolic) leaps into the unknown are encapsulated by her description of how, aged eight, she watched experienced swimmers dive from the top board into the swimming bath: 'I wanted to follow suit, and since I couldn't yet swim, I let the lifeguard tie a rope round me and I plunged down into the water. My courage has never really failed me, and neither did it later when – after a row with Wedekind – I sprang without warning into the river Spree.'[99]

Conclusion

As her leap into the Spree suggests, a captivating, but terrifying, quality of Tilly Wedekind was her desire to defy gravity, without always having a life-line around her waist. As we have seen, the very process of writing *Lulu: The Role of My Life* seems to be her attempt to construct a kind of 'psychological life-line', which led to the banishing of her depression. And yet – in typically elliptical style – she also describes the immense power of playing Lulu in a production of *Earth Spirit* in 1917: 'I seemed to be flying from a dark cage towards the light. I surpassed even myself, I was sovereign and elated, without restraint or the weight of the earth.'[100]

So 'Lulu' is both the role *of* Tilly's life – in that it released her aerial, spiritual quality – and the role *in* her life – in that it lay at the centre of her earth-bound depression. The web is tangled. The answers are as ambivalent as the character herself. When writing of her self-poisoning, Tilly provides a striking image, one which in many ways serves as a neat metaphor for her own process of negotiating her life through the act of autobiographical writing. Describing her recovery in hospital, she tells of the affect on her skin, as the poison gradually works its way out of her body: 'The skin on my hands had made itself as hard as parchment. One day I could pull it off like a pair of gloves. The lines of my hands were on them. … Underneath was new skin as tender as a baby's.'[101]

In many ways, Tilly's autobiography reflects the dried-skin gloves: it is 'made' from her, her life-lines are upon it, and yet the 'authentic self' remains somewhat elusive. Throughout the book, her writing is understated, dryly humorous in many places, often non-linear (there are few dates included), and startlingly detached from deeply emotive situations. She reveals explosive personal issues: then she frames, contains, and diffuses them by the simplicity of her writing style. The result is that the 'real' part of her, the new skin underneath, remains tantalisingly evasive. As with Lulu and as indeed with autobiography in general, we are offered a mask onto which we may project an interpretation and beneath which we can detect nuances, but the real flesh-and-blood is caught only in momentary glimpses. The result is that no solid conclusions can be drawn: to some extent, elements of Tilly's personality enabled Wedekind to project onto her the qualities that he both admired and feared in women, and with which he had infused the character of Lulu. And to some extent, Tilly colluded with him. She was both his professional 'bringer of fortune' through the incarnation of his plays, and his personal destroyer, as her charm and talent fuelled his self-consuming jealousy and fear. At the age of eighty-one, the note upon which Tilly ends her autobiography is both touching and implicitly self-mocking. Having unlocked the cause of her depression by tracing it back to her playing of Lulu and renegotiated her 'authentic self' through the process of writing her autobiography, she reveals her unerring desire to explore identity through performance: 'I now had the great desire to act in the theatre again.'[102] In 1970, a year after *Lulu: Die Rolle Meines Lebens* appeared in Germany, Tilly Wedekind was dead.

Notes

1 Such creations include Kadidja in *Censorship* (1907), Lamia in *The Stone of Wisdom* (1909), Franziska in *Franziska* (1911) and Delilah in *Simson* (1914).

2 Frank Wedekind, *Diary of an Erotic Life*, trans. W. E. Yuill, ed. Gerhard Hay (Oxford: Basil Blackwell, 1990).

3 Elizabeth Boa, *The Sexual Circus: Wedekind's Theatre of Subversion* (Oxford: Basil Blackwell, 1987).

4 Donald Rayfield, *Anton Chekhov: A Life* (London: HarperCollins, 1997), Jean Benedetti, *Dear Writer, Dear Actress* (London: Methuen, 1996), Michael Meyer's *Strindberg* (Oxford: Oxford University Press, 1987) and Eivor Martinus's *Strindberg and Love* (Oxford: Amber Lane, 2001) are among the studies which acknowledge the importance of these romantic and professional entanglements.

5 Tilly Wedekind, *Lulu: Die Rolle Meines Lebens* (Munich: Rütten + Loening Verlag, 1969). All quotations from the autobiography included in this chapter appear in my own translation. With the exception of an extract translated by

Nick Hern in *Theatre Quarterly* 1: 2, April 1971 (London: Eyre Methuen), the book has yet to appear in English translation.

6 *Pandora's Box* (*Lulu*), screenplay by Ladislaus Vajda from *Earth Spirit* and *Pandora's Box*, directed by G. W. Pabst, produced by George C. Horsetzky for the production company, Nero Film A.G., first shown in Berlin in February 1929.

7 Joanne Whalley Kilmer (Almeida Theatre, London, 1991, directed by Ian McDiamid who also played Dr Schön), Susan Lynch (Cambridge Theatre Company, 1992, directed by Nick Phillippou) and Anna Friel (Almeida Theatre, London, 2001, directed by Jonathan Kent).

8 Tilly cursorily mentions playing the title role in *Maria Stewart*, directed by Hermine Körner at the Kammerspiele, Maximilian Straße, Berlin (and Lulu in *Pandora's Box*, both productions staged in the 1920s), as well as Kirstin in *Miss Julie*, the mother in Hauptmann's *Michael Kramer*, and Mrs Higgins in *My Fair Lady* (all in the 1930s).

9 Brief romances or intense friendships existed after Wedekind's death: a significant relationship was developed between herself and the doctor and writer, Gottfried Benn (1886–1957), whom Tilly met when they were both forty-four and with whom she had a seven-year friendship. Their letters, written between 1930 and 1955, were published in German in 1986.

10 Sidonie Smith and Julia Watson (eds), *Women, Autobiography, Theory: A Reader* (Madison: University of Wisconsin Press, 1998), p. 5.

11 The Max-Planck-Institute was founded in Munich in 1917. In 1966 its name was changed to the Max-Planck-Institute for Psychiatry and its research was expanded to cover all major areas of psychiatry and basic research in related sciences. In many respects, Tilly was something of a 'guinea pig' in undergoing her medical treatment.

12 Tilly Wedekind, *Lulu: Die Rolle Meines Lebens*, p. 293.

13 Karl Kraus, dramatist, social critic, aphorist and poet, published a periodical entitled *Die Fackel* ('The Torch'), among the contributors to which was Frank Wedekind.

14 Tilly Wedekind, *Lulu: Die Rolle Meines Lebens*, p. 294.

15 Estelle C. Jelinek (ed.), *Autobiography: Essays in Criticism* (Bloomington: Indiana University Press, 1980): 'Introduction: Women's Autobiography and the Male Tradition', p. 15.

16 Ibid.

17 Tilly Wedekind, *Lulu: Die Rolle Meines Lebens*, pp. 63–4.

18 *Earth Spirit*, Act 1 Scene 3 between Lulu and the painter Schwarz, demonstrates something of Lulu's simple allure. Frank Wedekind, *The Lulu Plays and other Sex Tragedies*, trans. Stephen Spender (London: Calder and Boyers, 1972), p. 29.

19 The following impassioned speech immediately precedes Lulu's impulsive shooting of Dr Schön in Act 4, Scene 8 of *Earth Spirit*: 'I've never in the world wanted to be anything but what I've been taken for, and no one has

ever taken me for anything but what I am. You're trying to make me put a bullet through my heart. I'm no longer sixteen years old, but I think I'm still too young to put a bullet through my heart.' (Ibid., p. 97.)

20 Act 1, Scene 1 of *Earth Spirit* reveals Lulu's utter self-awareness. Ibid., p. 19.

21 Lulu's act of murdering Dr Schön is the epitome of violence.

22 As Prince Escerny says of Lulu's dancing in Act 3, Scene 2 of *Earth Spirit*, 'When she dances her solo she is intoxicated with her own beauty – seems to be idolatrously in love with it.' (Ibid., p. 69.)

23 Lulu's implicit theatricality is laced through most of her encounters with men, as illustrated by her exchange with the artist, Schwarz, in Act 1, Scene 4 of *Earth Spirit*. Ibid., p. 28.

24 Tilly Wedekind, *Lulu: Die Rolle Meines Lebens*, p. 298.

25 Barbara Kosta, *Recasting Autobiography: Women's Counterfictions in Contemporary German Literature and Film* (Ithaca: Cornell University Press, 1994), p. 37.

26 'Towards the end, Paula had got into the habit in the afternoons of going into the small room at the back of the apartment ... Then she shut herself in. Shortly after, Dora heard a bloodcurdling scream ... You could hear gurgling groans from inside ... Paula lay on the floor. Half a bottle of cognac stood on the chest of drawers – empty – and a note lay next to it: "Forgive me – for God's sake, don't save me." The walls were splattered with blood. She had slashed her throat and wrists with a razor blade.' (Wedekind, *Lulu: Die Rolle Meines Lebens*, p. 105.)

27 'My family never told me that my mother's death was suicide, but really I assumed it.' (Ibid., p. 165.)

28 Ibid., p. 239. During Wedekind's life time, Lila Breda had played opposite Tilly and Wedekind as 'the heavenly lover' in *Franziska*. She had developed a romantic relationship with the doctor, Gottfried Benn, who was later to become Tilly's close friend.

29 Tilly Wedekind, *Lulu: Die Rolle Meines Lebens*, p. 188.

30 Barbara Kosta suggests that 'the historical significance of *Verständigungsliteratur* in the 1970s must be seen primarily in its creation of a public forum. Women's texts facilitated a support system and provided a realm for personal confrontation.' (Barbara Kosta, *Recasting Autobiography*, p. 47.)

31 Ibid., p. 47.

32 Tilly Wedekind, *The Lulu Plays*, pp. 88–9.

33 Wedekind's 'persecution mania' is illustrated in Tilly's account of an incident when Wedekind's illegitimate son, Erwin, came to visit them in Berlin – she lent him one of her costume ties which later sent Wedekind into a frenzy. (Tilly Wedekind, *Lulu: Die Rolles Meines Lebens*, pp. 115–16.)

34 'The worst part of the story was that for the rest of his life, Frank reproached me for [the tie incident]. At every opportunity he would begin on it again. Frank knew that people often described his displays of anger as persecution mania. Now people call the same thing complexes.' (Ibid., p. 156.)

35 Pandora was created from clay by Zeus and Hephaestus as a punishment for Prometheus's stealing of fire. Each of the Olympians gave their mortal creation a different gift and talent, thus each god and goddess 'completed' her, much in the way that Lulu's lovers in the Lulu Plays 'complete' her.

36 Gaea is Mother Earth, believed to be the daughter of Chaos and the mother of all creatures. She tends to be referred to as the Mother of other Gods, without having any specific myths attached to her.

37 Tilly Wedekind, *Lulu: Die Rolle Meines Lebens*, p. 294.

38 The battle between Logos and Eros (or Sexus) lay at the heart of the nineteenth-century 'Woman Question', which was debated by philosophers, dramatists, artists and social commentators. Elizabeth Boa's chapter on 'Wedekind and the "Woman Question"' in *The Sexual Circus: Frank Wedekind's Theatre of Subversion* provides a useful context and overview to the key ideas and theorists, taking the argument back to J.G. Fichte's *The Science of Rights* (1796). See Elizabeth Boa, *The Sexual Circus*, p. 181.

39 'They lay me on the bed. Frank pressed twenty Marks into the boatman's hand and asked him to keep quiet … And the boatman and the landlady both kept their mouths shut.' (Tilly Wedekind, *Lulu: Die Rolle Meines Lebens*, p. 64.)

40 Mary Elizabeth Place, *The Characterisation of Women in the Plays of Frank Wedekind* (Unpublished PhD thesis, Vandabilt University, 1977, DAI-A 38/03, p. 1427), p. 188.

41 Shortly after their marriage in 1906, Tilly was to appear in Barnovsky's production of Wilde's *The Ideal Husband* in Berlin, playing opposite the dashing Harry Walden. Tilly recounts that Frank didn't want her to do the production and threatened to leave. 'I had just got married, I was expecting a child and my husband was leaving me after barely four weeks!' (Tilly Wedekind, *Lulu: Die Rolle Meines Lebens*, p. 82).

42 Tilly writes that on one occasion when Wedekind failed to find letters she had placed for him in a parcel he accused her of 'indecency' – 'With what right do you come and go from my house? – Frank Wedekind.' Her response was just as assertive: 'With what right? With the right of a faithful spouse, with the right of a caring mother, with the right of a devoted partner, who has helped to find success for his plays, success which had been denied them for years!' (Ibid., p. 134.)

43 Tilly Wedekind, *The Lulu Plays*, *Earth Spirit*, Act 2, Scene 1, p. 38.

44 Ibid., Act 3, Scene 9, p. 78.

45 Efrat Tseëlson (ed.), *Masquerade and Identities: Essays on Gender, Sexuality and Marginality* (London: Routledge, 2001), pp. 163–4.

46 See Lulu to Schon, in Wedekind, *The Lulu Plays*, *Earth Spirit*, Act 3, Scene 9, p. 77.

47 Ibid., Act 4, Scene 7, p. 90.

48 Lulu's inability to answer Schwarz's questions in Act 1, Scene 7 of *Earth Spirit*, 'Do you believe in a creator?', 'Have you no soul?', 'Have you ever been in

love?', illustrates her spiritual 'muteness'. (Tilly Wedekind, *The Lulu Plays*, *Earth Spirit*, p. 34.)

49 In Act 1 of *Earth Spirit*, the Pierrot portrait stands unfinished on an easel; in Act 2, it hangs over the mantelpiece in a rich brocade surround; in Act 4, it appears on an ornamental easel, with a reproduction antique gilt frame. It ornately adorns a gaming salon when Alwa restores it in *Pandora's Box*: and appears as a rolled up canvas in the final act. As Peter Skrine points out, the manner in which each of Lulu's admirers displays the painting reveals something about their attitudes to its subject matter. Peter Skrine, *Hauptmann, Wedekind and Schnitzler: Macmillan Modern Dramatists* (Basingstoke: Macmillan Educational Ltd, 1989), pp. 88–90.

50 Tilly Wedekind, *Lulu: Die Rolle Meines Lebens*, p. 48.

51 Ibid., p. 171.

52 Ibid.

53 According to Tilly, Wedekind later used the picture to make one of his most overt statements of apology and forgiveness to Tilly. (Ibid., p. 190.)

54 This was even the case with Reinhardt's production of *Spring Awakening* in 1906 at the Berlin Kammerspiele: 'Wedekind himself could not imagine a production in which the boys' parts were played by actors. Therefore, he suggested to Reinhardt that girls could play the boys. Reinhardt thought the suggestion was ridiculous, so decided against it. He knew better. He cast the parts with his young and very gifted actors, as well as with a few who were still at drama school.' (Ibid., p. 98.)

55 Ibid., p. 121.

56 Mary Ann Doane, *Femmes Fatales: Feminism, Film Theory, Psychoanalysis* (London: Routledge, 1991), p. 25.

57 Tilly Wedekind, *The Lulu Plays, Earth Spirit*, Act 4, Scene 1, p. 82.

58 The only reference to sex in *Lulu: Die Rolle Meines Lebens* is subtle and relates to the losing of her virginity. (Tilly Wedekind, *Lulu: Die Rolle Meines Lebens*, p. 17.)

59 Tilly's description of the actress Elisabeth Bergner (1897–1986) is particularly loaded with androgynous appeal: 'Bergner looked childlike and boyish, like a pixie or an elf, and with her tousled, chestnut-red hair, her big, dark pensive eyes, and her heart-stirring tiny shoulders, which always seemed tense with fear, she had the charm of a helpless and very troubled little girl, wherein her alert intelligence, her intellectual experience, and her burning energy were hardly perceptible. She must have been about twenty at that time but for a moment you could have taken her for twelve. She was unparalleled in Shakespeare's female roles, such as Rosalind and Viola in their pages' costumes, with her bashful laddish pluck and all the poetry of crafty innocence.' (Ibid., pp. 183–4.)

60 Ibid., p. 88.

61 Efrat Tseëlson, *Masquerade and Identities*, pp. 33–4.

62 Tilly describes how she had costumes from *The Ideal Husband* and *Emilia Galotti* adapted into society outfits and how she wore stage costumes at

parties and also lent them to friends for such occasions (Wedekind, *Lulu: Die Rolle Meines Lebens*, pp. 110, 229).

63 Wedekind's attention to costuming detail throughout the *Lulu Plays* is almost salacious, and not simply with Lulu's character.
64 Tilly Wedekind, *Die Rolle Meines Lebens*, p. 111.
65 See Frank Wedekind, *Diary of an Erotic Life*, p. 120.
66 Tilly Wedekind, *Lulu: Die Rolle Meines Lebens*, p. 177.
67 Discussed in Sidonie Smith and Julia Watson (eds), *Women: Autobiography, Theory: A Reader*, p. 18.
68 Ibid., pp. 20–1.
69 Tilly Wedekind, *Die Rolle Meines Lebens*, p. 279.
70 Ibid., p. 171.
71 Ibid., p. 186. This outburst relates to Tilly's secret arrangement in 1917 of a guest-appearance for Wedekind with the celebrated actress, Maria Orska, in *Earth Spirit* at the Theater in der Königgrätzer Strasse, Berlin. (Tilly Wedekind, *Lulu: Die Rolle Meines Lebens*, pp. 174–5.)
72 Tilly Wedekind, *Earth Spirit*, p. 97.
73 Tilly Wedekind, *Lulu: Die Rolle Meines Lebens*, p. 125.
74 Klaus Mann was a novelist, essayist and playwright. One of his most daring works was *Mephisto*, first written in 1936 and published in West Germany in the late 1950s, which comprised a scathing portrait of the Third Reich, written while he was in exile from Germany. In 1924, he and the Wedekinds' elder daughter, Anna-Pamela, were engaged.
75 Tilly Wedekind, *Lulu: Die Rolle Meines Lebens*, p. 246.
76 Ibid., p. 44.
77 Mary Anne Doane, *Femmes Fatales*, p. 22.
78 Tilly Wedekind, *Lulu: Die Rolle Meines Lebens*, p. 45.
79 Ibid., p. 175.
80 Ibid., p. 179.
81 Ibid., p. 158.
82 Ibid., p. 160.
83 Ibid., p. 187.
84 Ibid., p. 187. By contrast, one of Wedekind's most tender dramatic investigations of their marriage appears in the earlier play, *Franziska* (1911), in which Tilly played the eponymous female 'Faust'.
85 Tilly Wedekind, *The Lulu Plays*, *Earth Spirit*, Act 4, Scene 8, p. 97.
86 Ibid., p. 9.
87 Tilly reveals how Wedekind could only reach her through severity, 'such that I began to fear him as an unyielding teacher and trainer' (Tilly Wedekind, *Lulu: Die Rolle Meines Lebens*, p. 88.)
88 In 1887 Wedekind joined the Herzog Circus, working and touring as their secretary, during which time he wrote his *Zirkusgedanken*: 'Thoughts on the Circus'. Later, when in Paris, he spent two years (1892–94) working backstage at the circus.

89 Elizabeth Lott, *A Study of Frank Wedekind: Portrait of a Self-Styled Modern* (Unpublished PhD thesis, Columbia University, 1978, DAI-A 38/09 p 5640), p. 157.
90 Leroy R. Shaw, *The Playwright and Historical Change: Dramatic Strategies in Brecht, Hauptmann, Kaiser and Wedekind* (Madison and London: University of Wisconsin Press, 1970), p. 64.
91 David F. Kuhns, *German Expressionist Theatre: The Actor and the Stage* (Cambridge: Cambridge University Press, 1997), p. 55.
92 Jean Starobinski, *Portrait de l'artiste en saltimbanque* (Geneva: Editions d'art Albert Skira, 1970), p. 52, cited in Mary Russo, *The Female Grotesque: Risk, Excess and Modernity* (London: Routledge 1995), p. 44.
93 Ibid., p. 44.
94 Ibid., pp. 43–4.
95 Tilly Wedekind, *Lulu: Die Rolle Meines Lebens*, p. 118.
96 In the very names that Wedekind chose for his dramatic incarnations of Tilly there are immense reverberations and cultural signifiers. 'Lamia', for example, in Wedekind's *The Stone of Wisdom*, is the arch temptress in a play that deals with the reconciliation of the mind (logos) with physical longing (eros).
97 Sadism runs throughout Wedekind's writing. See Wedekind, *Diary of an Erotic Life*, p. 71. Note here the reverberations with Act 1, Scene 5 of *Spring Awakening* in which Wendla implores Melchior to beat her with a switch (Tilly Wedekind, *Spring Awakening*, trans. Edward Bond (London: Methuen, 1997), p. 16), and Act 3, Scene 9 of *Earth Spirit* in which Lulu goads Schön: 'Strike me! Where is your whip? Strike me across the legs ...' (Tilly Wedekind, *The Lulu Plays, Earth Spirit*, p. 78.)
98 Tilly Wedekind, *Lulu: Die Rolle Meines Lebens*, p. 86.
99 Ibid., p. 17.
100 Ibid., p. 178.
101 Ibid., p. 191. There is a striking similarity between Tilly losing her skin and a snake sloughing its outer layer: as Wedekind describes Lulu in serpentine terms in the Prologue of *Earth Spirit*, 'She coils herself with strong squeeze round the tiger'. Tilly Wedekind, *The Lulu Plays, Earth Spirit*, p. 11.
102 Ibid., p. 299.

7

TROUBLING IDENTITIES: CLAIRE DOWIE'S *WHY IS JOHN LENNON WEARING A SKIRT?*

Gabriele Griffin

Introduction

Troubling identities have been and has been at the centre of much recent women's performance work,[1] projecting the ambiguities that the phrase itself bespeaks grammatically. For 'troubling' may either function as an adjective, referring to identities that are troubled, or as a transitive or intransitive verb in which case the phrase raises four possibilities, namely those of troubling one's own identity; troubling another's/others' identities; being troubled by one's own identity; and being troubled by another's/others' identity.

Implicit in these possibilities are also their opposites, that is *not* troubling one's own or another's/others' identity, and *not* being troubled by one's own or another's/others' identities. The multiplicity of meanings thus inherent in the phrase 'troubling identities' constitutes an apt way of describing Claire Dowie's work since it is centrally concerned with unsettling and unsettled identities, and specifically issues of troubling gender identities.[2] As such it has been in dialogue both with theoretical developments of the 1990s, in particular with queer theory as articulated in the work of Judith Butler, and with socio-cultural events that have shaped public perceptions of gender identity. I therefore want to begin this chapter with a quotation from the *Guardian*, one of Britain's leading broadsheet newspapers, which under the heading 'Trouser woman agrees payout' carried the following story in March 2000:

> The woman who won her claim for sexual discrimination against the Professional Golfers' Association after being sent home to change her trousers for a skirt has agreed compensation in an out of court settlement, it was announced yesterday. Judy Owen, 39, of Solihull, West Midlands, had been expected to win tens of thousands of pounds after her victory at a Birmingham employment tribunal earlier this year.[3]

I begin this chapter with this story for the following five reasons: firstly, it highlights the degree of gender normativity that continues to be imposed on female subjects, a coercion which it is hard to believe is still going on in the twenty-first century in a supposedly enlightened Western country. Secondly, it reveals the disruption or trouble the female subject causes to those gendered regimes as two male-centred institutions, a professional association and an employment tribunal, representative of the law, take up contradictory positions regarding the enforcement of these regimes. Thirdly, it indicates the resolution of this state of contradiction through economic appeasement which functions, effectively, as a displacement of the need to interrogate the socio-cultural norms that were enacted in the original demand on the female subject to perform her femininity through her appearance. Fourthly, the story presents a 'real-world' variant of a phenomenon which Dowie addresses in her monologue *Why is John Lennon Wearing a Skirt?* but which some female audiences can find difficult to accept. As Dowie herself said: 'Even with something like *John Lennon* some women get really angry because you're pointing out to them where they've been coerced and they blame me for it. It's threatening to them and they're sitting there pulling down their short skirts.'[4] Lastly, I begin this chapter with this story because in the heady world of postmodern subjectivity in which normativity and transgressivity dance merrily together, the female subject in question, as this story shows, keeps colliding with material realities which defy both transgressivity and normativity as the subject, asked about her identity, negotiates her way across the floor by trying to elide, or is it appease, both.

But is it possible for her to do so on *her* terms? This is the question I wish to pose as I discuss Dowie's wonderful stand-up theatre piece, *Why Is John Lennon Wearing a Skirt?*, published in 1996, in a gesture of long-overdue recognition of the central role Dowie has played in British performance work, particularly in the arena of gender and sexual politics which some might describe as queer.

Dowie's one-handers such as *Why is John Lennon Wearing a Skirt?* (hereafter *John Lennon*) and *Leaking from Every Orifice*, its sequel, present themselves as (auto)biographical pieces through the use of first person narratives, the seeming self-sameness of the 'I' of the monologues and the performer; a language which is at once informal, colloquial, intimate, interactive with, and interrogative of the audience; a disarming use of humour that encourages bonding between the audience and the performer and invites identification; and through their loosely chronologically strung-together episodic structure. Here, apparently, is a young woman, Dowie, the performer, regaling the audience with her history of gender confusion. But performance is, of course, always citation, and as such instantly troubles the I-dentity of character and performer. If I perform me performing me, we are in the world of deconstructionist traces where there is no self-sameness, only the infinity of the split, endlessly (re)enacted in a Sisyphian attempt to approximate the self. When Judith Butler, in *Bodies that Matter*, describes the 'forcible citation of norms'[5] which she regards as underlying performativity, she simultaneously suggests that the iterativity of that performativity offers opportunities for transgression, for tweaking those norms that seek to enchain us in specific prescribed gender performances. Dowie's *John Lennon* explores precisely how this is done and generates a highly nuanced notion of identity in which fixity and fluidity coexist and are, indeed, generative of the gender confusion which informs Dowie's narratives and performance. This chapter interrogates, *inter alia*, what the specific nature of that gender confusion is or, more precisely, whether or not 'gender confusion' is indeed what Dowie's piece is concerned with.

The enactment of the gendered self

The opening sequence of *John Lennon* establishes the splits which haunt Dowie's monologue. Appearing on stage '*wearing school uniform*' she immediately '*address[es] the audience*' whilst '*show[ing] off [her] uniform*' with: 'This is me at fourteen.'[6] Here we have a temporal split between the present – the on-stage performance – and the past – a version of the former self – presented like a photograph complete with the visual clues (the school uniform) to authenticate that past. We also have a split between the performing self – the subject of the performance, the 'I' – and the performed self – the object of the performance, the 'me'. That split is both sustained and subverted by the metadiscourse through which the performing self discusses the performed self. For whereas conventionally the realist stage allows only for one self to be present, envisaging the melting of the performing self into the performed self, here the split is deliberately sustained, thus imbuing the metadiscourse of the performing self as the agent of the performance with the authority that stems from hindsight – the present looking back upon the past – akin to the authority of the omniscient narrator in the realist novel and suggestive of some teleological development about to unfold. There is also a split between narrative – the metadiscourse of the performing self about the performed self – and performance within performance – the enactment of the performed self – both within the overarching frame of the performance as such. Lurking behind/beneath/beyond the performing and performed selves – what in the terms of the linguist Ferdinand de Saussure might be described as the signifier and the signified – is the referent, the actual person towards whom the performing and performed selves seem to gesture. Here we have another and more complex split between the on-stage persona and the real-life person whose relation with each other eludes us even as we seek to solidify it into a source of meaning.

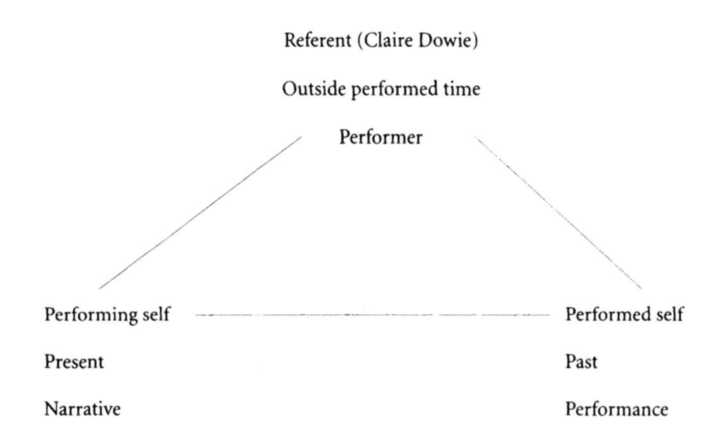

This triangular figuration is not stable throughout the monologue. Rather, the positions established within it slip and slide, especially those of the performing and the performed self, as Dowie moves from metadiscourse to direct dialogue, thus interspersing metadiscourse or narrative 'about' with inhabiting the moment narrated, making the past present through reproducing, as direct speech, past conversations as if they were happening now, and enacting the self she was. This movement from distance to immediacy, of the past into the present, of the performing self into the performed self, which effectively collapses the splits detailed above into one space, person/a, sets up – as a consequence of this fluidity – the liminal identity that Jon McKenzie describes as 'a mode of embodied activity whose spatial, temporal, and symbolic "betweenness" allows for dominant social norms to be suspended, questioned, played with, transformed.'[7]

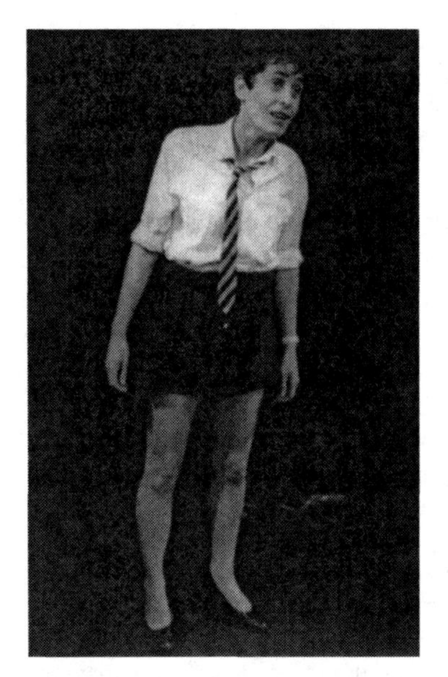

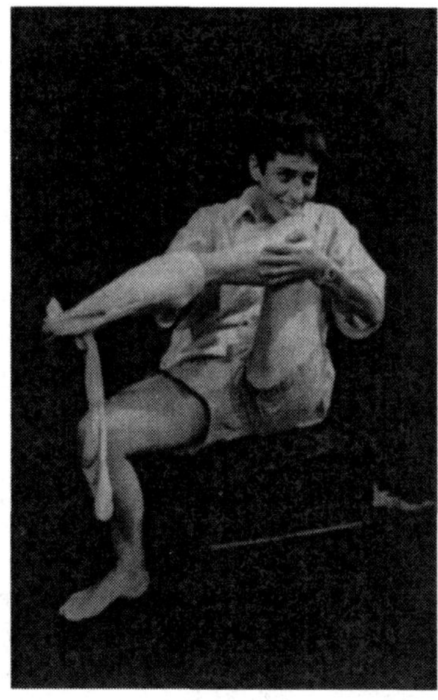

11 and 12 Claire Dowie in her performance piece, *Why is John Lennon Wearing a Skirt?*

Questioning norms

The dominant social norms to be questioned – but not suspended or transformed – are those associated with gender, specifically with the *enactment* of gender as opposed to a particular corporeal materiality. It is that questioning which provides the dynamic of the narrative and the performance, and which fills the gaps between the performing and the performed self. From early on the persona is caught in a binary world divided into private/public; fantasy/reality; inner self/appearance; individual self/social self; girl/boy. The narrative of *Why is John Lennon Wearing a Skirt?* concerns the persona's repeated attempts to reconcile her private sense of self with her public persona, to live her public self as closely aligned to her private self as she can manage. That attempt opens up contradictions and tensions between what is revealed and what is concealed, between the visible and the hidden, between the real and the imaginary. The top half of the school uniform, shirt and tie for boys and girls alike,[8] sets a gender agenda which is then contradicted by the bottom half where boys and girls are carefully distinguished through girls wearing skirts and boys wearing trousers. That dress code, combining the potentially androgynous with the highly gendered, in turn conditions behaviours that are also highly gendered. Dowie cites and enacts the 'knicker factor' – the issue of girls having to behave in such a manner that their knickers do not show but having to do so in clothing that is in a sense designed to reveal knickers unless one acts in a very constrained manner – as one of the instances that divide girls and boys along gendered lines in preparation for teenage courtship behaviours that reinforce stereotypical gender roles.

Dowie's monologue (re)produces Butler's notion of gender as construct,[9] consisting of repeatedly enacted performances involving a series of interlocking gender sign systems that include dress code, behaviour (meaning both how the body is posed and enacted by the individual) and interpersonal social styles, ways of interacting with others. As the persona's friends from school, her gang, turn into teenagers, their self-presentation begins to change:

> we went around in a gang, tomboys, until these walked into the classroom (*Takes out pair of tights from satchel and holds them aloft.*) ... (*Puts tights on as talking.*) I thought they looked silly, I thought they looked cold. I said to [my friend], What are you doing for heaven's sake that's the sort of thing my mum wears, and she's practically forty-six.[10]

Soon all the persona's friends are wearing tights, and her protests are countered with, 'why don't you just grow up, you stupid boy!'[11] Not only do the other girls begin to dress differently, they also begin to act differently. They no longer want to play physical games such as 'wrestling'or 'football', they become passive and decorative, and begin to 'snog' boys. The persona sums this process of transformation up with the words, 'girls just don't seem to have fun any more, I mean, they giggle a lot, but they don't do anything'.[12]

This sequence illustrates several key aspects of Dowie's engagement with gender. It highlights the importance of dress for gender identity. Indeed, dress is one of the key props used in the performance of this monologue[13] – it is, *inter alia*, through dress changes that Dowie as performer transforms herself on stage in front of the audience into the persona and the various people that the persona engages with. In Brechtian manner Dowie thus enacts gender as construct, as a situated bodily practice, revealing its devices to the audience as part of the performance. That process of revelation has several meanings, only one of which is to underline the performativity of gender *per se*. The other aspect of this on-stage transformation is to show that the persona *can* 'do it', that is that she can do gender, indeed inhabit different versions of gender as demanded or desired. She understands, as do her peers and the audience, exactly what is required to do gender both in its normative version and as transgression against such normativities. As such, she models for the audience the 'choices' open to her to conform or to transgress. Dowie thus literally shows the audience that gender is performance, based on a shared understanding of what the various components that make up any one performance of gender mean. She both speaks of that performance and enacts it. This process distinguishes her from the 'hysteric' who does seemingly without knowing, whose corporeality expresses what she cannot bring to mind.[14] Instead Dowie, as performer, retains the psychic and corporeal integrity of the rational subject that acts as the guarantor of self as agent/subject. The knowing appropriation of the cultural accoutrements of the two specific genders, which liberates gender from corporeal specificity, points both to the authenticating function of those gender signifiers and to their non-essential nature. Dowie thus signals the provisionality of gender, its temporal specificity, its very enactedness which also therefore means that *it can/could be done differently*. The tights which she puts on as she discusses them signify a specific version of femininity, understood as such both by the friends referred to in the monologue and by the audience watching. If the audience did not understand these conventions the monologue would cease to make sense. Dowie's performance thus points to the sociality of gender performance, its reliance upon social recognition for its meaning and effectiveness. She also stages Butler's description[15] that 'to be a woman is to have *become* a woman, to compel the body to conform to an historical idea of "woman," to induce the body to become a cultural sign, to materialise oneself in obedience to a historically delimited possibility, and to do this as a sustained and repeated corporeal project.'[16] Butler revises the idea of the 'project' into one of 'strategy' to suggest that there is no 'originating force of a radical will' but rather, that one responds to a 'situation of duress'.[17] The historical idea of 'woman' referred to by Butler is encoded in Dowie's monologue through the reference to the mother and her age as the comparative position to the friends who start to wear tights. It signals the friend's insertion into a pre-existing order and set of signs, 'an act that has been going on before one arrived on the scene'.[18]

Acting 'the boy'

The persona's rebellion against this action takes the form of refusing that insertion and choosing instead to adopt the position of 'boy'. Part two of the monologue, which provides further, and indeed iterative, accounts of the persona's quest for an inhabitable self, offers an explanatory exposition of her choice to enact 'the boy': 'I realise I have been learning from four, from three that the only thing I can do, the only thing I can aim for, the only thing that's accepted and applauded is manhood, is to be a man. And I'm not. But I practise ...'.[19] Having understood the devaluation of self that femininity entails, the persona chooses not to identify with that devalued position but instead, an understandable strategy, decides to inhabit masculinity, the privileged signifier. Whilst revealing femininity and masculinity as constructs, the persona underwrites the meanings ascribed to those constructs through her self-insertion into the male order where she can, to some extent, 'carry off' the 'boy' but not the 'man' to whom, in any event, she does not aspire.

That 'choice' reflects the binary gender structure which delineates conventionally available gender options and which structures the persona's deliberations regarding gender roles. Although the word 'choice' is invoked here and the persona makes a choice of sorts when she enacts 'the boy' her situation is one of duress, to refer back to Butler, since the conventional feminine gender performances available to her do not approximate the self she wants to inhabit. Her refusal to enact femininity constitutes a critique of that position. However, as a biological girl[20] the persona in fact lacks the choice suggested by the seeming availability of the two cultural gender positions, masculinity and femininity, for they are already aligned with specific material corporealities, and her corporeality being that designated 'girl', she is expected to '*become* woman' as Butler puts it, to enact femininity rather than masculinity. Throughout the monologue the binarism of femininity and masculinity is referenced to investigate habitable gender positions. The monologue makes clear how difficult it is to think outside those categories – the persona adopts 'boy' as the preferred position – the prevalent gender categories seem to be all she has to play with. Taken as a whole, then, Dowie's performance may be read as a critique of gender regimes that leave no option but co-option.

Negotiating difference

The discrepancy between the persona's gender enactment and her corporeality, derived from the disjunction between the self she wants to be and the identity which from her perspective attaches to enacting femininity, constitutes the underlying theme of the monologue. As the persona is repeatedly confronted with the social unacceptability of manifesting gender incoherence, presenting and enacting a gender seemingly at odds with her corporeality, the persona develops several strategies to mediate between her desire to be a particular self and the demands to live within the accepted socio-cultural constraints of the gender role assigned to her. One of these strategies is to pass, a high-risk activity since being 'found out' carries with it social sanction.[21] Passing is also very difficult to perform as the persona finds.

> One day I was sitting on the bus going to school and a fluffy pink little girl was sitting opposite with her mummy ... And she looked at me then said in a really loud voice for the whole bus to hear, she said, 'Mummy, why is that boy wearing a skirt?' ... and I said in an equally loud voice for the whole bus to hear, 'My dear girl, I am not a boy – I am John Lennon!' That's told her I thought, and the rest of the world come to that.[22]

There is then a scene shift, leaving the audience to imagine what happened following on from the exchange. The exchange in the bus itself both elates and debases the persona for the girl's 'loud voice' is clearly intended to effect public humiliation by drawing attention to the persona through the tone and the content of what is said. As Butler points out, 'gender is a performance with clearly punitive consequences ... those who fail to do their gender right are regularly punished ... The historical possibilities materialised through various corporeal styles are nothing other than those punitively regulated cultural fictions that are alternately embodied and disguised under duress.'[23] The persona's bravura response to the little girl's attempt at public humiliation, a falling into excess through claiming for herself not only masculinity but famed masculinity, is simultaneously an assertion of self and a resistance to being humiliated by the event.

The persona is not the only one who experiences the punitive dimension of doing gender. In the school the 'cold' look of the tights interacts with the new behaviour her friends display – no longer do they act in a physically unfettered manner; instead, they stand around and spend their time enacting femininity, becoming passive and decorative in the process, signalling their submission to heteronormativity. Through *doing* they *become*, thus fulfilling the gender destiny heteronormativity has in store for them. Being physically uncomfortable is part of the price paid for this submission, and adopted for the sake of the reward which is social approval within the heterosexual contract. The persona, unwilling to submit, becomes socially isolated, her (now) former friends increasingly uninterested in associating with her. She thus suffers the punishment of social isolation for failing to comply with the prevailing gender norms.

Fantasy in actuality

The encounter on the bus is one of several narrated and enacted during the monologue in which the persona is pulled up short and faces, so to speak, a social reality check when she is confronted head-on with the social unacceptability of her gender performance. The context for these events is always similar and points to the key strategy, fantasy, which the persona employs in order to negotiate between her sense of self and the contours of socio-cultural permissibility within which she has to function. Both part one and part two of the monologue start with the representation of such a fantasy, the hidden private narrative through which the persona seeks to reduce the discrepancy between how she thinks of herself and what she is expected to be like. Thus at school she transforms her gang into the Beatles: 'Secretly I named my friends Paul, George and Ringo, but I never told them (I'm not stupid), they just seemed to act like Paul, George and Ringo and that was good enough for me. I was John, of course, although you wouldn't think so to look at me dressed like this [in school uniform]'.[24] The persona continues her fantasies in young adult life. For instance, she 'improves' on the reality of her job situation packing cans in a factory by imagining first that she is a member of MI6 'working on a decoding machine'[25] and then that she is a Russian spy. But, as the opening sequence of part two states, 'It's hard to get a job in Russia, everybody knows that. Especially if you're a resistance fighter. Packing cans in a factory might seem dull, boring and brain wasting, but I like it, I prefer it, gives me all day to think – and plan the revolution.'[26] The narrative cleverly shifts between fantasy and reality, between the imaginary identity the persona ascribes to herself to get through her day and which she fully understands as such, that is as imaginary, and the actuality she knows. Thus she understands that it would not be socially acceptable to reveal to her friends that she thinks of them as the Beatles, and she understands that being a resistance fighter in Russia is a difficult position to inhabit. It is through the articulation of that understanding that the persona signals to the audience her grasp of the conventions which govern the socio-cultural norms she is trying to resist. The persona's fantasies are thus explicitly held in check by an understanding of the actuality of the structures the persona inhabits. Simultaneously, the persona avoids being 'written off' as deluded since her metadiscursive appraisal of her situation, always mediated by humour, asserts the rational subject.

Nonetheless, supplementing actuality by fantasy to sustain a sense of self is a high-risk strategy because of the problematic of how to sustain the illusion for the sake of the self whilst at the same time maintaining the boundary between actuality and fantasy for the sake of others. At the point where fantasy spills over into actuality, where private fantasy is made manifest within a public social context, it places the persona outside the social order, endangering her position within the socio-economic context in which she operates. Thus at one point while she is working she strikes up a friendship with another woman worker:

> I knew from the beginning that she thought I was a boy and I never did anything to correct her. In fact I went out of my way to make myself look more boyish. Did I fancy her? No, not really, it wasn't about that. She fancied me, that's what it was about. She made me feel good-looking, attractive, wanted, and I was myself, that's what it was about. She fancied me for what I was – till her friend put her straight of course which embarrassed and annoyed me.[27]

The episode[28] recounted is strongly reminiscent of the Jennifer Saunders case.[29] As in other situations where the persona allows herself to play to the imaginary identity she has established for herself, inhabiting the role of 'boy' until the point when fantasy and actuality collide in sociality, and actuality, meaning certain forms of heteronormativity, are asserted through the social, here emblematised both through the 'friend' who puts the woman straight and through the breakdown of the friendship with the woman who mistook the persona for a boy. As Butler states: 'there are strict punishments for contesting the script by performing out of turn or through unwarranted improvisations'.[30] The persona's enactment of 'the boy' becomes one such unwarranted improvisation at the point where her ascribed biological gender identity is revealed.

The process of inhabiting her fantasy repeatedly follows the same trajectory: a micro-social scenario is presented in which the persona has to act in ways that contradict her sense of herself. To deal with this dissonance, the persona identifies with a character or an imaginary version of herself which, though at odds with heteronormativity, approximates to her sense of self. Fantasy and actuality then collapse, either inadvertently or in an act of deliberation on the persona's part. Indeed, in the episode mentioned above it is clear that the persona, in what one might describe as an act of radical will, encourages that collapse. However, sociality, the affirmation of self through/in the social, explodes that unity, re-asserting the heteronormative order and propelling the persona outside that order. Sociality, the monologue argues, is bought at the expense of self, for to subscribe to sociality means to submit to certain orders and socio-cultural norms, and to inhabit an identity as defined by those norms. If such submission is perceived to be unproblematic, that is if the demands of conventional gender performance are internalised to the extent that they 'appear as the natural configuration of bodies', then submission to heteronormativity is not at issue, even if, and despite the fact that 'the association of a natural sex with a discrete gender and with an ostensibly natural "attraction" to the opposing sex/gender is an unnatural conjunction of cultural constructs in the service of reproductive interests'.[31] If, however, dissonance is experienced between the sense of self and a prescribed gender performance, strategies to manage that dissonance are required and, as Dowie's play suggests, these are usually high risk and very difficult to sustain effectively.

Beyond gender binarisms?

The persona in *John Lennon* is, however, not put off by her repeated collision with conventional gender norms. Sacked from her job in the factory for allowing her fantasy to be articulated publicly – she salutes her boss military-style, pretending to be in a camp[32] – she looks for other jobs and spaces in which she can be what she wants to be. Her fantasies and her arguments with gender normativity indicate the problematic of the gender binarisms offered by contemporary western culture as sites for identification, as well as the site restrictions which structure both what the persona rejects – femininity – and what she seeks to be – a 'boy'.[33] The persona's narratives regarding femininity project the clichés which rule cultural norms of what constitutes being a woman: 'Don't want to be thought of as a tart or a chick or a bird or a doll, a babe, a skirt, piece of crumpet, or even as a nice girl'.[34] 'Doing woman' for the persona means not doing the things she really enjoys, whilst pandering to men's expectations of acting as their sex object and general drudge. She refuses that role but, as the monologue suggests, it leaves her with virtually no options since her gender universe consists only of femininity and masculinity, strictly aligned to ascriptions of corporeal identifications according to which she should be what she refuses, namely a chick, a doll, possibly even a nice girl.

The persona seeks to deal with the dilemma of dissonance through moving across diverse social fields one of which is 'the women's movement' which in the monologue takes on rather unitary dimensions. There she expects difference to be welcomed and heteronormativity to be refused. But the fantasy of what feminism means which the persona builds up prior to attending a women's meeting – a fantasy that fuses actual interventions which women undertook such as setting up women's refuges, with imaginary behaviours designed to put men in their place and give women control over their situation and bodies – evaporates when the persona, in response to women articulating their hatred of men, asks, 'Doesn't anybody hate women?'[35] The persona states that she does not want to be the kind of woman – 'kind and gentle and understanding and supportive and patient and democratic and nurturing and reasonable and non-aggressive and helpful and self-sacrificing and fair-minded and co-operative',[36] which is one version of femininity now associated with a particular feminist ideal of femininity of the 1970s, and which effectively relied on the reclaiming, re-writing, and re-valuing of the meaning of that femininity as 'not in the service of men' but 'for the benefit of women'. The persona repudiates the desirability of that femininity through her assertion that she does not want to be that kind of woman, and through articulating her desire to be a boy:

> Doesn't anybody just love what men do and want to do it too? Isn't there anybody here who's insanely jealous that they weren't born a boy? That they weren't born with the opportunity to do anything they wanted to do without having to apologise or justify or explain or feel guilty or awkward or feel like a freak or be ridiculed or persecuted or ostracised or wait till it's fashionable?[37]

The persona engages in a high-risk strategy here in her quest for her social space, for to speak of jealousy for not having been born a boy means also speaking of the penis envy – not literally necessarily, but metaphorically certainly – that has structured the hetero-psychoanalytic imaginary of gender identity and has been the object of sustained critiques by feminists.[38] Where the third question in the quotation above – about being able to do anything one wants to do – shifts away from a gendered territory to a gender-neutral terrain,[39] the first two questions reveal the problematic of a gender economy that only allows for two positions, and ask for identification with the position – masculinity – that many feminists have, of course, explicitly rejected. It is thus not surprising that the persona finds herself again ejected from the social space where she thought she might find her place. In its representation of feminism, Dowie's monologue effectively argues that feminism's reclamation of a certain kind of femininity does not explode the gender normativities which she would like to reject, that ontology is aligned to ideology, and that the tolerance levels for divergence are very limited indeed, including in feminist spaces. Dowie's persona as boy inhabits the betweenness that the limitations inherent in conventional gender roles generate, repeatedly driven into a position of awkwardness and embarrassment as she herself acknowledges by refusing to comply with the narrow ontological definitions available to her within the social. There is still the absence of a third term that would move her beyond the conventional gender binary.

The monologue from this point in particular engages with a debate which was very prominent from the late 1980s through the 1990s, namely the issue of gender binarisms and their significance. These binarisms were interrogated by the emergence of queer, rising out of a rejection of certain forms of lesbian feminism, the reclamation and renewed engagement with particular styles of doing gender among lesbians[40] from the 1950s and 1960s, specifically butch-femme.[41] Their interrogation also meant their gradual abrogation as the performative nature of gender became increasingly rehearsed.[42] However, that performativity brought with it certain issues, specifically the question of the relationship between 'doing' and 'being'. Whereas the concept of 'playing with gender' foregrounds and emphasises doing, Dowie's monologue problematises that notion through suggesting that being and doing are complexly intertwined. Her persona is able to do gender – after all, she enacts it on stage, changing from portrayals of femininity to portrayals of mascuinity, and all of them equally convincing which is, of course, part of the monologue's argument about the doing of gender – but Dowie's persona does not want to do or be the only gender conventionally readily available to her. In a rapid-fire account, the persona works her way through the gender encounters she has to negotiate and her responses to these:

> I got chatted up by a lesbian – No, I'm a boy, you know. Got invited to women only meetings by feminists – No, I'm a boy, you know. Got coerced into a discussion about sexual politics and women's problems by a right-on liberal man – I'm a boy, you know ... I get annoyed at people who think it's a problem and want to put me straight, I get annoyed at people who think I'm some sort of traitor to some kind of Cause ... I am a boy.[43]

The persona here asserts an ontology which her morphology belies – hence the attempts by others to intervene. But her quest for a place to be her self is a quest for the actualisation of an ontology and not a morphology. Significantly, her quest is not a function of some morphological dysphoria, or about sexual preference, or gender dysphoria in its conventional sense. In that respect it moves beyond the conventions of transsexualism, transgender, and lesbian/gay identities as conventionally configured. Her quest is about the search for ontological integrity,[44] for being able to act in accordance with what the persona feels her self to be. Within the gender binaries available to her, the 'boy' approximates most closely to that ontology, not as a morphic entity (although she 'does' that morphism, for instance when she works in the factory) but as the lived reality, the ontological position, she wants to inhabit. But the sedimentation of gender norms is such that the persona finds herself repeatedly rejected as a consequence of the ontology she invokes to identify herself with.

Identity as sociality

The monologue makes the key point that identity is fundamentally a social phenomenon, deriving its significance from the meaning it has within social interaction, a meaning which is constructed, reinforced and sustained through that sociality. In that sense, what is in the persona's head, so to speak, never matters until it collides with social reality – itself a construct, just as what is in the persona's head, but underwritten by social consensus about gender normativities. These require a congruity between morphology and gender performance, assigning female to femininity and male to masculinity. However, the persona's sense of self is at odds with that demand. She has a very clear sense of self – a self that wants not to be constrained and accountable – but cannot align that ontology with the gender performance that femininity demands. To achieve ontological integrity for her means adopting the performance 'boy' as the closest approximation to the sense of self she has. But the adoption of such a performance – since it is at odds with her morphology – places her outside social convention and invites social sanction. The monologue as form serves to reinforce that social sanction in the form of isolation which the persona suffers since the performer stands alone on stage, separated from the audience that through their inhabiting of a single space, the auditorium, is invited to experience the coming together in the social that is denied to the persona and only achieved at the point of performance.

Dowie's monologue details the quest for a social space in which to inhabit a particular sense of self. Its starting point is not ontological uncertainty but an ontological certainty at odds with conventional gender roles. One might argue that Dowie's persona constitutes a failure within heteronormativity of genderisation, or the process of acculturation into a particular gender, since the persona's preferred identification is with 'the boy', not the 'fluffy pink little girl' which is meant to be her destiny. Apart from pointing to the privileged positions boys occupy in contemporary culture, the monologue does not engage with the question of how such genderisation fails, what enables its transgression and/or prevents the persona's full inauguration into her feminine role. Gender roles in the monologue are presented as such, that is as roles which some understand as performances, thus allowing for the possibility of different kinds of roles that might be played, and others accept as given. Here the monologue as a form reveals itself to be particularly appropriate for the interrogation of identity since its focus on the single individual suggests the ontological coherence and unity which conventional gender norms and indeed realist theatre demand but at the same time allows for the explosion of that coherence through the enactment, by one performer, of diverse versions of the self: past, present, feminine, masculine, performing self, performed self and so on. The monologue thus enables a particular performance of gender performance.

The unsettling of normative identities which is at the centre of Dowie's performance is also the ground on which possibilities of difference are validated. The preferred difference enacted in the monologue, 'the boy', however, is itself one born under cultural constraints and invested with gender specificities that include the pre-sexual, the adventurous, the adolescent, being ungrounded in social and other obligations. The desire for that position is itself a testimony to the sedimentation of gender norms that seem impossible to shrug off. Dowie's play thus offers both a critique of conventional gender roles and the assertion that they are inescapable.

Identity matters

In Dowie's play identity emerges in conventional terms as the quest for ontological integrity, consisting of a congruity between one's sense of self and how one (inter)acts in the world. Identity is constructed as achieved through a process which entails enactment in line with a specific sense of self and social acceptance as validation of that performance. In the case of the persona, her sense of self is imbued with ontological certainty but the quest for ontological integrity is both continuous and iterative, requiring a repeated social re-situating since ultimately the search is, in fact, not for a specific identity but for a social space for that identity, for a context in which the identity that is performed is not in question. Sociality thus becomes the arbiter of performance, the context which both necessitates and validates performance and therefore self.

In Dowie's monologue, an imaginary sociality – the people the performer conjures up for her audience as the interlocutors of her past gender performances – is juxtaposed with the sociality of the audience, and a relation is produced between the two in which their judgements of the persona's gender performances are pitted against each other. *John Lennon* reproduces the logic of the privilege of the male signifier – the persona, after all, wants to be a 'boy' and performs 'boy' as the preferred self. For the viewing audience one issue that impacts upon their reading of the persona's gender performance is how to understand that performance. As the performed self traverses various socio-cultural sites it seems that her preference for 'the boy' is not a politically motivated one but is personal – and though the personal is the political, the political that seems to emerge from the personal here is the affirmation of the male order, homosexuality and sexual indifference, to quote de Lauretis.[45]

One might argue, with Elin Diamond, that Dowie (here taking the place Irigaray occupies in Diamond's discourse), 'links the phallus to (Platonic, model-copy) mimesis: the female, lacking the organ of privilege, unable to symbolise her fantasies and desires in a male symbolic, is positioned as mirror to the male, reflecting back to him – thereby demonstrating the truth of his centrality – his own image, his Self-Same'.[46] That self-same can be reflected in two different ways: through the embrace of conventional femininity and through the adoption/(re)production of masculinity. The latter is of course the persona's strategy and, in the form of mimicry, it undermines the authority of the male symbolic since successful imitation prises the signifier and the referent apart, suggesting their provisional adherence rather than their emblematisation of some fundamental truth. Women, the monologue suggests, can have it too, albeit at a price. As Diamond, referencing Plato, puts it: 'women's theater writing has been able to decenter ideal Forms with false offspring'.[47] The difficulty with that use of 'false offspring' is that it continues to wed signifier to referent since it gestures towards a regime of truth and falsehood that claims the authenticatibility of some versions over others. One might argue that Dowie's monologue supports that position in as much as those who subscribe to the gender regime depicted and resisted by the performing self would regard the performed self, 'the boy', as the false offspring of the regime of masculinity, 'the little girl masquerading as the "little man"'.[48] However, the monologue also asks the audience, through its juxtaposition of the actual audience with the imaginary one, to take up positions in the gender stakes and to consider what gender performance, indeed what notion of identity, to subscribe to. In the process the performing self knowingly transgresses various ideological positions regarding gender regimes including a conservative one subscribing to the immutability of gender; a feminist one recovering conventional gender stereotypes as positive attributes of femininity rather than as signs of inferiority; a lesbian feminist one demanding congruity between the rejection of a heteronormative gender regime and sexual practice.

Indeed, the persona's performance of 'boy' repeatedly raises questions about her sexual identity which, the monologue suggests, is fluid since she is open to relationships with women and men. It is, in fact, not the issue of sexual identity or of a specific object of sexual desire that drives the persona but the opportunity to enact the sense of self she inhabits. Sex or sexual activity plays only a minor role in the persona's quest for a social space for her self. From a lesbian feminist perspective this is the most difficult aspect of Dowie's play since it suggests a lack of a specific kind of ideological commitment, precisely the point of debate between lesbian feminism and queer.[49] The play ends with the persona engaging in a relationship with a man who 'hates men' just as the persona 'hates women', who also does not want to inhabit conventional gender roles, and by whom she gets pregnant. Together her boyfriend and the persona 'invent characters', '[find] ambiguous positions' and have 'sex. And it was wombless, to us in our heads.'[50] But the gender and identity games they play, seeking to move beyond conventional gender roles, are put into question when conventional gender reality asserts itself through the persona's pregnancy. Instead of the social, it is now the corporeal that disrupts the persona's sense of self. The persona's ambivalence about her pregnancy, wanting it and not wanting it, culminates in the monologue's ambiguous ending, with the persona stating: 'And I thought, "No, I'm not going to play their games, I'd rather just drop my womb and be a boy, it's much more fun."'[51] No change there then, one might say.

This ending reveals cyclicity as the key structure of the monologue. It is realised not only through the iterative experiences detailed by the persona, the sameness of the experiences the persona undergoes, but also through the invariability of her desired identity of 'boy'. The opening of the play, gesturing back towards a past self which through this very gesture suggests the possibility of development, is mirrored by its ending when the persona still wants to be the boy she aspired to as an adolescent. The narrative's cyclicity in turn is mirrored by the foregrounding of the cyclical experiences associated with the female body through the persona's pregnancy. It suggests a closed world with an enclosed world within (the womb), an inescapability which is both affirmative of a certain ontological certainty and undermining of the possibility of change. De Lauretis makes the point that '"sexual difference" is the term of a conceptual paradox corresponding to what is in effect a real contradiction in women's lives: the term, at once, of a sexual *difference* (women are, or want, something different from men) and of a sexual *indifference* (women are, or want, the same as men)'.[52] Taking up an argument by Luce Irigaray she goes on to suggest that 'the phallic regime of an asserted sexual difference between man and woman'[53] – the regime represented in Dowie's *John Lennon* – is predicated upon 'a complete indifference for the "other" sex, woman's'.[54] The singular nature of this regime leads to a situation where 'there will be no female hommosexuality, just a hommo-sexuality in which woman will be involved in the process of specularising the phallus, begged to maintain the desire for the same that man has'.[55] It is through the evacuation of the 'erotic from the discourse of gender' that Dowie's performance of 'the boy' moves from the homosexual to the hommosexual, thus recovering the sexual indifference of the heterosexual social contract. If one takes the view that to aspire to the position of 'boy' seemingly outside an erotic order is to invest in the hommosexual rather than in the homosexual, then the key critique of Dowie's monologue is that it ultimately underwrites heteronormativity. But if one views the performance of 'boy' as a reverse discourse figuring as an '"oppositional appropriation" of dominant representation', then one arrives at the 'struggle over interpretation' which 'is a constitutive process for marginal subjectivities, as well as an important form of resistance'.[56] The absence of a teleological narrative underlying Dowie's monologue and its ambiguous ending allows for that struggle to occur within the audience, for readings of submission as well as of resistance.

Notes

1 For a useful overview of women's/feminist performance work which indexes how closely Dowie's work fits into that paradigm see Jeanie Forte, 'Women's Performance Art: Feminism and Postmodernism', in Sue-Ellen Case (ed.), *Performing Feminisms* (Baltimore: Johns Hopkins University Press, 1990), pp. 251–69.

2 Three collections of her plays have appeared to date: *Why Is John Lennon Wearing a Skirt? and Other Stand-Up Theatre Plays* (1996); *Easy Access (For the Boys) and All Over Lovely* (London: Methuen, 1998); and *The Year of The Monkey and Other Plays* (London: Methuen, 2001). All are concerned with questions of identity, gender performance, the impact of heteronormativity on the non-compliant individual, and gender role play and expectations in close relationships that are often, but not always, familial.
3 'Trouser woman agrees payout', *Guardian*, 14 March 2000, p. 6.
4 Claire Dowie, 'Claire Dowie', in Heidi Stephenson and Natasha Langridge (eds), *Rage and Reason: Women Playwrights on Playwriting* (London: Methuen, 1997), p. 160.
5 Judith Butler, *Bodies That Matter* (London: Routledge, 1993), p. 233.
6 Claire Dowie, *Why Is John Lennon Wearing a Skirt? and Other Stand-Up Theatre Plays* (London: Methuen, 1996), p. 36.
7 Jon McKenzie, 'Genre Trouble: (The) Butler Did It', in Peggy Phelan and Jill Lane (eds), *The Ends of Performance* (New York: New York University Press, 1998), p. 218.
8 Although potentially androgynous, the conventional ascription of shirt and tie to the male gender articulates the gender privilege that accrues to men which dictates that men's wear is the norm as school wear (education traditionally being conceived of as education *for men*) and which drives the persona to adopt a masculine position. As Joanne Entwistle, discussing the suit, suggests: 'this body [the male one] is normative within the public sphere, it has come to represent neutrality and *dis*embodiment'. See Joanne Entwistle, 'The Dressed Body', in Joanne Entwistle and Elizabeth Wilson (eds), *Body Dressing* (Oxford: Berg, 2001), pp. 33–58, p. 53.
9 At the end of the 1980s and the beginning of the 1990s questions of gender consolidated into various forms of public discourse, both creative and theoretical. It is within that context that *Why is John Lennon Wearing a Skirt?* was first presented at the Edinburgh Festival in August 1990.
10 Claire Dowie, *Why Is John Lennon Wearing a Skirt?*, pp. 36–7.
11 Ibid., p. 37.
12 Ibid., p. 38.
13 Entwistle discusses the significance of the dressed body in relation to subjectivity. Her very interesting deliberations do not extend to an exploration of the inter-relationship between the dressed body and bodily demeanour. However, it is the relation between the two that is the focus of Dowie's performance.
14 See Hélène Cixous and Catherine Clément's elaboration of the hysteric in *The Newly Born Woman*, trans. Betsy Wing (Manchester: Manchester University Press, 1986).
15 Judith Butler, 'Performative Acts and Gender Constitution: An Essay in Phenomenology and Feminist Theory', in Sue-Ellen Case (ed.), *Performing Feminisms* (Baltimore: Johns Hopkins University Press, 1990), pp. 270–82.

Butler explicitly draws on Simone de Beauvoir's *The Second Sex* in this analysis.

16 Ibid., p. 273.

17 Ibid.

18 Ibid., p. 277.

19 Claire Dowie, *Why Is John Lennon Wearing a Skirt?*, p. 54.

20 To use that phrase – biological girl – is not to reify or naturalise biology here but to suggest the cultural primacy of biology, for the ascription of a biological sex initiates expectations regarding gender role performance, and the 'debunking' of any such performance always refers back to biology/ morphology to validate that 'debunking'.

21 See Carole-Anne Tyler, 'Passing: Narcissism, Identity, and Difference', in Elizabeth Weed and Naomi Schor (eds), *Feminism Meets Queer Theory* (Bloomington: Indiana University Press, 1997), pp. 227–65, for a critique of 'passing as a politically viable response to oppression', p. 227.

22 Claire Dowie, *Why Is John Lennon Wearing a Skirt?*, p. 53.

23 Judith Butler, 'Performative Acts and Gender Constitution', p. 273.

24 Claire Dowie, *Why Is John Lennon Wearing a Skirt?*, p. 35.

25 Ibid., p. 49.

26 Ibid., p. 51.

27 Ibid.

28 In *Amazons and Military Maids* (London: Pandora, 1989), Julie Wheelwright explored 'women who dressed as men in pursuit of life, liberty and happiness' as the subtitle so aptly put it. The period between the late 1980s and the early 1990s was one in which cross-dressing was the object of much debate as part of the re-thinking of gender identities during the period. Famously, Marjorie Garber's *Vested Interests* (New York: Routledge, 1992) appeared during that time. A number of plays were performed/published during that period which dealt with cross-dressing, see Gabriele Griffin and Elaine Aston (eds), *Pulp and Other Plays by Tash Fairbanks* (London: Harwood Academic Publishers, 1995); and Gabriele Griffin and Elaine Aston (eds), *Subversions: Playing with History in Women's Theatre.* (London: Harwood Academic Publishers, 1997).

29 In September 1991 eighteen-year-old Jennifer Saunders was charged with indecent assault upon two teenage girls. Disguising herself as 'Jimmy', Saunders had successfully played 'the boy', seducing girls with whom she worked and engaging in sexual activities with them. The girls claimed not to have realised that she was a girl. Writing about the case, Wheelwright maintained, 'in the end, cross-dressing proves to be an unsatisfactory alternative since it often forces women to caricature male virility and fear their feminine self'. Julie Wheelwright, 'Girls Will be Boys', *Guardian*, 24 September 1991: 35.

30 Judith Butler, 'Performative Acts and Gender Constitution', p. 282.

31 Ibid., p. 275.

32 Claire Dowie, *Why Is John Lennon Wearing a Skirt?*, pp. 47–8.

33 There is no space here to go into the choice of 'boy' as the identity adopted by the persona as her self of choice is clearly aligned to the Peter Pan myth of the eternal youth. The fantasy element that underlies the Peter Pan story is vividly re-cast in Dowie's monologue as the persona's world of make-believe, her only way of being her self.
34 Claire Dowie, *Why Is John Lennon Wearing a Skirt?*, p. 44.
35 Ibid., p. 59.
36 Ibid.
37 Ibid.
38 See, for example, Teresa de Lauretis, *The Practice of Love: Lesbian Sexuality and Perverse Desire* (Bloomington: Indiana University Press, 1994).
39 It is, of course, not gender-neutral in the sense of the persona aligning that opportunity with masculinity, but the question itself is asked in a gender-neutral fashion whilst the previous two questions raise gendered issues.
40 For a useful discussion about the relationship between lesbianism and feminism, pertinent to Dowie's representation of her persona's experiences, see Cheshire Calhoun, 'The Gender Closet: Lesbian Disappearance under the Sign "Woman"', in Martha Vicinus (ed.), *Lesbian Subjects: A Feminist Studies Reader* (Bloomington: Indiana University Press, 1996), pp. 209–32.
41 This revival/reclamation was initially particularly strong in the US where it became associated with writers such as Joan Nestle, for example, who brought out *The Persistent Desire: A Femme-Butch Reader* (Boston: Alyson Publications, 1992).
42 A good example is the emergence of the drag king as a cultural phenomenon in the late 1990s. See Del Volcano and Judith 'Jack' Halberstam, *The Drag King Book* (London: Serpent's Tail, 1999).
43 Dowie, *Why Is John Lennon Wearing a Skirt?*, p. 60.
44 The publication of performer and writer Kate Bornstein's *Gender Outlaw* (London: Routledge, 1994) heralded a new era in debates about gender dysphoria since Bornstein revealed that transsexual surgery is not necessarily the answer to gender dysphoria – reconciling the body with an assumed ontological position does not necessarily mean that that reconciliation is achieved.
45 Teresa De Lauretis, 'Sexual Indifference and Lesbian Representation', in Sue-Ellen Case (ed.), *Performing Feminisms* (Baltimore: Johns Hopkins University Press, 1990), pp. 17–39.
46 Elin Diamond, 'Mimesis, Mimicry, and the "True-Real"', in Lynda Hart and Peggy Phelan (eds), *Acting Out: Feminist Performances* (Ann Arbor: University of Michigan Press, 1993), pp. 363–82, p. 364.
47 Ibid., p. 376.
48 Ibid., p. 369.
49 One viewpoint is presented in Sheila Jeffreys' *The Lesbian Heresy* (London: Women's Press, 1994). See also Elizabeth Weed and Naomi Schor (eds), *Feminism Meets Queer Theory* (Bloomington: Indiana University Press,

1997). A pertinent stage version of some of the issues can be found in Valerie Mason-John's play 'Sin Dykes' in Valerie Mason-John, *Brown Girl in the Ring* (London: Get A Grip Publishers, 1999).

50 Claire Dowie, *Why Is John Lennon Wearing a Skirt?*, pp. 62–3.

51 Ibid., p. 65.

52 Teresa de Lauretis, 'Sexual Indifference and Lesbian Representation', p. 17.

53 Ibid., p. 18.

54 Ibid.

55 Ibid.

56 Ibid., p. 31.

PART III

AUTO/BIOGRAPHY, IDENTITY AND PERFORMANCE

8

LATINA THEATRE AND PERFORMANCE: ACTS OF EXPOSURE

Caridad Svich

> What are the Latina myths?
> Would they be the 'woman as whore/virgin' kind of myth,
> or real myths like the story of *La Llorona*?
> The Latinas who inhabit my plays are survivors,
> who have used their minds and bodies
> to determine their place in the world.
>
> (Migdalia Cruz)[1]

American Latina theatre and performance has been reconstructing Latina myths and investigating identities disguised, imagined and real for close to thirty-five years. In the world of stand-up and performance, comedians and storytellers like Marga Gomez and Carmelita Tropicana have explored the place of memory, cultural nostalgia and women's roles in undermining the traditional social expectations of what a woman can be, especially a Latina woman, in American society. Often using the confessional autobiographical model so dominant in many performance and storytelling traditions, performers manipulate and play tricks with the form, creating multiple versions of themselves and their 'true stories', thus reconfiguring the truth and spinning magic out of fictions. Latina playwrights, influenced particularly by the performance world that flourished in New York City in the 1970s and 1980s have found transformative ways to present their constructions of self using the dramatic form. Playwrights Migdalia Cruz, Cherrie Moraga and others have presented versions of themselves in their texts, often seeking to not only to reconstruct notions of femininity imposed by Latino and Anglo culture, but also to re-imagine their own history. Wrestling with various truths, these artists dissect the Latina body to lay bare the inequities of a culture that has forced the stereotyped image of the 'bombshell' on Latinas as its most powerful sexual model. Although it would seem as if that image ought to have lost its potency, it nevertheless remains at the centre of much Latina performance, either as myth, a reflecting gaze, a ghost of the present

Latina self, or as object of affection. Autobiographical readings play a crucial part in understanding Latina theatre and performance.

An autobiography is a record of a life written by the subject himself or herself. The many different kinds of autobiographical writings relevant here include letters, memoirs, diaries and journals preserved with autobiographical intent; formal, retrospective studies; and autobiographical fiction. The nature of autobiography changes significantly when it enters the world of theatre and performance, in part because the act of performance or transforming of a life into a theatrical event always creates a filter through which the audience read the work. Neil Simon, for instance, in his autobiographical trilogy set in Brighton Beach, New York invites the audience to witness his plays as thinly veiled documents of his life, but the plays themselves are carefully constructed pieces of fiction firmly rooted in the boulevard comedy tradition. Spalding Gray's solo pieces work on stage as moving objects of confessional literature, yet Gray's persona as a performer is a crafty creation several steps removed from his 'real' self. Alina Troyano, who performs and writes under the name Carmelita Tropicana, adopts different stage personas (male and female) to tell the story not only of her reconstructed memories of pre- and post-Castro Cuba, but also a veritable history of how the Cuban bombshell stereotype was created in the first place. The playwright Migdalia Cruz does not ask for straightforward autobiographical readings of her work from the audience, but instead infuses her plays with memories of her childhood growing up in the Bronx and allows the audience to guess as to whether what she presents is true to her life or representations of lives she has witnessed. Each artist works behind a veil because the act of performance necessitates that the work presented is seen through the lens of craft and composition: autobiography is altered on stage. Moreover, for Latina artists, the veil is made of a tougher fabric: patterns of immigration have skewed white American society's view of race and sexuality. Latinas have to struggle to be seen outside of the imagined racial and sexual binary structure of the United States, which emphasises the polar opposite of white/non-white and immediately places Latinas in the non-white category, regardless of their racial configuration. Latinas are primarily viewed as 'exotic creatures' and 'hot mamas' whose main function is to tempt and please a man. Commercial performers like Jennifer Lopez and Salma Hayek have to a large extent reinforced this 'Latin siren' image, adding to the difficulty for writers and performers like Carmelita Tropicana and Cherrie Moraga in telling their stories.

The veil covers our eyes/Covers our face
Shields us from the world:/The married woman's veil,
The child's veil,/And the mistress' veil.
One day the veil is lifted/And open eyes discover
A face, a body, a shadow/A world within our reach,
A world that reclaims/The silent daughters
Of more than one hundred years of vengeance.[2]

Latina playwrights

The names of Latina playwrights and storytellers are written on the evanescent walls of theatre history: Maria Irene Fornes, Cherrie Moraga, Migdalia Cruz, Carmelita Tropicana, Josefina Lopez, Carmen Rivera, Marga Gomez, Elaine Romero, Edit Villareal, Dolores Prida, Denise Chavez, Naomi Iizuka, Milcha Sanchez-Scott, Lisa Loomer, Silvia Gonzalez S., Monica Palacios, Ana Maria Simo, Anne Garcia Romero, Diana Saenz, Lillian Garrett-Groag, Silviana Wood, Lynette Serrano-Bonaparte, Amparo Garcia, Karen Zacarias, Cusi Cram, Estela Portillo Trembley, Rose Portillo, Nora Glickman, Coco Fusco, Nao Bustamante and so on. These names are both documented and left undocumented in the records of time. Latinas, Chicanas, Mestizas, Cubanas, Puertorriquenas, Nuyoricans and Creole – Latinas, whether born in the US or those who have chosen the country as their home, have been forging a distinct and often uncompromising theatre in the US and elsewhere for more than twenty years. Yet these voices remain relatively unheard or unacknowledged by the critics and a media and production system that continues to favour the Latino voice – if at all – over the Latina.

And I got up and the world was large/kicking to hold my breath
screaming ALL HELL/to those that held me
behind the veil door kitchen house/of my dreams and desires
ALL HELL NO MORE/I say with my loud mouth
and *mi sangre en llamas* (my blood in flames).
I am not your *dona*, your girl, your courtesan.
I will not sit behind your desk/ tearing behind my veil.
I am a body in flagrante/and I will not be held down.[3]

A remnant of the veil remains and Latinas in theatre, *Latinas al borde* (on the verge) negotiate new ways in which to make their voices heard.

The feminist and subsequent post-feminist movements have indelibly affected the creative work of Latinas, especially those active in theatre and performance since both inhabit public realms of experience and thus interact directly with society. Rebelling against Latino culture's inherent machismo (evident, even in the US community), its delicate but very real negation of ambi-sexuality and the expectation that its dramatists and storytellers should follow an exclusively linear model that favours the hero over the heroine, Latinas have created a theatrical literature that is, in part, based on defiance. The defiance is sometimes politically overt in the writing through the choice of subject matter and its presentation. Certainly, the work of Chicana poet/playwright Cherrie Moraga, which takes its cue from the 'actos' of Luis Valdez' Teatro Campesino, has as one of its driving components a militant attitude toward the unmaking of Latina myths and stereotypes that sometimes borders on the didactic. But often the defiance is itself presented in what could be deemed a veiled manner to the less cognisant eye. This is due to the fact that the very act of writing for Latinas, while not impossible, was made a forbidden one for such a long time in the Latino culture.

Twentieth-century feminist movements took the forbidden, the taboo, out of the act of writing, which is, after all, about the recording of memory, the textual inscription of the female body – and therefore, against the notion of historical erasure. Latinas began to reclaim the works of the religious mystics such as Santa Teresa de Avila, Sor Juana Ines de la Cruz and others as a way of acknowledging the tradition of writing of which we are a part and the large debt we owe to our forebears whose own obstacles were greater than any we could imagine. This act of reclamation was first taken by Latina poets, novelists and visual artists influenced by the burgeoning movement of writing and art-making often mistakenly identified as 'magic realism' that was then making its presence felt in Latin America and then later in the rest of the Americas and the world at large. Playwrights and storytellers found inspiration and strength in the works of these artists, and began to make plays and performance pieces that spoke directly to this newly 'liberated' Latina self.

> MEDEA: Oh yes, I've changed. I married you when I was still a girl, not a woman, but a girl with a girl's naivete who still looked for a father's protection. But that was long time ago. I am a woman. A Mexican woman and there is no protection and no place for me, not even in the arms of another woman because she too is an exile in her own land. Marry your child-bride. *A mi no me importa*. No, in that lies no *traicion*.

> *La traicion* occurs when a boy grows into a man and sees his mother as a woman for the first time. A woman. A thing. A creature to be controlled.[4]

Cherrie Moraga

A poet, editor and essayist as well as a playwright, Cherrie Moraga is a pioneer in the new generation of Latina playwrights. A former student of master playwright and teacher Maria Irene Fornes, Moraga's militantly lesbian and overtly political aesthetic marks what has become a significant phase of Latina playwriting in the US. Covering taboo subjects such as incest and sexual abuse with an unflinching gaze, Moraga constructs complex sexual and political paradigms on which the frames of her plays and meta-plays rest. Both inside and outside the work, she is playwright as activist, building on both Fornes' canon and the influence of Luis Valdez' Teatro Campesino. She also bridges, in plays like *Heroes and Saints* and *The Hungry Woman*, the world of poetry, where she has her roots as a writer, with more traditional Western conventions of theatre. Moraga traces aspects of her own life through her work. *The Hungry Woman*, for instance, is profoundly influenced by her own experience as a lesbian mother and the Anglo and Latino societal prejudices she had to face when trying to raise her child. In taking on the classic work *Medea* as one of her source texts, she transcends the personal story of the play with a more mythical one. Moraga seeks to record history, her own and that of others, and to reconsider it as well. What are the myths we have grown up with? What are the manners and behaviours that make a woman feminine? What are the shadows we live with as we create an identity? It is no accident that Moraga's poetic dramaturgy as well as that of her colleagues Migdalia Cruz, Naomi Iizuka, Cusi Cram and others revolves around the question of identity and the coming-of-age. This has been the touchstone of much of the work written by the children of immigrants. Rite of passage is the archetypal story told again and again. Moraga's fierce politics dig at the very heart of her tough and tender plays and poems. She writes the story of her life transformed for an audience, and the stories of her community. A grassroots artist, Moraga both records and documents and makes human the injustices and the hardships of men and women crossing the Mexican border, in particular, in order to find their way in the US. Like August Wilson, whom she greatly admires, Moraga seeks to write the unwritten history of her community, and thus leave a fictionalised but nevertheless accurate record of her time. Working from interviews, oral history texts, Aztec and Mayan myths, classical stories and 'pure' fiction, Moraga weaves complex stories where characters cross racial, sexual and class boundaries in a US culture that rarely acknowledges class, let alone the intricate ways a sexual and racialised self is constructed.

'Enacting the hybrid' is in fact one of the hallmarks of Latina theatre. Whether using the elliptical collage structure used by Maria Irene Fornes, or Moraga's metaphysical dislocations of cultural and gender identities it refuses to define itself as one thing and one thing only. This defiance of categorisation liberates the work from the very structures that seek to codify it for easy consumption. Drawing equally from Iberian and Latin American models – from Garcia Lorca to Borges to Valle-Inclan – Latina theatre incorporates the plasticity and fluidity of the body as its central locus, and offers it thus as an essential way of reading the work.

Marga Gomez

The daughter of a Cuban comedian and a Puerto Rican dancer, Marga Gomez makes her body the focus on stage: she is provocateur and animator, a rude MC and an offbeat heroine. Gomez began her career in the comedy clubs of San Francisco playing for a mostly gay audience. In the late 1980s she joined forces with five other Latino comedians to create Culture Clash, the acclaimed Latino theatre troupe. Although her primary instincts as a performer and writer belong in the world of stand-up, Gomez has turned to the dramatic form as a means of exploring more fully her childhood memories and the cultural lessons from her immigrant parents. Her solo pieces *Memory Tricks* and *A Line Around the Block* are coming-of-age pieces, and autobiographical in the most direct sense. The fictional line is thin in these pieces and Gomez seeks through their performance to truly document not only the world of her parents making a go of it in New York's Latino nightclub circuit in the 1950s and 1960s, but also her own struggles as a comedian and entertainer. The tension is always alive in Gomez's work between the stand-up energy of her beginnings as a performer and a desire to present a more self-consciously crafted piece of theatre. This sometimes uneasy tension exposes the seams in her writing and performing, and thus exposes her private self in a candid and refreshing manner. Gomez is a skilled, sharp performer who works in stand-up, theatre and film, yet in her dramatic solo pieces, in telling her stories and her parents' stories, her skill cannot mask the, at times, more confessional qualities. Unlike Spalding Gray, a confessional monologist, storyteller and actor, who has constructed a public persona so seamless it is difficult to imagine what the 'real' Spalding Gray is like, Gomez in a piece like *Memory Tricks* or *Jaywalker*, is both a crafted persona and an un-crafted one. Uncomfortable with playing one role and one role only, she reveals herself through performance. It is her voice and body that are her autobiographical stance, rather than exclusively her texts. In a culture that worships celebrity where we are always looking for the private self behind the actor's mask, Marga Gomez is both an embodiment of the culture's obsession and a trickster lightly mocking such an obsession. Moreover, her outspoken sexual stance marks her as one of the first acknowledged Latina gay performers to be successful in mainstream theatre. This is in part to do with Gomez's infectious charm as a performer as much as it is to do with the fact that her material, for all its vitality and frankness, is primarily commercial in its appeal. In her solo works, Gomez is the wacky, 'irreverent gal' who tells the audience her story straight-up without many mixed messages or resolutely complex signs for the audience to decipher. She is a populist entertainer and writer who uses her body as the place to locate her sexual desire and re-member her past.

Alina Troyano's Carmelita Tropicana

Fellow lesbian comic performer Alina Troyano's creation Carmelita Tropicana began her stage life in 1984 at the WOW Café in New York. Like Gomez, Tropicana is a stage persona devoted to both making sense of the past and exploring her sexuality. Unlike Gomez, Tropicana is firmly rooted in the performance art tradition. Her work is a mixture of cabaret, stand-up, vaudeville, melodrama and Cuban drag revues. Her pieces include the acclaimed *Milk of Amnesia*, *Memories of the Revolution* and *Candela*. They focus on how identity is constructed and more especially on the incongruities between the public self and the fantasy self. Tropicana is a composite of Troyano's grandmother, sister and mother. She is also her mother's memory of pre-Castro Cuba. From this rich composite, Troyano has created a character which can operate as an agent of memory: a time- traveller and time-walker who is a pastiche of the already faded words and images, faded yet again through handed-down stories, ill-remembered phrases and sharp bits of popular culture. The name she has adopted for her persona recalls the US brand name of Tropicana orange juice, and Cuba's famed nightclub *The Tropicana*. The juxtaposition of pop culture and old-style glamour from her parents' native island reflects Troyano's desire to explore the links between the culture where she has been raised and the one that is a part of her through her blood lines.

Her *Memories of the Revolution* is based on Troyano's father's stories, and as such it plays as an act of retrieval by the writer/performer. She is trying to piece together her past by re-enacting his. A three-act extravaganza, the piece is a parody of thriller dramas and Tropicana revues of the 1950s. Troyano plays Carmelita in a red sequined gown and platform shoes. She also plays the male character of Pingalito (literally 'little dick'), who is grossly enamored with Carmelita. Stories of the revolution weave in and out of this plot centred on raging desires, all things Cuban, tropical bombshells and imminent disaster. Within the aesthetics of camp, Troyano examines gender roles, the authenticity of femininity and the importance of imaginative excess. Planted firmly in the 'downtown' New York art scene, Troyano is a transgressive artist who uses elements of her autobiography to refashion memories of every B movie she has seen, every old Cuban pop song she has heard and of every male and female type that has been part of her consciousness. *Milk of Amnesia* focuses more on the split sense of identity US-born Latinas face. Growing up in the US with her parents' memories swirling about her, her own place of origin becomes more elusive as where she is in the present and where she might have been in the past, merge. The vision of Cuba past and present haunts her, and Troyano's piece, less flamboyant and high-spirited than her earlier work, is an attempt to represent the displacement of self which immigrant children feel. It is a haunting piece that allows Troyano to blend her natural sense of the outrageous with a more serious, less go-for-the-laughs approach to presenting her material. Above all, Carmelita Tropicana is Troyano's unique creation. Part Carmen Miranda, part torch singer, part wiseacre and master of the revels, Tropicana is Troyano's vision of herself through time. Her autobiography can be read consistently through Tropicana's never-ending quest to understand who she is, whom she loves and how the world is too small to contain her.

Migdalia Cruz

CITRONA: People say you can't get used to some things,
But you do. Like the smell of your own shit.
You sit in it long enough and you want to feel it in your legs.

> You smear yourself. Because it keeps you warm. It's familiar.
> It's like your family. My shit and urine is my company.
> I check it all the time. I look for signs of life. I look for light.
> I sleep with my face toward the light. I keep track of myself.[5]

Bronx-born and bred, Migdalia Cruz studied with Maria Irene Fornes in the fabled Intar Hispanic Playwrights Lab in New York in the 1980s and early 1990s. Obsessed with the female body and how it is often maligned and distorted by the male gaze, Cruz's intensely private, metaphorical plays are situated in the dark realm of desire where sex and suffering are linked. Experimenting with style and form in plays like *Fur*, *Miriam's Flowers* and *The Have-Little*, she offers a dramatic point of view as challenging as Moraga's, if less politically overt. In *Fur* Cruz re-tells the story of *Beauty and the Beast* in an imaginative and highly personal manner. The beast in question here is Citrona, a young woman covered in hair, who is treated like an animal by her captor/owner, a handsome man named Michael. Their dark, violent love story is played out against a soundtrack of Beatles songs and the observant eye of a young woman named Nena, who is in love with both Citrona and Michael. The play, like Cruz's earlier piece *Miriam's Flowers,* works on its own terms as well as working as an act of autobiographical translation. Cruz places aspects of her own life and personality into the work but transforms them in the telling. Many playwrights, Latina and otherwise, write plays which contain acts of exposure: moments, incidents, diary entries from their personal life placed on stage in characters' mouths and made part of the narrative of the play. The manner in which these acts of exposure manifest themselves theatrically break down the boundaries between fiction and reality. Cruz makes you guess which aspects of her work come from real life and which are wholly imagined. She does this by inserting her personal, private obsessions into the work in such a forthright manner that the characters seem to speak directly to the audience, directly and with an authorial voice. These acts of exposure, which are more apparent in the work of performance artists and comedians like Gomez and Troyano (because they are less interested in disguising their material through a fictional lens) are the autobiographical traces that link the theatre artists and the performance artists in the Latina world of artistic, live presentation. Cruz's body-specific plays owe much to the explosion of feminist pieces that came out of the storytelling and performance art world in the late 1970s and 1980s. The rise of the WOW Café in New York, for example, and its bold, often aggressively raunchy explorations of the female body in performance, and specifically the Latina body, as signified in the work of comic provocateurs like Marga Gomez and Carmelita Tropicana, created a lively synergy of artistic minds. Playwrights like Cruz and others began to take on the playful frankness and transparency of these performers' work and began to transform them through the prism of dramatic form we call 'a play'.

Cruz also goes a step further than Moraga in creating a new form, which she calls the 'plovel'. The plovel incorporates a narrative within the play, giving the work a novelistic feel in addition to the dramatic elements already present. Again, the notion of hybridisation informs the making of the work. Stylistic lines are blurred as the forging of a new kind of theatre is begun. But unlike the work of similar *pioneras* like

Sabina Berman and Jesusa Rodriguez in Mexico, Paloma Pedrero and Concha Romero in Spain, and Christina Escofet and Diana Raznovich in Argentina, Migdalia Cruz and Cherrie Moraga, and even Maria Irene Fornes have not found a public forum in the US equal to their talents. The work remains hidden behind an invisible veil of commerce, discrimination, sexism and homophobia both within and outside of the Latino community.

Whereas certain Latino voices are accepted and applauded more and more by the theatrical mainstream – writers like José Rivera, Octavio Solis, Edwin Sanchez and Nilo Cruz, as well as performer/writer John Leguizamo – the female counterparts to these voices, the writers that are speaking to the same generation, about the same issues and ideas in often more provocative and exciting ways, are routinely silenced or kept marginalised, finding their way into the public arena of academia or the underground theatres willing to 'risk' presenting their work. A US sociocultural climate of discrimination and sexism is one of the causes for this neglect of Latina voices, but there is more at play here than victimisation or patriarchal precedents.

Selling Latino culture into the mainstream

Certain Latino writers, like José Rivera and Nilo Cruz, have been accepted by the mainstream precisely because the manner in which they have chosen to 'sell' their work fits into an already established mode of US theatrical consumption. They have allowed themselves to be seen as indicative of the 'other' or the 'exotic', which is the most comfortable relationship US audiences have to Latino work, despite the fact that it is created in the US often by writers born in the US. Nilo Cruz's Pulitzer

Prize-winning drama, *Anna in the tropics*, for instance, was marketed in the US as a story set in the alluring, distant 'tropics' when the play is actually set in Tampa, Florida in the 1920s. Witness, moreover, the way in which a writer-performer like John Leguizamo has exploited the expected kitsch nature of his New York Hispanic culture and upbringing. Although his mockery is entertaining and his brilliance as a comic performer is without question, how he has chosen to present himself and his work demonstrates the receptiveness US audiences have for yet another variant of the Latin buffoon or outsider. The ghost of Ricky Ricardo haunts the US's relationship to Latino material.

Playwright José Rivera, for example, does not take issue with journalists and producers who choose to package his work as the 'Latino' product of a given theatrical season. A world-class writer, he has been eager and conflictingly so, to embrace the label of 'magic realism' applied to his work because it is a label recognised by an audience, whether or not the label is accurate in terms of the work being presented. By letting the work be defined by existing tropes, Rivera, Nilo Cruz and certain other Latino voices arguably reinforce the limitations placed on Latino work, despite the quality of their individual writing. Latina voices from the same generation have thus found their path more difficult because of the mainstream success of their counterparts, especially if they are trying to upend the notion of 'exoticness' or 'otherness' through their work.

This climate has also created another kind of Latina writer, one who has decided she should not be identified as Latina, and who works within the mainstream using mainstream models, often at the cost of co-opting her own vision. In plays like Lisa Loomer's *The Waiting Room* and Lillian Garrett-Groag's *The Magic Fire*, conventional dramatic structures are used to mask more progressive intentions, although in Loomer's play *Living Out*, the complex sociopolitical scenario established by the author enables the mask to be dropped. Their relative success in the US regional theatre movement, and at the same time, the works' lack of significant discussion within Latina theatre circles inside and outside of academia, points to a larger question that is embedded in the oppositional thinking that has defined Latina theatre as an Other in the US. What makes a Latina play Latina anyway?

I use both autobiography and imagination.
Truth and lies.
There is a transcendent quality about writing your own story.
I have a series of monologues that I perform about my father

and my relationship to being Bolivian
and when I perform them I understand more
about my feelings about Hispanic: my longing, alienation, joy.[6]

Haunted by a phantom *patria*, this writing speaks of exile regardless of whether the writer is born in the US or elsewhere. It is a writing filled with longing for a homeland that lives in the memory of ancestors, and stretches across the Americas, indebted to the bloody, complex history of colonisation, while at the same time embodying a post-colonial spirit. Syncretic in every sense, the writing fuses the sacred and the profane, pop culture and high art and a dizzying weave of languages and forms of text. Recipes, letters, diary entries, religious rituals, rituals of the body and hygiene, acts of performance and violence, songs and more standard dramatic scenes can make up the world of a play created from the ghost of a country or countries that live in the breath, body and mind of an individual Latina or Latino playwright. Exile is a condition, a state of being, and this writing while rooted in the Americas finds its link in the notion of diaspora. The act of fleeing is central to the understanding of Latina work, because it was and is created in flight, on the wing, in the liminal space where women and Latinas have been writing for centuries.

In the US, where theatre is an almost invisible presence, save for the commercial theatre's musicals and British imports, Latina theatre is practically non-existent in terms of the general populace's perception. This invisibility is due in part to mainstream culture's marginalisation of the Latina/o population in the US even though it remains its fastest-growing 'minority', as well as a history of neglect in the US's relationship with Iberia, Latin and South America. Although Latina/o music and art have been appropriated by and incorporated into the mainstream – witness the media explosion around Jennifer Lopez and Ricky Martin, our two contemporary 'Latin Bombshells' – Latina theatre, by virtue of its already marginal status, has been ignored where other 'minority' voices have been afforded a visible forum. The provocative nature of Latina work is perhaps one reason the mainstream refuses to fully acknowledge its presence. Sensual, frank, disruptive and often centred around the body in relation to issues of cultural scarring and trauma, the strongest Latina writing for theatre and performance confronts audiences and critics alike with visions that do not sit comfortably with what the mainstream will tolerate from its 'colourful' citizens, or what Latino theatre will tolerate from its *bellas señoritas*. It is also work that by its very nature calls into question old world versus new world tensions, still alive as the problems of the border, and Latin and South America attest.

In fact, the border as concept has created an ironic rupture in the discussion of Latina theatre. Whether an artist is referring figuratively to the actual border between Mexico and the US, or the more open-ended border between Latin America, the Caribbean and the US, the very fact that the US continues to be viewed as the geographic and economic power by which the artist defines herself is a point of contention that does not diminish with time. Identity politics and the subsequent rise of tribalism, as witnessed in the 1980s, made the 'border' the referent by which artists were able to establish their position. As the 1980s waned, the border became a concept that instead of uniting artists began to divide them. Seeing the US as the 'other', just as seeing the male as the 'other', justified polarity, but many artists of my own generation and younger find the concept limiting. As transgressors we are interested in erasing borders, breaking boundaries, creating work outside of the climate of opposition, while at the same time honouring and remaining responsible as artists, and therefore citizens, reminding our audiences of the violence that continues to haunt the Americas.

> She's carved into his nut-brown flesh, her face frozen in a divine smile,
> Her eyes half closed, her mouth forever shut,
> /her hands fused together fused
> In a stance of eternal rapture.
> She stands atop a mountain of flowers.
> The cholo turns and shifts his weight.
> The muscles of his back ripple beneath the skin,
> /and as he does this, the flowers open up and shiver with divine delight.
> god's coming.[7]

Naomi Iizuka and hybridity

Naomi Iizuka's plays are often centred around the idea of a haunting mythology, history and the ghosts of forgotten, marginal souls. Half-Japanese, half-Latina, she is one of many hybrid artists who uses her complex heritage to write multi-layered texts about living in the Americas. Her plays include *Polaroid Stories*, an adaptation of *Odyssey* told in the voices of street punks and runaways, *36 Views*, a sleek examination of Hokusai's *36 Views of Mount Fuji* and *Skin*, which transfers Georg Buchner's dark Teutonic allegory *Woyzeck* to a sunny southern California peopled with surfers, cops, sailors and Latina men and women barely surviving under the pressure of a discriminatory society. Iizuka's power lies in the strong, idiosyncratic conception of her stage worlds that feel like movies and play like dreams. Her acts of exposure are often found in her evocative, filmic stage directions, which read like journal entries and private ruminations on the everyday life around her. They are the authorial voice that inserts itself into the body of the text and forces an intimacy between the reader and the page, and the audience and performance. Often, directors will incorporate her stage directions as part of the performance, thus making the private feeling of these poetic fragments tangible to an audience. Like Migdalia Cruz, Iizuka is interested in creating texts which not only live as answers to other texts (Buchner, Homer and so on), but in creating a form which is closer to contemporary fiction than more traditional, conventional playwriting. Her work borrows from the journalistic experiments of William T. Vollman and William S. Burroughs and draws heavily on the compositional models offered by John Cage and the Sex Pistols. More recent work, of which *36 Views* is a part, is obsessed with exploring old-fashioned orientalism and how the West has been affected by the East. Iizuka sees herself as a universalist, and thus is separate from artists like Moraga and Migdalia Cruz, who seek to represent the stories of their specific Latina/o communities, and to be advocates for their communities. There is a fine line between the activist impulse and the purely artistic one. Iizuka is still discovering where her allegiances lie, or if her allegiances to community can be multivalent, and therein lies the power of her work. *Skin*, which remains her most direct and muscular piece of writing, is the body on which the rest of her plays lie. Fragmented, harsh, mysterious, transcendent, critical of authority and written with stark compassion for her doomed characters, the play is reminiscent of the work of Maria Irene Fornes. It brings to mind Fornes' *Mud* and her epic *What of the Night?* This master writer's influence is seen in the work of almost all the Latina theatre and performance artists, many of whom studied with her. Thus, *Skin* serves as both a bridge to the recent past in Latina writing through its Fornesian imprint, and as a marker for new Latina writing in the making and yet to be written.

Intersecting identities and the hybrid sensibility

Latina theatre fuses ancient or classical images from the Americas, while simultaneously offering an abstract, purely fictive reality. The intersection of identities is representative of a distinctly hybrid sensibility, which is at the core of Latina dramatic writing in the US, even as post-colonialism is starting to affect and change the direction of the work itself. What makes the work different from other hybrid sensibilities is its refusal to fully integrate its syncretic strands. Instead, cultural allusions, mythic images and symbols from the writers' personal iconic vocabulary co-exist on the same playing field, moving freely within the demands of a given text, with a fluidity that lays bare the very nature of being a hybrid American, thus questioning the very notion of 'assimilated' text. Beyond the central preoccupation with the body and how the male and female gaze, culture, religion and language demarcate it, Latina theatre is at a turning point in its still-young evolution. The trans-cultural model offered by writers like Naomi Iizuka and more commercial writers like Lisa Loomer let us build on our nascent past, as we redefine our unwritten history. The stereotype of the Latin bombshell may be a thing of the past, but the ability for Latina writers to play with that image now, even as it is being revived by the Salma Hayeks of this world, is one of the more fascinating trends in contemporary Latina theatre outside of the world of performance art, where the image of the bombshell has been dissected and sent up mercilessly for years. In fact, it is the incorporation of the body itself that is proving to be the next step for Latina theatre. Emerging playwrights like Karen Zacarías and Cusi Cram are beginning to look back – at history – for inspiration and models of dramatic writing. Looking outside to how the body interacts with the city, the state and the world – how the hungry Latina body, hungry of spirit and sex, makes itself manifest through political discourse and fully engages in either its emancipation or subjugation through layers of social strata – is the exciting brink on which the writing finds itself. Latina playwrights are not only owning up to their indigenous African, European and mestiza blood but also their pancultural Americaness through their use of language, metaphor and structure. Taking a cue from the venerable Cuban-born, US-based Maria Irene Fornes, they are allowing themselves to take on Chekhov, Brecht, Strindberg and Moliere as well as Kauffman and Hart, Tennessee Williams and Richard Foreman, without forgetting Gabriela Mistral, Helena Maria Viramontes, Cristina Garcia and a host of Latinas who have made their way in the life of letters just a tiny bit easier.

Fighting against the invisible veil placed on them by the will of culture and authority, they remain defiant in their quest to make our stories and voices heard, readily acknowledging the multiplicity of the many stories in their midst. There is no one Latina voice or identity.

They are Latinas *al borde*, not of a nervous breakdown, but of a long-brewing revolution where borders are dismantled and redefined for the next and the following waves of writers that will take their pains and lessons in stride.

> The veil is lifted/The face is lit
> A ray of light/In the center of the world.[8]

Notes

1 Migdalia Cruz, 'Honoring Mystery', in Caridad Svich (ed.), *Trans-Global Readings: Crossing Theatrical Boundaries* (Manchester: Manchester University Press, 2004), p. 71.
2 Caridad Svich, from an unpublished keynote lecture delivered on Latina Theatre at the University of Minnesota, MACLS Summer Institute, August 1999.
3 Ibid.
4 Cherrie Moraga, 'The Hungry Woman', in Caridad Svich and Maria Teresa Marrero (eds), *Out of the Fringe: Contemporary Latina/o Theatre and Performance* (New York: Theatre Commumications Group, 2000), p. 340.
5 Migdalia Cruz, 'Fur', in Caridad Svich and Maria Teresa Marrero (eds), *Out of the Fringe*, p. 80.
6 Cusi Cram, from an interview with Caridad Svich, 3 August 2000.
7 Naomi Iizuka, 'Skin', in Caridad Svich and Maria Teresa Marrero (eds), *Out of the Fringe*, p. 181.
8 Caridad Svich, from an unpublished keynote lecture delivered on Latina Theatre.

9

BEING HER: PRESENCE, ABSENCE AND PERFORMANCE IN THE ART OF JANET CARDIFF AND TRACEY EMIN

Jen Harvie

> Every part of me's bleeding. (Tracey Emin, blue neon light, 1999)

> I can't explain it but then the voice
> became someone else a separate person
> hovering in front of me like a ghost
> (Janet Cardiff, *The Missing Voice (Case Study B)*, 1999)

For feminism, the female autobiographical subject – the voice who claims, for example, she is bleeding – is at once both valuable and problematic. She is valuable because she testifies to lived female gendered experience, experience often characterised by marginalisation, oppression and struggle. However, 'she' is also problematic because of the potential essentialism 'she' ascribes to female identity and the potential homogeneity 'she' produces out of multiple and changing identities. As many feminists have long argued, an essentialised female identity risks ascribing to women apparently universal, timeless and unchanging characteristics – like being more sensual than rational and being nature to man's culture. These apparently intransigent – and often derogatory – characteristics are then difficult for the projects of feminism to interrogate and, so, to change.[1]

Autobiographical performance might be particularly at risk of being understood as essentialist because the performer is present and embodied in it. This presence may appear to invest the autobiographical narrative – as well as the essentialist link between body and gender – with especially resonant authority. On the other hand, the presence of the autobiographical performer may also provide opportunities for querying essentialist understandings of female identity as determined by the biological body by making that problematic body present and available for interrogation.

Work by many contemporary performers and artists deals productively with the problematics of female autobiography by engaging with autobiographical forms in ways that exploit their powers of testimony and simultaneously query their apparent essentialism. And many of these artists use themselves – and their audiences – as models and performers to exploit the particular potential of embodied performance to interrogate essentialism. Such contemporary performers and artists include Marina Abramovic, Mona Hatoum, Sarah Lucas, Orlan, Jenny Saville, Cindy Sherman, Jana Sterbak and Jane and Louise Wilson. This chapter will focus on the work of two such artists, both of whom have exhibited extensively internationally: Janet Cardiff and Tracey Emin.[2] While some might more readily classify this art as fine art rather than performance, it contributes to the concerns of this book and its fields in at least three key ways. First, it indicates the hybridising of art forms that is common in current art and performance practice, as well as women's autobiographical practices more broadly. Second, as the bulk of this chapter argues, it produces relationships between audiences and artists that are productive for particular feminist agendas. Finally, because several of its material features – particularly its uses of sound and space – are shared by more conventional performance, it can help us to think how these features might be deployed across performance to be most effective for feminism's projects.

Cardiff's and Emin's work is profoundly different, and I do not intend to argue otherwise. What I do aim to show is that both artists' work uses some similar strategies in different ways to achieve a host of enabling effects. The work practises two destabilising and re-arranging double movements. First, it posits the artists as both present and absent, here and there – bleeding and ghostly, to invoke my epigraphs. Second, it enlists both the artist and her audience to perform the work and so, to some degree, to assume the work's autobiographical identity. Both of these movements radically assert and de-stabilise female subjectivity with a range of productive outcomes. By exploring the female artists' presence, the work affirms female identity and explores women's subjective experiences, of intimacy and memory in particular; challenges the boundaries that delimit women's spatial and institutional mobility; and affirms experience as sensual and material, not only visual but also aural, spatial, tactile and olfactory. Simultaneously emphasising the female artists' absence, the work resists objectifying and commodifying its female artists and problematises an understanding of the body in particular as the origin of female identity. The work's first double movement between subjective presence and absence – between the artists' dichotomous self-articulation as 'me' and 'her' – thus articulates and explores the poststructuralist problematics of being a woman. It fulfils, in other words, Jane Gallop's still-resonant proposal that, for feminism, 'Identity must be continually assumed and immediately called into question.'[3]

This first double movement is made especially resonant for the work's audiences because of the second movement, that of authorial identity between the artist and the audience. Predominantly through its handling of narrative, organisation of space and even distribution of role, these artists' work compels its audiences in some ways to 'be' her, to occupy or perform the artist's – ambiguously present and absent – self. This places the works' audiences in the curious position of the present/absent artist, in the very problematic of subjectivity produced by the art. It is not only the artist who is both here and not here, testifying both for female experience and to the contingency of that experience: I experience those ambivalences myself as an audience to, participant in and performer of the work.

Here: presence in the work of Janet Cardiff

> *Presence*: The fact or condition of being present; the state of being before, in front of, or in the same place with a person or thing; being there ... [S]ometimes nearly = embodied self ... A person who is corporally present; usually with implication of impressive appearance or bearing.[4]

> In theatre, presence is the matrix of power.[5]

The work of both artists produces a strong sense of her intimate presence. As Philip Auslander has argued, a performer's presence can be seen to affect audiences in ways that are politically both productive and retrograde. Seen positively, the performer's charisma and sense of authenticity that are conventionally read as presence in theatre, other media and politics, are powerful and authoritative, working to persuade audiences and stimulate our emotional engagement with the performance. Put less positively, presence - here, charisma may be a better word - can also be seen as duplicitous and manipulative. For Derrida, the manifest here and now of presence is always a ruse.[6] Cardiff and Emin explore the power and problematics of presence in many of its nuanced guises. Here, I discuss three central outcomes of this use of presence: its affirmation of female identity; its challenge to boundaries of participation and activity delimited by gender; and its emphasis on the sensuality of experience.

Cardiff is a Canadian artist who now primarily produces installations and audio-recorded walks, often in collaboration with her partner George Bures Miller.[7] In Cardiff's walks, the audience member carries a discman and listens to a multi-layered recording which includes – among snippets of recorded music, partial narratives, and other sounds – Cardiff's voice describing the walk and directing the walker, as well as the sound of Cardiff's footsteps setting the pace. This essay considers her audio-recorded walk *The Missing Voice (Case Study B)* in greatest detail.

Commissioned by Artangel,[8] *The Missing Voice (Case Study B)* was originally available for collection, walk and listening from the Whitechapel Library in East London from 17 June 1999.[9] For the deposit of a piece of identification, the listener collects the discman with *The Missing Voice* disc. He or she is directed by a librarian to a spot at the back of the library in the Crime section and instructed to start playback of the thirty-nine-minute recording. A woman's voice begins to speak: she talks about a book on the shelf and reads aloud from it a passage in which a woman is pursued (the listener is instructed to take the book down and follow along with the reading). Using instructions and suggestions, the voice leads the listener upstairs in the library and down again, out onto the busy Whitechapel High Street, down a narrow alleyway, over to and up Brick Lane, through Spitalfields, into and out of a church, and finally into Liverpool Street Station (pictured in Figure 13). Here, the speaker finally abandons the listener to make her own way back to the library and return the disc and discman. Throughout the recording, the voice of a single woman – Cardiff – dominates: she reads aloud from the

13 Listener (right) overlooking the main concourse in Liverpool Street Station, London.

book, directs the listener's movement and observations – 'See the paint peeling off the ceiling' – makes observations – 'here's another banana peel on the ground' – and tells fragments of a narrative about a missing woman. Other voices – apparently that of a male police detective investigating the missing woman's disappearance, and the voice of a man who misses a woman – speak up intermittently. Ambient noises are both constant, such as the walking footsteps, and fade in and out: a fire truck roars down Whitechapel High Street, Asian music comes from shops on Brick Lane and a choir sings in the church.

The work is physically intimate and produces a sense of presence in ways typical of Cardiff's audio walks. Simultaneously recorded on at least two spatially separated microphones and played back in stereo on headphones, the playback produces a binaural effect:[10] the sound feels three-dimensional and the listener seems to inhabit Cardiff's space in her time. We hear her voice in our heads: 'To experience Cardiff's work', writes one reviewer, 'is to invite the artist's voice into one's head in a way that is eerie and intoxicating.'[11] We walk in time with her footsteps, because we are instructed to, also because maintaining her pace means our movement is synchronised with hers – we arrive where she 'is' when she does – and, for Cardiff, because we are physically affected by the sound.[12] We react to apparently ambient noises as she does, unable to distinguish between those that are actually occurring and those that are recorded. Reviewers observe: 'the car that came so fast behind me on Wentworth St. wasn't actually there';[13] and, 'one cannot properly determine whether the spoken words come from the soundtrack or from the real-time speakers'.[14] We are physically motivated by Cardiff: we follow her instructions or risk getting lost in the narrow, twisting alleyways of Spitalfields, disappearing like the missing woman in the narrative.

This sense of physical intimacy and presence is compounded by a sense of narrative intimacy. First, the listener is integrated into a narrative involving a missing woman: 'I believe she's still in this area', says a male voice. It is unclear who this woman is, she might even be the speaker; and considering that the listener is eerily conflated with the speaker, she may even be the listener. 'Choreographed by Cardiff's recorded voice, and walking in time to her footsteps', argues Rachel Withers, 'the listener's own body is inescapably identified (irrespective of gender) with the "woman of the crowd" at the heart of the piece.'[15] Secondly, the physical environment is intimately and subjectively invoked. As Gregory Williams observes, Cardiff's recordings focus on the marginal, the 'hidden corners and narrow passageways that normally receive scant attention'.[16] This audio tour comments not on the conventional material of a London guided walk – famous local inhabitants, major historic events, extraordinary criminal histories like that of Jack the Ripper – also local to the area of Cardiff's walk – but, to a large degree, on the daily and pedestrian – street furniture, banana peels, pigeons, other pedestrians – and the extraordinary but anonymous – the missing woman. These everyday minutiae insert the listener into the present time and place of the recording. But that time and place are disjointed – both now and not now, both here and eerily not here. For Williams, 'Cardiff acts as hypnotist, keeping the visitor off-balance and conjuring up a steady stream of associations that are as diverse as the participants' memories.'[17] The piece itself evokes memories – Cardiff's of the woman and of her sister and brothers – but it may also provoke the audience's memories by suggestion: the woman's voice says, 'sometimes when you read things/ it seems like you're remembering them'. Perhaps the most important aspect of *The Missing Voice*'s evocation of presence through narrative, though, is in Cardiff's mode of address. Admittedly, this is variable, but often she 'addresses the beholder as a "known" companion'[18] and as a good listener,[19] producing what Jennifer Fisher has called an effect of 'conversant space'.[20] In Cardiff's own words, 'I hope that my piece gives people a sense of knowing someone a little, even it if is only with a [*sic*] unknown voice, a missing one'.[21] The listener is hailed as an intimate confidant(e) of the speaker, and sometimes even as a witness to the speaker's unconscious, as the speaker recounts events that seem to be dreams and/or fantasies. Notice how Artangel's promotional photograph for the work visually suggests Cardiff whispers into her microphone (see Figure 14). *The Missing Voice*'s audience is incorporated into the physical, aural, and narrative worlds of the piece, worlds that explore personal conflict, memory, sexuality and the unconscious, and in which speaker and audience are ambiguously witness, victim and perpetrator.

This intense and many-layered evocation of the main speaker's intimate presence works productively to affirm female identity, to challenge boundaries of movement and behaviour delimited by gender, and to emphasise the sensuality of experience. Physically and through narrative, the piece acknowledges anxieties sometimes experienced by women in cities: the threats of being pursued, 'going missing' and feeling schizophrenic.[22] It challenges codes of access and mobility by talking in a library and 'being' a woman walking and observing in a city, historically the space of the privileged male *flâneur*. 'Together with Cardiff's observations in your ears', Claire Bishop argues, 'you feel invisible, part of another London

14 Janet Cardiff in promotional photograph for *The Missing Voice (Case Study B)*.

that the rest of the population can't see.'[23] Feelings, emotions, and anxieties are expressed in central urban public spaces, normally dominated by rationality, commerce and enterprise. The listener is let into a woman's intimate experience that is neither generalised nor mollified: the speaker is complex, expressive, bold, afraid, generous, intimate and active. Instead of allowing the visual to dominate, as it so often does within art circles and wider cultural circles, the aural dominates, and other sensual experiences are admitted too. What is heard may be rationally processed but may also seem to be experienced viscerally: the sounds of an approaching fire truck might make the listener move in from the kerb; the environment is experienced spatially and climactically – through movement and different weather conditions – as well as visually. As David Pinder points out,

> An effect of the soundtrack and especially of hearing the artist's first-person observations and her accompanying footsteps, as well as her instructions to turn this way or that, to wait here or to cross that road there, is to make you acutely aware of rhythm, pace, breath: of the practice of walking. It emphasizes the sensuousness of walking as a mode of apprehending the city that is tactile, aural and olfactory as well as visual.[24]

The impression of Cardiff's presence testifies to the importance of her gendered, spatial and sensual experience.

There: absence in the work of Janet Cardiff

While Cardiff's work produces a profound feeling of intimate presence, it simultaneously produces a sense of subjective absence. Thus, the affirmations of female identity produced by the impression of presence – including the triumph of transgressing gendered boundaries, and the promotion of sensual experience as meaningful – are all problematised by the effect of absence. The importance of this here is that it portrays women's experiences as not necessarily essential and unproblematically available to any audience, especially through a biological body. The sense of absence resulting from, amongst other things, the fact that the body of the artist/speaker is not actually present problematises the body as the origin of woman's meaning, recognises that 'knowing' 'woman' is difficult, and resists art practices' historical tendency to objectify not only their female subjects/models but also their female artists.

The Missing Voice (Case Study B) produces the impression of the woman's absence in many ways, beginning with its title and consistent narrative preoccupation with disappearance. The title tells us that a voice is missing, and one figure whose voice that logically could be is the missing woman of the narrative. The listener knows from what narrative is supplied that a woman is missing, but the narrative is so partial that the woman's absence may not only be understood but also *felt* by the listener. By concentrating on voice as opposed to body, furthermore, *The Missing Voice* precisely resists the voyeuristic access to women's bodies so endemic in Western art traditions, not to mention other visual media like film, which *The Missing Voice* playfully evokes through a soundtrack and narrative indebted to the conventions of film noir. Through the intrigue of its narrative, *The Missing Voice* produces interest in the enigmatic woman victim, but it frustrates access to her by ensuring that we never see her, nor learn what precisely happened to her, nor discover who she was. In fact, the listener never learns precisely who is who at all: is the missing woman the speaker? Who are the men who speak? And, importantly, who is the speaker: as Pinder points out, 'Cardiff's narratorial voice is not constant', producing 'differentiated and shifting perspectives' perhaps more accurately understood as 'multiple selves'.[25]

As Barbara Lounder comments, the title's 'missing voice' may further imply aphonia or loss of voice, a chief symptom of Freud's prototypical hysterical patient Dora from 'Fragment of an analysis of a case of hysteria' (the 'missing' *Case Study A*, perhaps).[26] This connection potentially identifies loss – or lack – of (female) voice as a possible effect of patriarchal culture and is reinforced with both humour and foreboding by *The Missing Voice*'s narrative implication that the missing woman has been abducted: 'he grabs me from behind/his hand over my mouth'.

Of course, it is not only the fictional missing woman of the piece who is absent, but also Cardiff herself, both as a character and as a material body. 'Even though there's always an autobiographical element to my narratives, like a baseline of truth', she explains, 'in each walk I blend a lot of fiction so that I'm always creating a new persona for myself every time.'[27] Further, like the woman at the centre of the narrative, Cardiff is unseen. Thus, while *The Missing Voice* may be sensual, the actual body of the artist is unavailable to either voyeuristic or physical appropriation. Further still, while Cardiff's voice may engage the audience, as a female Canadian voice it may also hold itself at a distance from listeners both male and British. Cardiff's voiceover is intimate and personal, but Ursula Deniflee notes it is nevertheless 'not confessional'.[28] Access to Cardiff is available but limited. And importantly, the limits placed on access to Cardiff are constructed precisely by her. In some ways Cardiff is the object of the art: her voice is its medium. But importantly she is also the active agent of the art: she has made the art, 'vacated' it, and left a series of commands which direct the audience, sometimes with great authority and even forcefulness.[29]

Finally, absence is produced in the piece by the very fact that it is recorded. The piece and its figures may appear to be 'real' and present(-time), but they are of course actually recorded and necessarily therefore unrecoverable. Hearing a recording of the past in a material and temporal present, the effect for *The Missing Voice*'s listener can be a strong sense of both 'being there' and being profoundly dislocated.[30] Writing on Cardiff's earlier audio walk *Chiaroscuro* (1997), John Weber observes, 'Like the camera and the video camcorder Cardiff also employs, the audio recorder seems to capture the world exactly, with a degree of verisimilitude that mimics "natural" perception. But all three technologies preserve slices of an unrecoverable past and thereby inevitably evoke absence as well as presence.'[31] Presence – especially Cardiff's – is keenly evoked in *The Missing Voice*, but it co-exists with her absence. The possibility of 'knowing' a woman and articulating her subjectivity is presented by the sensation of presence; however, the problematics of 'knowing' a woman and articulating her – culturally contingent – subjectivity are simultaneously invoked by her absence.

Here II: presence in the work of Tracey Emin

Tracey Emin was born in London to a British mother and a Turkish father, spent her childhood and early teenage years in the English seaside town of Margate and now lives and works in London. Her work is predominantly autobiographical, is prolific, and encompasses a vast range of forms, including monoprint and drawing, video, painting, embroidered blankets and furniture, writings, neon signs, assembled snapshots and memorabilia, installations and more.[32] Emin's work has been notoriously, consistently and often aggressively criticised for being narcissistic and self-indulgent, a criticism that suggests it is extremely limited in value to anyone other than Emin herself.[33] But as I aim to demonstrate here, first, there is value for her audiences in the work's self-reference and evocation of subjective presence, and second, the work does not simply – or, importantly, naïvely – evoke only Emin's presence; as with Cardiff's work, it evokes her absence as well. As Julia Watson and Sidonie Smith argue in their introduction to *Interfaces: Women/Autobiography/Image/Performance*, Emin's art 'both mimics and questions the notion of autobiography's authenticity, teasing the public as well as the art establishment about the limits and possibilities of the artist's re-presentation of the "real" life in autobiographical acts and about the women artist's essentialized narcissism'.[34]

Given its autobiographical emphasis, the sense of subjective presence produced in Emin's work is more consistently that of Emin herself, rather than that of a fictionalised persona like Cardiff's narrator in *The Missing Voice*. This sense of Emin's presence comes across, first and profoundly, in the autobiographical narratives that dominate her work. They are perhaps most obvious in her longer written texts, such as *Exploration of the Soul* (1994), from which she gave readings in a tour across the United States, and the shorter *Always Glad to See You* (1996). They are also evident in her videos, such as *How It Feels* (1996),[35] which describes her botched abortion and subsequent miscarriage, and *Why I Never Became a Dancer* (1995),[36] which tells of her sexual exploitation as a young teenager in Margate by men older than she was. But Emin's autobiographical narratives are present too in the scenes depicted in her drawings and monoprints (for example, the series *Illustrations from Memory* [1995]), as well as in the writings in these drawings, and in her appliquéd texts on blankets, furniture, and a tent, and in her neon signs. And they are there in her installations which are repeatedly about environments she has inhabited, both literally and metaphorically: the bed with its soiled linen, discarded knickers, and used contraceptive pill packets of *My Bed* (1998); the rebuilt Margate beach hut of *The Hut* (1999);[37] and the tent, covered inside with appliquéd names and writings, entitled *Everyone I Have Ever Slept With 1963–1995* (1995 – shown in an installation in the Tracey Emin Museum in Figure 15).

It is not simply because Emin's work is autobiographical in its content, however, that it produces such a strong 'aura of "authenticity"'[38] and sense of her presence; crucial too are the forms of her work as well as its modes of address. In her autobiographical narratives, Emin's address is consistently deeply intimate and starkly revealing, her stream-of-consciousness writing style enhancing the narrative effect of uncensored exposure. This effect is also articulated in much of her graphic work, particularly that which looks quickly executed, 'unedited and unpolished'[39] – like the monoprints, sometimes produced on 'found' paper, for example hotel stationery.[40] And it is produced in the graphic work that bears uncorrected 'errors', such as the spelling 'mistakes' and reversed letters that crop up in her monoprints in particular (the results, after all, of a process which produces a mirror image of Emin's original drawing and writing; for example, see *I see it thoe*, Figure 16).

Even the work that may not at first appear to be based in narrative conveys this sense of urgency, rawness, and immediate access to Emin. And this includes her work in more conventional media, including what Sarah Kent identifies as Emin's 'preferred medium', monoprinting: 'A sheet of glass is inked … the paper is laid on and a line drawing made. When the paper is peeled off, the ink attaches along the line so creating a mirror image of the drawing on the underside of the paper.'[41] Although the form itself is not intrinsically radical, the quality of Emin's monoprints is unusual and, in the opinion of several critics, it is a quality that conveys a sense of access – to her, to her unconscious, and to raw experience. For Matthew Collings, 'Those lines flow like magic, like they come from nowhere, and immediately describe what life is like for her.'[42] For Kent, 'Emin's lines look as if they have seeped through the paper unaided', giving the impression 'they are communications from elsewhere – from the other side of consciousness, or of the grave'.[43] Curator Philip Monk likens '[t]hese simple prints … to drawing in barbed wire'.[44] Whatever media Emin uses, Joanna Lowry contends, Emin's 'raw stories seem authentic because of their careless volubility, because they deny the censor, because they leave real traces in scribbles on paper and stitches on fabric, and ultimately because of their hysterical excess'.[45]

Although space may not at first appear to have the centrality in Emin's work and its production of a feeling of her presence that it has in

Cardiff's work, it is nevertheless important. Many of Emin's works are installations or environments, environments which are often intimate, and which contextualise both Emin and her audience. By locating her bed in an art gallery, Emin at least partially transforms the gallery into her room, her private, domestic space into which the audience trespasses. Stepping into the tent *Everyone I Have Ever Slept With 1963–1995*, and lying down on its mattress in order to read the embroidered text on the inside of the tent, the audience quite literally positions itself among the names of the many people Emin has – again, literally – slept with, including her mother, her twin brother, her foetuses and her friends, as well as her lovers. The installation *The Interview* (1999) includes a 'video, monitor, two chairs, and two pairs of slippers',[46] and the audience must peer over the worn, wooden chairs (with the well-worn, furry slippers 'ready' at their feet) to watch the video of Emin wearing one costume interviewing Emin wearing another costume. The chairs and the slippers produce a site to be occupied, one that looks as if it might only recently have been vacated by the two Traceys of the video, if not another two Traceys again.

In some cases, this sense of entering and occupying an intimate shared space with Emin is produced by the whole space of exhibition.

15 *The Tracey Emin Museum*, 1996. Installation with *Everyone I Ever Slept With 1963–1995*, Tracey Emin.

This is true of The Shop, in Bethnal Green, East London, which Emin co-ran, and in which she co-exhibited, with Sarah Lucas in 1993.[47] It is also true of the Tracey Emin Museum (shown in Figure 15), another shop front, this time on Waterloo Road, South London, where she made and exhibited work from 1995–98. Emin's actual presence in these spaces makes, for many audiences, a profound difference to their experience of her work. 'The artefacts', writes Josephine Berry,

> have not been completely severed from a now absent origin, but merely set at a distance from it. That origin, Tracey Emin, constitutes the museum and refuses us the possibility of treating the artefacts as displaced and parentless. The artworks obtain a dual status being both objects of scrutiny, reminiscent of the museum artefact, and components of a continuous, living fabric which is the artist.[48]

Although it was not 'her' exhibition space in the same sense as The Shop and The Tracey Emin Museum, *Exorcism of the Last Painting I Ever Made*, Emin's 1996 solo exhibition at the Galleri Andreas Brändström, Stockholm, also produced a pervasively Emin-ated environment. Here, she spent 'two weeks incarcerated in a room built within the gallery where she would eat, sleep and make the exhibition', naked, and with '[s]ixteen fish-eye lenses set into the wall enabl[ing] the public to watch her at work'.[49] The gallery became not just a gallery, but her studio, her home, as well as – perhaps – the audience's peep show, a point to which I return below.

Even in exhibitions where Emin's works occupy their space according to more conventional rules of presentation, they are often contextualised by a sense of her presence. Paula Smithard points out that in exhibitions that include one or more videos, for instance, Emin's voice pervades the space.[50] And in any exhibition which includes the installation *Leaving Home* (1999) – whose materials are a 'metal tub, gin, two keys, two suitcases, chains, spool of thread'[51] – the gin filling the tub produces a pervasive odour evoking Emin's many stories of drunkenness, not to mention her role as a model for Sapphire Gin.

As we saw with Cardiff's art, the evocation of a sense of Emin's presence in her art brings about a host of productive effects. In Emin's work, the material traces of her presence – from the stained bedclothes of *My Bed*, to the bloodied tampons and pregnancy tests of *The History of Painting* (1998),[52] to the declaration of the neon sign *Every Part of Me's Bleeding* (1999) – testify especially to the visceral embodiment of lived female experience. Pervasively, her work speaks her experience of visceral – especially sexual – pleasure and pain. Her pleasure in sex and

16 Tracey Emin, *I see it thoe.*

in embodied experience is articulated, for example, in the neon signs *Kiss me, kiss me, cover my body in love* (1996) and *Fantastic to Feel Beautiful Again* (1997).[53] Her physical pain is related in the video *How It Feels* and its narrative of her failed abortion and miscarriage, and in her monoprint *Don't Just Leave Me Here* (1997), which shows a solitary naked woman, prostrate, backside-up, apparently vomiting on a kerb.[54] As these examples indicate, Emin's work constantly reiterates the ambivalent feelings of self-love (by another name, the narcissism her detractors accuse her of) and self-loathing that she has felt, but also that she has been made to feel in a patriarchal culture where, for example, women are both idolised and vilified as sexual objects.

Emin's art transgresses gendered boundaries primarily by being about – and showing in galleries of fine art – the embodied experiences of being a woman. By showing materials made taboo through their gendered and scatological associations – bloodied tampons, pregnancy tests – Emin challenges fine art gallery protocol not to mention what Watson and Smith call 'the traditions of masculinist art-historical practice'.[55] This challenge is enhanced by Emin's perhaps less spectacular but pervasive exhibition of materials which are mundane and often domestic: worn slippers, snapshots, blankets stitched from recycled fabrics, and monoprints rendered on post-it notes.[56] Emin's practice also challenges the usual spatial separation of the labour of the art maker and the display of her fine art. By making her art *in* gallery spaces, Emin closes the decorous distance from labour that is assumed and performed by most gallery spaces, their dealers and curators, and their audiences and buyers. She also challenges the objectivity assumed by most gallery spaces and performed through their white walls and closely observed conventions of display. Even in exhibitions where she is not present, the apparent rawness of her art, as well as the handmade quality of so much of it, attests to her labour – not to mention her pleasure, suffering and pain. Emin's practice further challenges the conventional separation of the (usually female and passive) model and the (usually male and active) artist by being both and exhibiting herself as both. In her naked display at the Galleri Andreas Brändström, Emin may have set herself up as a spectacle in a kind of peep show, but she did so self-reflexively. The display was not that of a passive model; rather, she was an active artist/worker/model. Emin's photographs of the event show her painting, eating, mixing paints, reading the paper and lying on a mat in familiar life model poses. The model is active. Emin's title for these photographs, *Naked Photos – Life Model Goes Mad* (1996),[57] attests to this, but it attests also to the cognitive dissonance the viewer may experience in seeing the photos: a model who is *doing*, the title suggests, must be read as mad. 'She still opens herself to our gaze', argues Kent, 'but there is a condition attached; we have to acknowledge that her sexuality is hers to offer, not ours to take.'[58]

Finally, Emin's presence in her work attests to the sensuality and materiality of experience. It does so in her narrative affirmation of the scatology of women's experiences and in her related choice of materials, as discussed above. Like Cardiff's work, Emin's work also attests to the multi-sensual nature of experience, not only its visible aspects, but also its textures, sounds, smells, and occupation of space. Although her audience is not invited to touch her objects the way they are Cardiff's installations, many of her objects, especially the textiles, are distinctly textured and three-dimensional. Her exhibitions have sound from her videos, may have the smell from her gin, and they are spatial, placing their audiences in relation to her spaces, her tent, her bed, and her hut. To convey her sensual experiences, Emin's art works, precisely, sensually.

There II: absence in the work of Tracey Emin

As in Cardiff's artwork, however, Emin is not only profoundly present in her work, she is also absent. Again, this absence prevents her from being wholly objectified in her artwork and it prevents her audience from understanding her – and the womanhood she may represent – as wholly knowable, especially through the female body and its traces.

Emin's absence is best seen in the common disjunction between *what* her work appears to attest – that it comes immediately and directly from Emin – and *how* her work must really express itself in production – taking time and labour to be made. While Emin's work may seem to speak directly for her, to stand in for her, even to *be* her, it does not speak directly, it mediates; it is not unmediated expression, it is cultural practice. As Jan Avgikos notes, Emin's 'passionate, handwritten phrases – "Every Part of Me's Bleeding"; "My Cunt is Wet with Fear"' – are mediated through 'cool blue neon':[59] the passionate message is mediated through an electronic medium, a cool colour and – perhaps most tellingly – third-party, technological production methods. The same is true, if less obviously so, of Emin's quilts and other textile montages. Her quilts – for example, *Mad Tracey from Margate, Everyone's Been There* (1997)[60] – appear spontaneous due to their intimate, disjointed, and 'misspelled' revelations and 'homespun' materials. Although low-tech, the production of these works too is laborious, time-consuming, and detailed. Even the monoprints are reflections or impressions of Emin's drawings, not the unmediated, 'real' thing. This is especially evident when there is a disjunction, or even a contradiction, between the print's statements, between, for instance, text written within the print during the printing process and text written outside of the print after printing. One 1998 monoprint, for example, shows the backside of a naked woman, apparently bent over at the waist. Two lines of monoprinted text above the figure read, 'I JUST DONT SEE IT THAT WAY.' 'I see it thoe', responds the title, added later (see Figure 16). Similarly, the very proliferation of Emin's artistic testimonies about herself in her serial self-representation suggest that there is no definitive autobiographical statement to be made: 'she' is at once painfully obvious, and changing, elusive and multiple. Emin's work may appear to provide direct access to her, but that is only part of the story. Her biology is always mediated through her biography,[61] and that is mediated and multiplied through materials, time, and labour.[62]

Being her

This split between a sense of the artist's presence in her work and a sense of her absence there is made even more resonant for these artists' audiences through our experience of being in the position of the artist and, sometimes, through our sense of *being* the artist. In other words, I, as the audience member, experience the artist's presence and absence in some ways as my own; I adopt and enact the artwork's dynamic subjectivities. Thus, the effects of the artist's double movement between presence and absence – the affirmation of female experience, the transgression of boundaries, the recognition of experience as sensual, as well as the problematisation of knowing 'woman' through 'her' body – are literally brought home to the audience. They are not simply effects to be understood, as it were, 'out there', but experiences to be understood and negotiated from within. Significantly this within is not in the (essentialised) body of the artist; rather, it is a discursively produced and so unstable inside. This shift of experience from artist to audience is produced in many ways; here, I consider briefly the effects of narrative, spatial organisation, and enactment.

In both artists' work, narrative functions partly to summon audiences into the position of the artist. In *The Missing Voice*, Cardiff – as represented by her voiceover – is not the listener insofar as she maintains a separate position, commanding the listener, making revelations to the listener, and so on. However, the listener is connected to – and conflated with – Cardiff through the network of possible equations and displacements that the narrative establishes. Cardiff describes a woman who has gone missing in a city, is being looked for, and may have worn a disguise, including a red wig. From her voiceover, we know Cardiff is wandering apparently somewhat randomly in the city, may be the woman being looked for, may be wearing a red wig, and may be being pursued or stalked (note her disguise in the promotional photograph, Figure 14). Her abrupt departure at the end of the disc certainly suggests she is trying to escape someone's pursuit. Finally, the listener is wandering the city, but according to a route that is certainly Cardiff's and which could, therefore, be the missing woman's. If anyone were pursuing Cardiff/the missing woman, would they know, watch, and even stalk this route? If so, could the listener be (mis)taken for the missing woman, the listener's appearance being read as another disguise? Cardiff's whispered commands and abrupt departures – in the church and train station – certainly produce a sense that 'we' are being pursued. All told, Cardiff could be the missing woman; so could the listener. The missing voice could be that of the missing woman; it could also be that of the listener.

This sense of the listener's conflation with Cardiff is, of course, vastly enhanced through *The Missing Voice*'s treatment of space and enactment. As the listener, I am made to feel I am standing in for Cardiff, walking in her footsteps, and hearing her voice in my head. I am also the one who functionally makes the observations Cardiff recounts but is not actually there to see or hear. Whatever actual material threat may be out there is a threat to me, not to the absent Cardiff or to the missing woman. I perform the walk. And if the walk is concerned with a missing voice, it is concerned also with a present listener without whom the walk would not happen. It is perhaps not insignificant that I must relinquish a piece of my own identification in order to borrow Cardiff's disc from the Whitechapel Library.

Audiences are integrated into Emin's narratives not by the triangulation Cardiff effects, but by the revelations Emin makes and the sense of intimate knowledge they produce. Emin describes and depicts intimacies and memories only she can know (as well as some she cannot know – like the experiences of the two sperm which fertilised her mother's eggs when she and her twin brother were conceived, as recounted in *Exploration of the Soul*).[63] By revealing these experiences, Emin effectively enlists her audience into her life – she 'gives' us her memories, 'gives' us her intimate knowledge.

Emin's work enhances this narrative effect for her audience by framing it within spatial experiences of intimacy and conflation. In her tent, we may lie with the names of everyone she has ever slept with, but we also lie on her mattress which reads, 'With myself, always myself, never forgetting.'[64] I sleep or lie with myself is the message of the text – and the tent – and it pertains for whoever might lie there, in Emin's spot. Throughout her gallery/museum/shop work, audiences occupy her spaces marked as both public and private. We are there as a public, but also with access to the private. Spatially, Emin's work leads her audiences into her private realms, into herself. Incorporated as, in some respects, the artist, Cardiff's and Emin's audiences not only experience a sense of identification with the artists' presence, but also with their absence. For these artists' audiences, the problematics of female subjectivity are both witnessed and enacted.

Being her, here and there

These artists' work simultaneously testifies to women's experiences and problematises both the apparent origins of that experience – the female body – and the authority of the testimony. The work affirms female experience but does not allow it to seem inevitable, and so unchanging. These are art practices that exploit the powers of presence but explore also the powers of absence. While, for some, they may not fulfil the most conventional definitions of performance, they do suggest several models of performance. For example, they propose ways of organising spaces of performance. Although many live performers might be reluctant to go to the extremes of absenting themselves from their performances that Emin and Cardiff do, these practices suggest ways performance makers might think strategically about using both their presence and their absence in their work. Perhaps most importantly, this work suggests productive ways of not only re-orienting audiences to the art, but producing a more active – making, performing – audience. These may be art practices where the artists are 'not here', but, significantly, the audience/participant/performer is here, performing and actively investigating the affirmations and problematics of female subjectivities.

Notes

1 For a summary of some of the feminist debates around essentialism see: Stevi Jackson, 'Theorising Gender and Sexuality', in Stevi Jackson and Jackie Jones (eds), *Contemporary Feminist Theories* (Edinburgh: Edinburgh University Press, 1998), pp. 131–46; and Natalie Stoljar, 'Essentialism', in Lorraine Code (ed.), *Encyclopedia of Feminist Theories* (London and New York: Routledge, 2000), pp. 177–8. I accept that my construction here of an essentialist/anti-essentialist binary opposition is problematically delimiting (see Janet Woolf, 'The Artist, the Critic and the Academic: Feminism's Problematic Relationship with "Theory"', in Katy Deepwell (ed.), *New Feminist Art Criticism: Critical Strategies* (Manchester: Manchester University Press, 1995), pp. 14–19); I use it for its polemical brevity and force. For an overview article on feminism and art that is detailed, suggestive and frequently considers issues of essentialism, see Peggy Phelan, 'Survey', in Helena Reckitt (ed.), *Art and Feminism* (London: Phaidon, 2001), pp. 14–49.

2 Between 2000 and mid-2003, Cardiff had solo exhibitions (sometimes in collaboration with her partner George Bures Miller) in Munich, New York, Montreal, Rome, Venice and London, and Emin had solo exhibitions in Berlin, London, Munich, New York, Amsterdam, Oxford and Sydney.

3 Jane Gallop, *Feminism and Psychoanalysis: The Daughter's Seduction* (London: Macmillan, 1982), p. xii.

4 *Oxford English Dictionary*, 2nd edn, Vol. XII (Oxford: Clarendon Press, 1989).

5 Philip Auslander, *From Acting to Performance: Essays in Modernism and Postmodernism* (London and New York: Routledge, 1997), p. 63.

6 See, for example, Jacques Derrida, *Speech and Phenomena and Other Essays on Husserl's Theory of Signs*, ed. and trans. David B. Allison (Evanston, IL: Northwestern University Press, 1973).

7 For detailed information on Cardiff and her work, see Carolyn Christov-Bakargiev, *Janet Cardiff: A Survey of Works Including Collaborations with George Bures Miller* (New York: P.S.1, 2001), and the website, *Janet Cardiff*, www.abbeymedia.com/Janweb/jan.htm.

8 Artangel is dedicated to commissioning artists to engage with London's architecture. For more information see the company website, www.artangel.org.uk, and their book, Gerrie van Noord (ed.), *Off Limits: 40 Artangel Projects* (London: Merrell, 2002).

9 The piece was originally available from the Whitechapel Library from 17 June–27 November 1999. Further funding has enabled the library to continue to lend the piece indefinitely. A package containing a compact disc of the work, a book with an essay by curator Kitty Scott, a biography, stills from a video by George Bures Miller, photos by Gerrie van Noord and a book jacket printed inside with the transcript of the spoken text is also available to purchase from Artangel: Janet Cardiff, *The Missing Voice (Case Study B)*, eds James Lingwood and Gerrie van Noord (London: Artangel Afterlives, 1999). All further references to the text of *The Missing Voice* are to this CD and printed text. A transcript of the CD is also printed in Christov-Bakargiev, *Janet Cardiff*, pp. 116–19.

10 *The Oxford English Dictionary* defines binaural as: 'a system of sound reproduction that uses two separated microphones and two transmission channels to achieve a stereophonic effect; esp[ecially] one in which the sound is delivered to each ear separately by earphones' (*Oxford English Dictionary*, 2nd edn, Vol. II (1989)).

11 John Weber, 'Present Tense' (SFMOMA Catalogue, 1997). Rpt. at 'Present Tense' www.abbeymedia.com/Janweb/weber.htm.

12 In interview, Cardiff has said, 'one of the main things about my work is the physical aspect of sound. A lot of people think it's the narrative quality but it's much more about how our bodies are affected by sound. That's really the driving force.' In Meeka Walsh (introduction) and Robert Enright (interview), 'Pleasure Principals: The Art of Janet Cardiff and George Bures Miller', *Border Crossings: A Magazine of the Arts* 20: 2 (78, May 2001), p. 35.

13 Claire Bishop, 'Missing Voice', *Flash Art* (November–December 1999), p. 119. Rpt. at www.abbeymedia.com/Janweb/bishop.htm.

14 Gregory Williams, 'The Voice of Author/ity', *PAJ: A Journal of Performance and Art* 20:2 (59, 1998), p. 63.

15 Rachel Withers, Review of *The Missing Voice (Case Study B)*, *Artforum International* 38: 4 (1999), p. 157.

16 Gregory Williams, 'The Voice of Author/ity', p. 63.

17 Ibid.

18 Jennifer Fisher, 'Speeches of Display: The Museum Audioguides of Sophie Calle, Andrea Fraser and Janet Cardiff', *Parachute: Art Contemporain/ Contemporary Art* 94 (1999), p. 30.

19 Barbara Lounder, 'Janet Cardiff', *Parachute* 71 (1993), p. 41.

20 Fisher refers to *Chiaroscuro* (1997), Cardiff's eleven-minute binaural audio walk through and telescope installation in the San Francisco Museum of Modern Art (Jennifer Fisher, 'Speeches of Display', p. 30).
21 Janet Cardiff, *The Missing Voice*, p. 66.
22 Monica Biagioli, 'Janet Cardiff: *The Missing Voice (Case Study B)*: An Audio Walk', *Artfocus* 68 (2000). Rpt. at *Artfocus Online*, www.artfocus.com/JanetCardiff.html.
23 Claire Bishop, 'Missing Voice'.
24 David Pinder, 'Ghostly Footsteps: Voices, Memories and Walks in the City', *Ecumene* 8: 1 (2001), p. 5.
25 Ibid., pp. 5–6.
26 Barbara Lounder, 'Janet Cardiff', p. 40; Sigmund Freud, 'Fragment of an Analysis of a Case of Hysteria [Dora]', in *Case Studies 1* (London: Penguin Freud Library, Vol. 8, 1990), pp. 31–168.
27 Janet Cardiff in Corinna Ghaznavi, '*Les Pistes sonores de Janet Cardiff*/Making Sound Tracks', *Art Press* 269 (June 2001), p. 51.
28 Ursula Deniflee, 'The Case of the Missing Voice', *Make: The Magazine of Women's Art* 85 (1999), p. 25.
29 Gregory Williams comments on his experience of Cardiff's 1997 creation *Walk Muenster*: '*Walk* Münster required a willingness to follow instructions from the artist and relinquish a measure of free will ... Like the tone of the work's title (*Walk, Münster*!), the instruction primarily took the form of a series of commands, delivered by Cardiff in a voice that alternated between sensuous and sinister' (Gregory Williams, 'The Voice of Author/ity', pp. 62–3).
30 For a consideration of the disorientation produced by the walk, especially in the days following the terrorist attacks on New York's World Trade Center on 11 September 2001, see Sarah Gorman, 'Wandering and Wondering: Following Janet Cardiff's *Missing Voice*', *Performance Research* 8:1 (2003), pp. 83–92; p. 87.
31 John Weber, 'Present Tense'.
32 An extensive list of Emin's solo and group exhibitions is listed on her webpage on the website of the White Cube art gallery, 'Tracey Emin', www.whitecube.com/artists/bio/te.html. Further information about her work, writings on it, and a list television programmes in which she has participated are available in her book, Tracey Emin, *Tracey Emin: I Need Art Like I Need God* (London: Jay Jopling, 1998), pp. 66–7. See also a recent collection of critical essays on her work: Mandy Merck and Chris Townsend (eds), *The Art of Tracey Emin* (London: Thames and Hudson, 2002).
33 Examples are recorded in, for example: Deborah Cherry, 'On the move: *My Bed*, 1998 to 1999', in Merck and Townsend (eds), *The Art of Tracey Emin*, pp. 134–54; and Marcus Field, 'Emin for Real', *Modern Painters* (Autumn 2002), pp. 112–17.
34 Julia Watson and Sidonie Smith, 'Introduction: Mapping Women's Self-Representation at Visual/Textual Interfaces', in Sidonie Smith and Julia

Watson (eds), *Interfaces: Women/Autobiography/Image/Performance* (Ann Arbor: University of Michigan Press, 2002), pp. 1–46, p. 4.

35 This video is partially described in Josephine Berry, 'Wearing Sleeve Feelings: "How It Feels" at the Tracey Emin Museum' (1997, www.art-bag.net/contd/liner/emin.htm) and in Esther Pierini, 'Tracey Emin', *Flash Art* 197:3 (November–December 1997), p. 102.

36 The text of this video is reproduced in Tracey Emin, *Tracey Emin*, pp. 28–9.

37 Jan Avgikos writes, 'One need only look at the broken-down wooden shack transported from the English seaside to Emin's New York gallery (*The Hut*, 1999) to know that something bad happened to her there.' Jan Avgikos, Review of Tracey Emin exhibition, Lehmann Maupin, New York, *Artforum International* 38: 2 (October 1999), p. 139.

38 Julia Watson and Sidonie Smith, 'Introduction', p. 2.

39 Ibid., p. 1.

40 For example, two monoprints reproduced in *Tracey Emin* and possibly titled *Room Service* and *Room Service II* (n.d.) are printed on stationery reading 'Renaissance Hotels and Resorts' (Tracey Emin, *Tracey Emin*, pp. 22–3).

41 Sarah Kent, 'Tracey Emin: Flying High', in Tracey Emin, *Tracey Emin*, p. 34.

42 Matthew Collings and Carl Freedman (ed.), 'Just How Big Are They?', in Tracey Emin, *Tracey Emin*, p. 58.

43 Sarah Kent, 'Tracey Emin', p. 34.

44 Philip Monk, *Hypermnesiac Fabulations* (Toronto: The Power Plant, 1997), p. 12.

45 Joanna Lowry, 'Intimate Distance: Art in a Confessional Culture', *Contemporary Visual Arts* 18 (1998), p. 39.

46 'Tracey Emin: *Every Part of Me's Bleeding*', www.artseensoho.com/Art/LEHMANNMAUPIN/emin99/emin3.html. This site also includes a photograph of a detail of the installation. A photograph with more detail appears in *Artforum International* 38:2 (October 1999), p. 138, adjacent to Jan Avgikos' previously cited review of *Every Part of Me's Bleeding* at Lehmann Maupin, New York, which describes the installation.

47 Numerous photographs of The Shop appear in Tracey Emin, *Tracey Emin*, pp. 68–9.

48 Josephine Berry, 'Wearing Sleeve Feelings'.

49 Sarah Kent, 'Tracey Emin', p. 31.

50 Paula Smithard, 'It's a Tenuous Line Between Sincerity and Sensationalism', *Make* 76 (June/July 1997), p. 28.

51 'Tracey Emin: *Every Part of Me's Bleeding*', www.artseensoho.com/Art/LEHMANNMAUPIN/emin99/emin1.html.

52 A photographic detail of this piece is shown on the website of the exhibition 'Tracey Emin: *Every Part of Me's Bleeding*', at Lehmann Maupin, New York, www.artseensoho.com/Art/LEHMANNMAUPIN/emin99/emin2.html.

53 These are shown in Tracey Emin, *Tracey Emin*, pp. 54–5.

54 Ibid., p. 15.

55 Julia Watson and Sidonie Smith, 'Introduction', p. 4.

56 For a brief comment on Emin's use of snapshots, see Joanne Lowry, 'Photography, Video and the Everyday', *Creative Camera* 347 (August–September 1997), p. 16.

57 A selection of these photographs is reproduced in Tracey Emin, *Tracey Emin*, cover and pp. 38–9.

58 Sarah Kent, 'Tracey Emin', p. 31.

59 Jan Avgikos, review of Tracey Emin exhibition.

60 A photograph of this quilt appears in Tracey Emin, *Tracey Emin*, p. 43.

61 Jennifer Allen, 'De Vaginæ Eloquentia', *Contemporary Visual Arts* 20 (1998), p. 35.

62 The first double movement in these artists' works between presence and absence is enhanced through numerous forms of disorientation – spatial, aural, visual, temporal and ontological. Cardiff's mapping is distinctly arbitrary, leading her listener on a quest for banana peels as much as the missing woman, and moving eerily from past to present, from fantasy to reality. Emin's treatment of site is disorienting, instantaneously displacing her audience from gallery to bedroom. Cardiff's work is especially aurally disorienting, blurring the distinction between recorded and real sound. Emin's work can be especially visually disorienting, in the apparently random montage of phrases on her quilts, and in the lurching perspective produced in her monoprints. Both artists' work produces temporal disorientation: Cardiff's audio-walk 'splices flashback and present action' (Withers, review of *The Missing Voice*, p. 63); and Emin treats events that are long past and recent with the same voice of immediacy. Ontologically, both artists conflate fact and fiction. Cardiff's walks create 'semi-fictitious environments' by mixing real material environments with subjective observations and fictional characters (Williams, 'The Voice of Author/ity', p. 62). Emin trades on the truth of her experiences and their confession in her art, but in so doing, she not only *is* herself, she *makes* herself as a persona and a celebrity, one who makes art but is also a model for Sapphire Gin and Vivienne Westwood. (A Westwood advertisement featuring Emin is reproduced in Chris Townsend and Mandy Merck, 'Introduction: Eminent Domain: The Cultural Location of Tracey Emin', in Merck and Townsend (eds), *The Art of Tracey Emin*, p. 8.)

63 Quoted in Sarah Kent, 'Tracey Emin', p. 34.

64 Ibid., p. 36.

10

PERFORMING LESBIANS: CONSTRUCTING THE SELF, CONSTRUCTING THE COMMUNITY[1]

Deirdre Heddon

> Oppressed people resist by identifying themselves as subject, by defining their reality, shaping their new identity, naming their history, telling their story. (bell hooks)[2]

I write this at the beginning of the twenty-first century when the proposal of a gay bishop has entirely split the international Anglican Church; and when Section 28 has only just this year been removed from the English statute books.[3] I write this at a time, then, when the lesbian or gay subject is still struggling for their right to be.[4] I also, however, write this at a time when, in theory, the notions of self and community are thoroughly – and I would argue, rightly – problematised.

The 1980s witnessed a flurry of various published anthologies that were primarily concerned with making visible the details of gay and lesbian lives. Such anthologies included *Inventing Ourselves: Lesbian Life Stories*, *The Coming Out Stories* and *The Lesbian Path*.[5] Throughout the 1990s there appeared to be a similar flurry of theatrical activity in Glasgow bearing a strong resemblance, in terms of aims and content, to these published anthologies. One difference between them, of course, was their medium of representation, and it is this difference that I aim to elucidate in this chapter.

Biography

In 1995 7:84 Theatre Company (Scotland), working with the charity Scottish Aids Monitor, devised *Talking Bollocks* – a show that might be considered a 'community autobiography', drawing as it does on the life stories of its participants, gay men with little or no previous experience of theatre. The overwhelming success of this show prompted the company to devise a follow-up in 1998.[6] At the same time, Natalie

Wilson, co-director of the *Talking Bollocks* projects, decided that there should be a female equivalent, and with the gay and lesbian theatre company, mct, devised a sister show, *Fingerlicks*.[7] As with the *Talking Bollocks* performances, *Fingerlicks* proved to be a huge hit, reaching almost capacity audiences and prompting mct to produce *Fingerlicks 2* in 1999.[8] Finally, in 2000, 7:84 and mct combined forces to create *Just Pretending*, a project which appropriately involved both lesbians and gay men.[9]

All of these performances share certain characteristics, not least that their focus is on the experiences of being gay or lesbian, with those experiences drawn directly from the life experiences of the gay and lesbian performer-participants. One other shared feature of *Talking Bollocks*, *Fingerlicks* and *Just Pretending* is that their genesis is to be found in the gay and lesbian arts festival Glasgay.

Glasgay, launched in 1994, has become the UK's largest such festival, and is now an annual fixture in Glasgow's calendar.[10] That this festival is held in Glasgow, and not London, or indeed Manchester, both of which have sizeable gay and lesbian 'villages', is worth noting. One effect of Glasgay is that it has placed the gay and lesbian subject firmly within various real and representational frames. As the adage states, 'We're here ...' Wilson, commenting on the popularity of *Fingerlicks*, implicitly references the more typical absence of lesbian representation: 'audiences were wanting to see more of this type of work, wanting to see their lives on stage'.[11]

Of course, mct and 7:84 were not the first companies to represent gay men and lesbians in Scotland,[12] and the sheer variety of performances available in Glasgow, particularly following its hugely successful stint as European City of Culture in 1990, is noteworthy. Appreciating the diversity of cultural experiences, it is also to be acknowledged, however, that representations of gay and lesbian subjects within the theatrical frame remain infrequent events. The representation of Scottish gay men and lesbians is rarer still.[13] Glasgay, even if only once a year, attempts to redress that balance. Throughout the two week festival, most major venues in the city play host to some event programmed as part of Glasgay, ranging from art exhibitions, to performance art, to music, to clubs, to poetry and literature readings. At the 2003 Glasgay, there were over 40 events, with artists invited from New York, Toronto and South Africa. The programme included Diamanda Galás at the Scottish Concert Hall, a dramatisation of Louise Welsh's crime thriller, *The Cutting Room*, at the Citizens Theatre, the Ballet Trockadero at the

Theatre Royal, and Ursula Martinez's *OAP* at the Centre of Contemporary Art.

Context

The highly visible backlash against the repeal of Section 28 in Scotland provides an illustrative example of the continuing prejudice against gay men and lesbians in Scotland. Section 28 referred to Section 28 of the Local Government Act of 1986, amended in 1988 with a new Section, 2a, which provided that, 'A local authority shall not (a) intentionally promote homosexuality or publish material with the intention of promoting homosexuality; (b) promote the teaching in any maintained school of the acceptability of homosexuality as a pretended family relationship.'[14] The establishment of the Scottish Parliament in 1999 enabled the Section to be repealed in Scotland in June 2000, but not before an impassioned 'Keep the Clause' campaign was mounted by those opposed to its repeal. In a press release of October 1999, for example, headlined 'No to gay lessons for Scottish school children', the Christian Institute Scotland stated that some '70% of Scottish men believe that homosexual practice is wrong', claiming to reproduce this statistic from a comprehensive 1994 study (the year before the first *Talking Bollocks* performance).[15]

The intended repeal of Section 28 also prompted Stagecoach tycoon, Brian Souter, to stage a private referendum, polling Scottish people on whether they thought the Section should be retained. More than a million Scots voted to keep Section 28 (87 per cent of those who voted), whilst approximately 166,000 desired its repeal. This private 'referendum' was widely dismissed by Scottish Parliamentary representatives but the fact that one million people *had* bothered to make their opinion known, and that this opinion was in support of, rather than against, Section 28, is not insignificant.

In the same year, Mori Scotland interviewed a sample of adults for the *Sunday Herald*, to determine public attitudes towards homosexuality.[16] Thirty-three per cent of those polled agreed with Cardinal Winning's description of homosexual relationships as 'a perversion'; 14 per cent indicated that if schools were to be allowed to discuss homosexuality, they should 'teach children that homosexuality is wrong, and should not be tolerated as a way of life'; while 24 per cent responded that schools should 'teach children that homosexuality is wrong, but should be tolerated as a way of life'. According to these figures more than one in three people in Scotland, in the twenty-first century, continues to believe that 'homosexuality is wrong'.[17] Another poll, undertaken by the National Centre for Social Research in the Summer of 2000, reports similar findings: '39% of Scots think that homosexuality is "always wrong".'[18]

While *Talking Bollocks* and *Fingerlicks* were performed prior to these polls, the attitudes represented by them are precisely the ingrained and everyday attitudes that the performance events were responding to. Within such an atmosphere of intolerance, the need for community and the insistence upon the gay or lesbian self's right to be, becomes imperative rather than academic. It is this culture of homophobia that prompted so many shows to take as their foundation the real stories – the lived lives – of actual gay men and lesbians. Using their own voices, the performers have the means to talk back, to insist, and to challenge. Importantly, the voices heard here are voices of gay men and lesbians living in Scotland, and that cultural location is as recognised and as important as any sexual identity.

Like the earlier published anthologies these performances seek to represent the marginalised and often objectified gay men and lesbians, allowing them to be – or become – subjects. In the remainder of this chapter, I wish to place one of these performances, *Fingerlicks* (1998), beside the published works in order to ask what difference (this) performance potentially makes to the representation of 'lesbian' selves.

Different stories

Anthologies of personal narratives written by lesbians implicitly challenge the assumption that a heterosexual identity is the only, or only legitimate, identity. These autobiographical narratives suggest other lives and other life-paths, providing a different model for a life than that of normative heterosexuality. Through figuring this 'other' subject, they also reveal the presence of that dominant hetero-normative narrative. 'Rendering lesbianism natural, self-evident, original, can have the effect of emptying traditional representations of their content, of contesting the only apparent self-evidence of "normal" (read heterosexual) life course.'[19]

On a very simple level, the stories told extend the range of stories available. Being part of discourse they also extend the range of lives available to be lived. As Liz Stanley insists, stories are preoccupied with a 'literary and political re-shaping of language and thus consciousness'.[20]

The fact that the stories are told by self-identified lesbians is also politically crucial. These 'lay' stories challenge the historical 'expert's story' of the dysfunctional, immature, not fully developed, inverted homosexual, or the alternative 'clergy's story' of sinful and unnatural behaviour. In Ken Plummer's words, the 'sexual stories of authority – given to us from on high by the men in black frocks and white coats – are fracturing in the face of *participant stories*'.[21] Through their stories, then, the storytellers not only claim identities for themselves, but they may also attempt to rewrite what those identities mean. These stories are not guilty confessions, but are most typically celebrations – celebrations of being here, of presence. The act of writing enacts the writer, bringing her in to existence, as matter. And her life story as something that also matters; that has a right to be read.[22] The writer of the lesbian autobiographical narrative is a subject in her own story, rather than the medical or psychiatric object of interest. For Biddy Martin, the personal narratives

> are responses to the at least implicit questions of what it means to be a lesbian, how lesbianism figures in a life, what it means to come out. In a stricter sense, they are accounts of the process of becoming conscious of oneself as a lesbian, about accepting and affirming that identity against enormous odds, including, of course, the authors' own resistance to the label.[23]

Not only do such narratives debunk expert knowledge, these stories and their tellers also provide possible role models, perhaps prompting further coming to voice. Stories, then, have an inspirational, educational, and consciousness-raising purpose and might indeed have real effects on the future lives or life-courses of their witnesses. This potential affect of the story is its social role.[24] 'These stories work their way into changing lives, communities and cultures. Through and through, sexual story telling is a political process.'[25]

Importantly, the stories told are also stories that serve to strengthen the idea of the lesbian community. As Plummer writes, stories 'gather people around them', while for Bonnie Zimmerman they are 'instrumental in creating networks and community'.[26] Plummer also identifies a dialectical movement between communities, politics, identities and stories, as communities and stories feed 'upon and into the other'.[27]

This relationship between stories and the construction of selves and communities is one that needs to be recognised. Communities, as most often conceived, operate through a process of inclusion/exclusion. In order to have a community, there must be a boundary separating those who belong from those who do not (and the former relies on the latter). Shared narratives are one process of erecting and maintaining a boundary. The repetition of the 'proper narrative' becomes an identification badge for community members, and simultaneously a process through which the community is maintained. Deviations from the proper narrative threaten any community established on the grounds of an assumed sameness. As such, deviations are prohibited. Those telling the wrong story may well find themselves ejected or barred from the community, whilst those unable to tell the proper story will be excluded from the outset. It is against such a reductive and dangerous concept of community based on sameness that Diane Elam proposes a coalition politics based on a groundless solidarity[28] and Biddy Martin figures a community as being *achieved* rather than assumed. Judith Butler's critique of the 'feminist community' is an apposite illustration, worth remembering: 'Through what exclusions has the feminist [lesbian] subject been constructed, and how do those excluded domains return to haunt the "integrity" and "unity" of the feminist [lesbian] "we"'.[29]

The 'proper narrative'

Whilst the anthologies of personal narratives are not singularly 'coming-out' stories, they are often so, representing that moment of coming-into being a lesbian. Plummer has identified common features of the coming-out story, which include 'the use of some kind of causal language, sense of linear progression, [they] talk with unproblematic language and [they] feel they are "discovering a truth"'.[30] Or, in Martin's terms,

> many of the coming-out stories are tautological insofar as they describe a process of coming to know something that has always been true, a truth to which the author has returned. They also describe a linear progression from a past shrouded in confusion or lies to a present or future that represents a liberation from the past. Coming out is conceived, then, as both a return to one's true self and a desire and a movement beyond distortion and constraint, grounding identity and political unity in moral right and truth.[31]

Plummer similarly identifies in the coming-out story a sense of self-consciousness about the self, about identity, 'which scans the past life for clues to one's sexual being. There is a sense of identity … hidden from the surface awaiting clearer recognition, labelling, categorising'.[32] Of course, the telling of stories about oneself is part of the construction of an identity for that self, rather than its mere presentation or recording. Barbara Ponse's empirical research, undertaken in the 1970s, led her to posit the existence of a 'gay trajectory' within the lesbian community.[33] This operates much like a narrative trajectory – unfolding in time, complete with a beginning which leads to a middle which in turn leads to an end. Ponse has identified five recurring components of the trajectory, which can occur in any order. These include being aware of a difference from some assumed norm, which is subsequently identified as same-sex attraction, the identification of same-sex attraction as belonging to a type of person, the application of that label to the self, the seeking out of others who share that self-identification, and the experience of a same-sex relationship. It is through and within this narrative – what could now be called a performative narrative – that the 'self' that 'is' categorically lesbian comes into being. (Presumably those who identify as heterosexual have no need to be 'self' conscious, and therefore do not construct an equivalent 'straight trajectory'). For Ponse, this narrative is the 'biographic norm of the community' and as such is the one most frequently told.[34]

Reading through the anthologies, this narrative is indeed evident. If there are auto/biographical norms operating within the lesbian and gay community, which arguably construct such a community, then these already existent and dominant narratives are surely implicated in the construction of one's own story – and in turn one's own sense of identity. The frame in and through which the self is constituted is already there.

The gay and lesbian auto/biographical norm is itself not immune to or divorced from wider narrative imperatives. The notion of a gay trajectory aside, Plummer acknowledges that the coming-out stories 'fit so well into the widely-held narratives of taking a journey, suffering and finding a home, [that] it is easy to see why they have become so pervasive. There is a fit; they sit well with what we already know.'[35]

For Plummer, then, the coming-out story is not specific in its formula, since it contains *generic* elements of modern stories: 'There is always a *suffering* which gives the tension to the plot; this is followed through a crisis or turning point of *epiphany* where something has to be done – a silence broken; and this leads to a *transformation* – a surviving and maybe a surpassing.'[36]

The ways in which lesbians make sense of their experiences, and of whom they are, are influenced by the existence of such dominant patterns of story telling. Added to such general dominant models, within *autobiographical* storytelling there are also dominant models, themselves patterned on this novel form, with its linear progression and its narrative drive to resolution. In summary, then, lesbian autobiographical narratives work between various models: the dominant model of autobiography, the dominant model of lesbian auto/biography, which may be oral in form, and the dominant model of narratives *per se*.

Dominant narratives, of course, do not function in isolation from reality, but very much inform and affect, rather than simply represent, the lived. The dominant narrative of sexuality in the contemporary Western world is that one *has* a sexuality – and specifically a singular sexuality. It is precisely this dominant narrative that the stories in lesbian anthologies often seek to represent. Writers' representations of their lesbian sexuality are appeals for inclusion within this dominant narrative, rather than challenges to it.

These generic stories, conforming to and performing the dominant and/or lesbian 'auto/biographical norm', might well limit what stories can be told about being lesbian, or anything else. Each time this normative narrative of what it is to be lesbian is recited, which includes Ponse's key narrative components, the more difficult it becomes to imagine, propose, recite or live other lives. Further, there is no acknowledgment, by the writers, of their own involvement in the construction of their identity, through *their* use of discourses – including the scientific, medical or genetic discourses of 'innate sexuality'. For Martin, 'these narratives tend to erase the individual's and the group's active participation in their formation as social beings ...'[37] Experiences and their *interpretations* are figured as essences and incontrovertible evidence. In these stories the often confusing, lived experience of sex and sexuality, the contested boundaries and binaries, the contradictions, the contingencies, the contexts, are erased or ignored in the name of the 'truth' of sexual identity. In these *individual* stories there is then, ironically, too often a *sameness*.

Lesbians performing

Recognising the potentials and limitations of published anthologies of personal narratives, I now want to turn to the performance, *Fingerlicks*. Aware of the lack of representations of lesbians in theatre, in general, and in Scotland, in particular, mct's aim for the production was that it should 'reach out' to lesbians. The intention was that it should function as the ground upon which to bring different women together, and to find ways for these women to use theatre to 'work together and collaborate together and to discuss experiences and find common grounds and find the differences'. On a practical level, it was hoped that the participants would acquire new skills, enabling them to 'put their life in front of an audience'.[38]

Despite the difference in the medium, which may indeed *make* a huge difference, there are structural and thematic similarities between *Fingerlicks* and the aforementioned published anthologies. *Fingerlicks* is performed by eight performers, each of whom has at least one moment in the spotlight to enact her story (with other participants playing other roles as necessary). Each of the stories is 'discrete', being self-contained. No single story unfolds throughout the performance, unless one considers the composite picture that is composed by these individual stories as being a larger story. The lives recounted here are all about 'being' a lesbian, and are all told from that perspective. For Wilson, 'the uniqueness of the group is the diversity of the lesbians involved. The common denominator is that they all have little or no experience of drama and have come together to create a theatre piece. The women come from all walks of life and by being together on stage they create a microcosm of the spectrum of lesbian sexuality.'[39]

Features identified by Martin and Plummer are uncannily present in some of the stories presented in *Fingerlicks*. Alba's story is illustrative, beginning as it does with a quote from William Shakespeare's *Hamlet*: 'To thine own self be true.' Alba's narrative figures a journey in which Alba, supposedly on the path towards her self, endures much pain, including rape by her former husband. By the end, however, we are in no doubt that the outcome is worth the pain endured. Matching Plummer's template, there is suffering, a turning point of epiphany, and a transformation, leading indeed to a surviving and a surpassing.

> He raped me. There was no struggle, no shouting, no screaming, no crying. Because that was what he wanted. I knew he could take nothing else from me than he had done over the past 20 years. I was in control. I may have lost a relationship with two of my sons because I'm a lesbian. I may have lost all my material goods. I may be in conflict with my religion. But I've regained my self respect. I own all my triumphs, all my successes, all my mistakes. I've had more sex in the last 18 months than in the past 20 years and it's been fantastic. I know who I am. And to thine own self be true.[40]

Alba's journey, narrated directly to the audience, is one that travels from despair to freedom, and the story appears to employ a very definite narrative trajectory. However, the route taken is less linear than circular, as Alba *returns* to what she believes she always was. This return is literally remarked in her text, through the repetition of the first and last line: 'To thine own self be true.' Alba's story, then, in line with Martin's insights, is less one of development than of *rediscovery*.

This narrative trajectory is equally evident in Caroline's story. Caroline begins by reflecting on herself as an eight year old going to visit her Aunty Bessy with her mum and dad. Aunty Bessy lived with Aunty Charlotte, 'in a posh house, with a big garden, and a cat'. Her mum said that the two aunties were just very good friends. Caroline remembers they both wore trousers, and the only other woman she knew who did that was Ivy Diddle. (Tellingly, this name had become a euphemism for lesbians in the place where Caroline lived. Her older sister had even told her that 'Aunty Bessy and Aunty Charlotte are Ivy Diddles'.) The narrative then tracks forward to Caroline, aged eighteen.

> C: [*Miming being on phone.*] Right – I need to go. Bye. I was eighteen. I needed to be on the phone for hours. I had to know where we were going that weekend. Who fancied who. What to wear. And I wanted to be part of the group. I loved clothes. Makeup. I was a young woman and was feminine. And I liked it. [*A., a female friend, enters.*] Hi, I've started night-school for shorthand and typing, it's next door to a pub called Vintners – Clyde Street. Do you want to go for a drink?
> A: Yeah, ok.
> [*They walk, music and lights – 'I am what I am' plays, as they enter 'pub'.*]
> A: Is this a gay bar?
> C: Well, there's plenty of men, but we're the only women.
> A: No we're not. They're women over there.
> C: They're women?
> A: Caroline, this is a gay bar. *They* are lezzies.
> C: Really? They look like men. I thought lezzies liked women?
> A: Well, that one likes the look of you.
> C: *I'm* not going to be like them.
> [*She covers her mouth quickly as she realizes what she has just blurted out.*]

Mirroring Alba's story, Caroline, in spite of her supposed awareness of her attraction to women, gets married, has a child, and endures an unhappy and abusive marriage. She then meets a woman and her story ends with the declaration:

> We've been in love for seven years now. My son and I live with Brenda. Same village, same avenue, same neighbours. Just a different life. And I know I never had a choice – I'm a lesbian. I always have been. I no longer

> feel any guilt or shame. I'm good. I'm happy. I'm happy about who I am. I've got a nice garden, I've got a posh house, I've got three cats. And Brenda and I, we're Ivy Diddles.

As with Alba, Caroline has made a journey, from a 'wrong' choice to the only possible, therefore 'right', choice. And just as Alba's story ends with the same line it began so too does Caroline's story tie beginning and end through the repeated motif of 'Ivy Diddle'. In both stories, traumatic difficulties are encountered and overcome, with the happy ending assured. Indeed, to become what they have always been is the only possible way that the happy ending can be achieved; otherwise they would be denying who they are.

In both these examples Martin's tautology – *coming to know something that has always been true* – is explicit. Caroline 'had no choice' about being an 'Ivy Diddle'. In spite of her heterosexual marriage, she has returned to that which she always was. Similarly, Alba has also returned to her 'true' self, which is her lesbian self. This return to a 'truth' simultaneously suggests that the life previously lived, prior to this return, was an aberration, an untruth, an inauthentic life. Here then, we witness Martin's 'movement beyond distortion' and towards 'liberation', the inscription of the moral right.

Both Alba's and Caroline's rendering of the past is typical of the coming-out story, as the past is sifted for clues that point to the present lesbian identity – clues which verify the authenticity and authority of that identity. In Alba's story, she fondly remembers herself as a schoolgirl, admiring other girl's bodies in the school-showers. In Caroline's story, the transformative forensic activity uncovers trips to the gay bar: 'Well, I went to Vintners every week … Why? I wasn't sure. Yes, I was, I was attracted to women.' Caroline first states she did not know why she went to the gay bar, and then insists that she did know. Two Carolines are perceptible here, the Caroline of the past who denies acknowledging her sexuality, and the Caroline of the present who reclaims that sexuality, who rereads previous events from the place of the present; from the present, secure, lesbian identity. Whilst the Caroline of the past claims that she 'wasn't sure', the Caroline of the present interprets that unsureness as denial, and cancels it out by being absolutely sure now, about what she *really* felt or knew then. In this narrative, it is not that she was not a lesbian then. In fact, she was one, but could not admit it. This reinterpreted past is the proof of who she is now. She is who she evidently always was. Any gap between was and is becomes erased through this reinterpretive act and any tension between then and now is also negated through ascribing authority to the present Caroline. The Caroline standing in front of us is the one who definitively knows the truth about who she is and was. This is the real Caroline. Her past, which includes her heterosexual past, is brought into line with the present, serving to provide a solid ground for this present, a ground upon which this act of reinterpretation is itself enabled. The act of remembering, then, contains within it a dialectical movement, as past and present become mutually dependent, supportive and regenerative. Such reinscription of course enables the production of a coherent narrative told by a unified narrator. The 'proper narrative' is recited here; the lesbian community, constructed on the secure grounds of stable sexual identity, remains unthreatened. The separating wall between 'us' and 'them' similarly remains in place, unbreached.

Performing lesbians

Acknowledging that some of the tales told in *Fingerlicks* mirror dominant narrative structures, I would be doing an extreme disservice to the production, its creators, and its audiences, if I failed to recognise that within *Fingerlicks* there are other sides to the story. Stanley challenges Martin's criticisms of lesbian coming-out anthologies by suggesting that though it is 'easy to dismiss coming out stories for their lack of sophistication in theorising "self" and its relationship to collectivities and identities' such criticism does not recognise that coming-out anthologies enable a dialogue. The readers of anthologies are *active* readers, and as such they contrast the stories read with their own experiences, rather than just consuming them unquestioningly. Readers 'read between, above, and beyond the lines'.[41]

The criticism frequently made of personal narratives that Stanley takes to task here is that they unproblematically assume a referentiality between experience and the writing of that experience. For Stanley, criticisms such as this are, at the outset, misplaced, since the primary import of these anthologies is their 'fundamentally *political* character'.[42] Set within a context of intolerance, the political character of *Fingerlicks* is of course primary. However, the performance does also play ambiguously, though strategically, with the referent. One reason that performers so frequently use personal material as a resource is that its assumed relationship to the 'real' affords it a particular power. Believing that something really happened, invests it with a political urgency; as witnesses to this event that did really happen, we are implicated in it, must change the reality, must stop it happening again and so on. Such is the potential effect of an appeal to the real. However, one cannot, of course, ever represent the real. It is always a *re*presentation. And many performers, whilst activating the power of the auto-biographical mode, simultaneously place the referent into a situation of instability, prompting us to question the status of what we see. Bobby Baker, for example, evidently plays herself as a persona, so is not, then, in fact playing herself;[43] Tim Miller makes it explicit that his autobiographical performances can be nowhere near to the lived mess of his experience.[44]

Certain representational forms used in *Fingerlicks* prompt referential readings. A frequent mode of delivery is the direct address – seemingly unadorned, straight to audience. We appear to see before us Alba, who tells us her own story. Alba plays Alba, Caroline plays Caroline, Seg plays Seg. The assumption of referentiality is also encouraged by the minimal mise-en-scène. The stage is mostly bare, and the performers ostensibly appear to be wearing their own clothes – that is, they do not seem to be wearing costumes. (Of course, they are – that of the everyday). Taken together, the effect suggests a denial of theatricality. (Which is, of course, a carefully stage-managed effect.) What we see appears to be raw, and there is perhaps a certain assumed correlation, or slip, between raw and truthful and the *real thing*. In an interesting comparison, Jon Dovey arrives at a similar conclusion in his study of 'first person media', stating that: 'the low grade video image has become *the* privileged form of TV "truth telling", signifying authenticity and an indexical reproduction of the real world; indexical in the sense of presuming a direct and transparent correspondence between what is in front of the camera and its taped representation'.[45]

The fact that the performers are not professional actors also appears to provide some ground for the assumption that what they are sharing is therefore implicitly closer to the real and authentic, or in Dovey's words, 'amateurishness [is read as] a guarantee of truth'.[46]

In tension with such assumptions, however, is the unavoidable fact that what we see before us is a *performance*, that the women are on a stage, at some distance from us, *performing*. The use of stage lighting and music make this even more evident. In contrast to the images consumed via the television monitor, the apparatus of the medium is here always apparent. We see it. Even without a lavish set, or costumes, the theatrical frame which separates us from the performers is always present. And what takes place within this frame are enactments. This is not a documentary, situated in supposedly real time. This is Caroline re-enacting her story, these are women playing other characters, including men. Finally, the very constructed nature of the stories, the presence of the narratives, the neat resolutions, the recurring motifs and repetition of key phrases, the carefully managed comic timing, make the status of these *stories* apparent. It is difficult, sitting in a theatre, to mistake a representation for the real. And it is evident, in the shaky, nervous voices of the non-professional performers, that this act of representation is hard work. As Wilson states, the performers have 'actually moulded and shaped one of their experiences into something creative'.[47]

Astutely aware of the political potential afforded by theatre, *Fingerlicks* capitalises on the shared space and time of the live theatrical experience through strategically incorporating what might be called shared symbols. These act as gelling agents for spectators, in the service of community construction. In the performance, the use of assumed shared signs include geographical or site related symbols, such as the Vintners bar, recalled by Caroline. As Glasgow's first gay bar, which has since been demolished, Vintners is a powerful symbol not only of a local geography, but also local history. These symbols, then, are not just general lesbian symbols, but more importantly are culturally specific, and would only hold significance for a local population. Location and sexual identity become implicated in each other. This significance is made tangible in the live theatre event, as members of the audience reveal their connection to and with the local, through laughter, head nodding, whispering to companions and so on. The awareness of shared local knowledge potentially induces a powerful sense of community cohesion – a community that is bound both by geography and sexuality. On the other hand, this cohesive tactic carries an implicit risk, as it excludes those who do not share the knowledge. The focus on the local, as with the focus on sexuality, necessarily confronts its own limitations – the non-transferability of the symbols.

Other, more general, symbols include those taken from contemporary British popular culture. The story enacted by Lynne includes a re-enactment from the soap opera, *Brookside*, a programme that, in the late 1990s, had particular interest for many British lesbians.

> P: At the age of 14, Lynne was confused and very glued to the box.
> [*'Brookside' music plays. P and A come on stage together. Lynne watches them from the armchair.*]
> A: Margaret, I've got something to tell you.
> P: What is it Beth?

This 'excerpt' from the soap culminates with Beth and Margaret indulging in a long, deep kiss. The clapping and cheering from the auditorium is immediate and sustained, causing the performers to take a pause before continuing with their stories. Such a response is presumably an indication of the recognition of the reference. Moreover, the fact that the two women who re-enact *that* kiss, live onstage, are self-identified lesbians rather than actresses acting as lesbians, probably added to the spectators' pleasure.

Finally, another form of symbol used variously throughout the performance is that of the expected scenario, which, precisely because it *is* predictable in its content, again enables a sense of shared experiences and knowledge. Whether these scenarios are true and are based on actual events is irrelevant. Their status is as lesbian *folklore*, and like folk stories, they engender a sense of the folk, of community, whilst at the same time, perhaps assuming that community. At a live theatre event, one is *with* the folk, sharing the experience.

In *Fingerlicks*, the inscription of lesbian folklore occurs just after the participant, Seg, has come out to her parents. Prior to revealing her sexuality, she tells them that she no longer wants to train in Physical Education. Upon learning of her lesbianism, her mother asks her whether she is mad: 'Throwing your life away like that. Is it this gay thing why you can't be a PE teacher?' Seg replies with one single word: 'Hardly'. For many who identify as lesbian, the myth of having a crush on the often assumed to be lesbian PE teacher is rife, and the mother's naivety here, alongside Seg's knowing answer, produces a wonderful comic moment. Providing you are in on the joke, of course.[48]

Further countering Martin's criticism of published lesbian anthologies, Stanley refers to the wide diversity of lesbian experience displayed in them, demanding that attention should be paid to the specifics of each story, rather than merely identifying the more obvious similarities in the narratives. Such attention would reveal the 'hints and more than hints of fractures and disagreements'.[49] Similarly, though it is possible to critique *Fingerlicks* for its inscription of sexual essences and the centrality of sexuality as an organising perspective, it is difficult to ignore the fact that there are eight different performers, with eight different lives, each performed in a different way. Though individual stories might contain moments of resolution, the presence of eight individual tales told in different modes results in an overall production that is neither seamless nor coherent. Alongside the narrative style of Alba's story there is the dramatic exposition of Caroline's story, punctured by Christabel singing her story, all of which are disrupted by short, comic, non-narrative interludes or sketches.

Similarly, while Alba's and Caroline's stories follow the predictable narrative trajectory, which leads the protagonist from silence to speech, from guilt to celebration, Lynne's story, by contrast, does not fulfil the demands of this convention. Admittedly, her story does start off on the typical path, but it refuses to stay there as she refuses to provide a closure to her narrative.

The story begins with the following statement, told by another participant:

> At the age of 11, Lynne began to wonder why she was different from her school friends.

Lynne's felt 'difference' is inscribed immediately and she tries to make sense of her feelings by seeking references from the culture around her, confirming Plummer's insights into the self-consciousness of the gay or lesbian self. Lynne finds the references she needs in the lesbian affair on *Brookside*, and in the confessions of Rikki Lake's guests. (This doubling of the confession – and its place in identity construction – is worth noting.) Advised by her older cousin to contact the Lesbian and Gay Switchboard, Lynne is told about their youth group. Being only fifteen, however, she has to get permission from her parents to attend, which obviously means that she has to come out to them.

> [Mother and father are sitting in the two armchairs, as if watching Television. Lynne approaches them.]
> Lynne: Mum, dad. Mum, dad, I want to ask you'se something.
> [Both ignore her.] Mum! [Dad turns TV off.]
> Mum: All right, what is it?
> Lynne: It's just that I'm going to a youth group on Monday.
> Mum: What kind of youth group?
> Lynne: I can't tell you.
> Mum: Well, where is it then?
> Lynne: I can't tell you that either.
> Mum: What do you mean, you can't tell us?
> Lynne: I just can't.
> Dad: Well, in that case you'll not be going.
> Lynne: Oh for god's sake, it's a lesbian youth group!
> [Father gets up, looks at her, and silently leaves the room. The mother then gets up and exits with this parting shot:]
> Mum: What have you done to us?
> [The scene ends with Lynne sitting down in one of the armchairs. She looks small, as she shrinks into the large seat. She sits with her hands by

her sides, and her head down, forlorn, and still. The lights fade on her down-turned head, so that she is left sitting in darkness. The track, 'She Screams in Silence', by Green Day, plays this scene out.]

Lynne's story does *not* end happily. But what is revealing and important about this story is that, as yet, there *is* no narrative ending. Instead, there is a pause. Lynne is the youngest participant in *Fingerlicks*. Unlike the other women, she does not yet have a secure lesbian present from which she can look back and reinterpret or rewrite her past. She does not have the benefit of hindsight, nor the reassurance that things will be all right. Here, there is no distance between the bad past and the good present. In life, her sexual story has not been resolved, and so she cannot provide a neat resolution here. Lynne's story appears to capture the moment of the present, and the uncertainty of the present, before it has become a narrated, past, event. And this present is *here*, in front of us – this *is* the teenager Lynne that we are witnessing. This is also, I would argue, the privileged moment of live theatre, and its aptness as an autobiographical medium.

Complicating this somewhat, and further fracturing the linearity of the performance, the fact that Lynne *is* here, in front of us, *telling* this story, *here and now*, perhaps does inscribe some sort of resolution. What she says and where she says it from are not quite in synch; what we hear and see are slightly different. This is, again, of course, the potential of theatre. Whilst her performance shows a young woman screaming in silence, that same performance *is* the scream made loud. That is, her involvement in this project is itself some sort of outcome. This is true of all the participants in *Fingerlicks*. The ultimate sign of the performers shift from guilt, or self-loathing, or rejection, or confusion, to acceptance, celebration and affirmation, is their presence in this production. And the production does not merely reflect, but actively enables the *practice* of this acceptance, celebration and affirmation. In this sense, it is performative.

Arguably, the performers in *Fingerlicks* are as affected through the telling of their stories as much as the spectators are affected through seeing them. Talking out demands an agency, and in the moment of performing, that agency is both experienced and perceived. Who knows what real effect Lynne's participation in *Fingerlicks* will have on the actual paths her life now takes?[50] Performances such as these do not merely report on experiences, but they may alter future experiences. So the future life becomes implicated by the reporting of the life already lived. Involvement in these productions necessarily becomes a part of the life-story, rather than merely commenting upon it. Although the lights come down on an isolated, rejected and abjected Lynne, her presence here bears witness to the fact that this is *not* where this story actually ends.[51]

Of course, one of the greatest differences between *Fingerlicks* and the published anthologies of lesbian experiences, is that the former is a collaborative process, involving the material presence of live bodies in shared space. The process of *Fingerlicks* was one that lasted six months, with the women working together on a weekly basis to collectively create the show. At the end of the piece, the eight women line up, side by side, and each one recites a single phrase from her story. These phrases, like the women saying them, stand alone, and although the words are spoken side by side, they do not automatically add up to any cohesive statement. Instead, the words are reminders of the diverse stories and experiences that have been shared. Lynne's phrase, for example, is 'She screams in silence', and Caroline's is 'We're Ivy Diddles'. However, the very last phrase of *Fingerlicks* is spoken by all of the women, simultaneously:

> Together. Fingerlicks.

This final line figures a community arrived at without imposing a sense of closure and resolution onto the production. Instead, what we are left with is an image of a group of women who have come together, for *this* project. This project, and in turn our witnessing of their stories, has only been possible through their shared participation. What is brought into focus at the end, then, is *the project, Fingerlicks*, and the shared experience of this, rather than a single, shared experience of being a lesbian. Perhaps this ending of *Fingerlicks* suggests, by example, the possibility of navigating a path between the powerful but potentially dangerous authority of individual experience and the *active creation* of communities. Here, at the end, *Fingerlicks* is the community.

And it is at the end of the night, in the theatre bar, or on the street outside the venue, or on the route home, that the tangible difference of live theatre makes its potential felt. For after the event the dialogue begins, as individual spectators speak their shared moments, differences, disagreements, aspirations and hopes to each other. This, then, is the potential dialogic quality of autobiography, as identified by Stanley.[52] But more specifically, this is the dialogic opportunity particularly afforded and prompted by the collaborative nature of theatre, which demands, in most instances at least, an audience.[53]

Notes

1 The research for this chapter was supported by the Arts and Humanities Research Board, UK.
2 bell hooks, *Talking Back: Thinking Feminist, Thinking Black* (Boston: South End Press, 1989), p. 43.
3 Section 28 (2a), 1988, was only finally repealed in England by the House of Lords in July 2003.
4 The fact that there has been an appointment of a gay bishop anywhere, and that Section 28 has finally been repealed does, however, show some kind of shift.
5 See Margaret Cruikshank (ed.), *The Lesbian Path* (California: Angel Press, 1980); Hall Carpenter Archives Lesbian Oral History Group, *Inventing Ourselves, Lesbian Life Stories* (London: Routledge, 1989); Julie Penelope Stanley and Susan J. Wolfe (eds), *The Coming Out Stories* (Massachusetts: Persephone Press, 1980).
6 *Talking Bollocks*, The Citizens Theatre, Glasgow, 4–5 November 1995; *Talking Bollocks – Unzipped!*, Ramshorn Theatre, Glasgow, 1–4 November 1998.
7 *Fingerlicks*, The Arches, Glasgow, 4–8 November 1998.
8 *Fingerlicks* 2, The Ramshorn Theatre, Glasgow, 24–25 June 1999.
9 *Just Pretending*, Tron Theatre, Glasgow, 27–28 October 2000. 7:84 was established in 1973 under the artistic direction of John McGrath. At the time of writing, the Scottish Arts Council has announced that it is likely to withdraw the company's core funding in 2005, making the future of 7:84 uncertain. mct stands for 'mollie's collar and tie', old euphemisms for gay men and lesbians. The company was launched in 1996 and Artistic Director Christopher Deans wanted to specifically address Scottish gay identity: mct was the first Scottish gay and lesbian theatre company, but its existence was short-lived and the company was disbanded in 2000.
10 As befits the cultural shift in perceptions of 'identity', Glasgay marketed itself in 2003 as a 'multi-arts festival for multi-sexual people and their friends'.
11 Natalie Wilson in interview with the author (London, 2001).
12 One company in Glasgow, whilst not identifying itself as a lesbian or gay theatre company, did consistently include gay or lesbian characters in its new writing. Clyde Unity Theatre operated throughout the 1980s and 1990s, producing shows such as *Mum, Dad, There's Something I've Got to Tell You* (1986), *Killing Me Softly* (1987), *A Little Older* (1992) and *Accustomed to her Face* (1993).
13 The idea of 'Scottish' identity is as problematic as the idea of a lesbian or gay identity.
14 In 2000 Mrs Strain and the Christian Institute brought a lawsuit against Glasgow City Council, claiming that the Council had violated the Section by funding events 'promoting' homosexuality. Such events included Glasgay and mct productions. The lawsuit was eventually dropped, following a hearing and an agreed settlement.

15 www.christian.org.uk/scotland/pressreleases/1999/october_29_1999.htm, consulted 17 November 2003. The study from which this statistic is taken is A. Johnson *et al.*, *Sexual Attitudes and Lifestyles* (London: Blackwell Scientific Publications, 1994).
16 www.mori.com/polls/2000/sh000121.shtml. Consulted 16 November 2003.
17 The National Centre for Social Research states that the figures reported for Scotland are 'almost identical to that found by the British Social Attitudes survey in England'. www.natcen.ac.uk/news_ssa_pr2001.htm, consulted 16 November 2003.
18 www.natcen.ac.uk/news_ssa_pr2001.htm. The rhetoric of these polls is surprising. The statistic from the National Centre for Social Research actually reads '*Just* 39% of Scots think that homosexuality is "always wrong"' [my emphasis].
19 Biddy Martin, 'Lesbian Identity and Autobiographical Difference[s]', in Bella Brodzki and Celeste Schenck (eds), *Life/Lines: Theorizing Women's Autobiography* (London: Cornell University Press, 1988), p. 85.
20 Liz Stanley, *The Auto/biographical I: The Theory and Practice of Feminist Auto/biography* (Manchester: Manchester University Press, 1992), p. 116.
21 Ken Plummer, *Telling Sexual Stories: Power, Change and Social Worlds* (London: Routledge, 1995), p. 138.
22 Wilson, who has worked with both the men in *Talking Bollocks* and the women in *Fingerlicks*, reports that one of the main differences between the two groups was the effort required to persuade the women that their stories did, indeed, matter, and that people would be interested in them. Interview with the author (London, 2001).
23 Biddy Martin, 'Lesbian Identity', p. 83.
24 Ken Plummer, *Telling Sexual Stories*, p. 25.
25 Ibid., p. 144.
26 Ibid, p. 174; Bonnie Zimmerman, 'The Politics of Transliteration: Lesbian Personal Narratives', in Estelle B. Freedman, Barbara C. Gap, Susan L. Johnson and Kathleen M. Weston (eds), *The Lesbian Issue – Essays from Signs* (Chicago: University of Chicago Press, 1985), p. 261.
27 Ken Plummer, *Telling Sexual Stories*, p. 87.
28 Diane Elam, *Feminism and Deconstruction: Ms. En Abyme* (London: Routledge, 1994).
29 Judith Butler, 'Contingent Foundations: Feminism and the Questions of "Postmodernism"', in Judith Butler and Joan W. Scott (eds), *Feminists Theorize the Political* (London: Routledge, 1992), p. 14.
30 Ken Plummer, *Telling Sexual Stories*, p. 82.
31 Biddy Martin, 'Lesbian Identity', p. 88.
32 Ken Plummer, *Telling Sexual Stories*, p. 33.
33 Barbara Ponse, *Identities in the Lesbian World: The Social Construction of Self* (London: Greenwood Press, 1978). Ponse's 'gay trajectory', produced in 1978, reads from a twenty-first century perspective as limited and old-fashioned.

34 Ibid, p. 125.
35 Ken Plummer, *Telling Sexual Stories*, p. 60.
36 Ibid., p. 54.
37 Biddy Martin, 'Lesbian Identity', p. 85.
38 Natalie Wilson, in interview with the author (London, 2001).
39 Natalie Wilson, cited in Press Release for *Fingerlicks*, 20 October 1998.
40 No published performance script of *Fingerlicks* exists. All citations are taken from my transcript of a documentational video recording of the performance (Arches, Glasgow, 5 November 1998), supplied by the director, Natalie Wilson.
41 Liz Stanley, *The Auto/biographical I*, p. 116.
42 Ibid, p. 119.
43 See Dee Heddon, 'Performing the Self', *M/C: A Journal of Media and Culture* 5:5 (2002), www.media-culture.org.au/0201/Heddon.html.
44 See my article '*Glory Box*: Tim Miller's Autobiography of the Future', *New Theatre Quarterly* XIX:3 (75), August 2003, pp. 243–56.
45 Jon Dovey, *FREAKSHOW: First Person Media and Factual Television* (London: Pluto Press, 2000), p. 55.
46 Ibid., p. 62. There is only one review of *Fingerlicks*, and in this there is no comment on the non-professional status of the performers. Reviews of *Talking Bollocks,* however, specifically mark the relationship between 'amateur' and 'truthful'. Colin Donald writes, for example, that 'the fact that [*Talking Bollocks*] is delivered by brave amateurs gives it a directness, honesty and charm' (*Scotsman*, 30 November 1996),whilst Minty Donald reflects that it is the 'loud and proud confidence, a tell-it-like-it-is honesty, [that] is really what's at the heart of 7:84's performance' (*Herald*, 16 May 1996).
47 Natalie Wilson, interview with the author (London, 2001).
48 Interestingly, in the only review of *Fingerlicks*, the reviewer (a heterosexual male), comments on the humour of the piece, writing that it is 'much, much funnier than *Talking Bollocks*'. This would suggest that certain symbols are shared beyond any so-called lesbian constituency. However, it does appear that the humour that Keith Bruce most responds to is that connected to the cultural setting, rather than the lesbian folklore.
49 Liz Stanley, *The Auto/biographical I*, p. 116.
50 The performers' openness regarding their sexuality and their decisions to publicly talk about their real life experiences did cause something of a backlash in the press, as Robert Thomson reports in the *Herald*, 4 December 1998.
51 This gap between the narrated events and the time of narration also serves to trouble any assumed referentiality or easy reflection between life and its representation.
52 Bobby Baker has also commented on this potential aspect of autobiography, a seemingly monologic form, to engender dialogue. Plagued by anxiety about appearing to be self-indulgent, Baker was relieved to learn that following her

show, *Box Story* (2001), spectators tended to be swapping their own life stories, rather than commenting on the one they had just witnessed. Baker, interview with the author (London, 2001).

53 This a somewhat idealistic conclusion but I maintain that the challenge for all autobiographical performance is to harness the dialogic potential afforded by the medium, using it in the service of difference rather than sameness.

11

RE(CI)PERTOIRES OF THE SELF: AUTOBIOGRAPHICAL ASPECTS OF BOBBY BAKER'S PERFORMANCE WORKS. BOBBY BAKER IN INTERVIEW

Catharine McLean-Hopkins

The main ingredient of any Bobby Baker performance is herself: her self as artist/performer/mother/shopper/patient/child or, soon to be, life guru. She represents her multiple identities through performed negotiations with food and domestic effects that are frequently sited in personally specific locations. She performs her selves through narratives of memory and anecdotes that cohere around performance structures and that have become, through multiple performance pieces, retellings of a repeatedly negotiated past.

Wearing her trademark, body-masking overalls and performance shoes, every performance opens with the lines: 'I am Bobby Baker. I am a woman. I am middle-aged.' Delivered with an apologetic, hesitant giggle in Received Pronunciation, this declaration locates the performance persona of Baker in the recognisable categories of white, middle-class, British womanhood. Her performance persona instantly strikes a comic note as she invites her audience to laugh with her.

The autobiographical ingredients that Bobby Baker draws upon in her work are more complex than just her bodily presence in the performative telling of her own story. Performance and the devising of performance appear to be a personal strategy for survival: she tackles vast personal questions about her own faith and belief systems and stages her internal conflicts with stunning levels of self-exposure. Her performances often reflect crises of thought or overwhelming emotion represented by a transgressive use of food as a painterly medium and framed by an imagery most frequently located in the uncelebrated world her own domestic domain.

Baker's use of food as a medium of representation signifies the domestic location of much of her performance work but was, in fact, her medium of choice whilst still an art student in the early 1970s. In both her art and her performance work the inevitable disintegration of food is a symbol of mutability representing the unstable and uncertain traces of a lifetime's work. Her use of food has frequently marked, through decay and change, the emotional intensity of her sense of loss and despair.

The transgressive use of personal sites as performance locations is a particularly telling strategy. From the use of a double sheet in *Drawing On A Mother's Experience* (1988) to her own kitchen or church, the use of personally relevant performance sites has framed and foregrounded the personal in her work. Baker's performance sites also reflect the importance to her of spatial composition in performance. In *Box Story* (2001) she framed her performance within the symmetrical architecture of her own church. The centrally located stained-glass window provided a backdrop for her large box /coffin/altar that was placed centrally, downstage, and flanked by the blue shoes that echoed the Madonna blue of her performance overalls, the window, the painted walls and a triptych. The completeness of this visual composition is at odds with a performance that reflects upon fate and tragedy. Just as the folded-up sheet of *Drawing On A Mother's Experience* hid the stains of painful emotions, the church in *Box Story* belies the unpredictability and lack of control at the heart of the most traumatic of Bobby Baker's autobiographical performances.

The juxtaposition of Bobby Baker's performance persona with the transgressive use of site and food whilst telling stories of her self combine to produce comic performances that, even as they explore the darkest moments of a life, find the humour in the absurdity.

The themes explored in Bobby Baker's performances come from an equally personal repertoire. Drawn from family relationships, motherhood, domestic events and skills, her performances have often been grounded in the hidden world of the home and the maternal. However an on going negotiation of her selves can be traced through from the early works to the most recent. Questions raised as early as *An Edible Family In A Mobile Home* (1976) seem to have some answers in the much later retrospective performance *Box Story.*

At the time of writing, Baker's next planned performance is removed from the domestic sphere altogether. *How To Live* (scheduled for November 2004) will be a self-help guide to life presented in the fashion of popular self-help programmes. The move to a wider platform, literally in the performance space of the main stage at the Barbican and

17 Bobby Baker in *Box Story* (2001).

thematically in a move away from the directly domestic, is a reflection of a new phase of life as the children whose birth stories are contained in *Drawing On A Mother's Experience* have reached adulthood. It will employ a familiar repertoire of performance strategies and be thematically centred on the view that a healthy society is dependent upon the ways in which its members treat each other.

The following text combines materials from two interviews recorded in July 2002 and April 2003. The interviews were recorded in Bobby Baker's studio in the garden of the North London home that was the site for *Kitchen Show* (1991). The studio contains relics from previous shows including the pink body form of 'the sister' from *An Edible Family In A Mobile Home.* Her studio shelves house past and future performance shoes (mostly pink) and a table is covered with recent paintings of bread in its various shapes and forms.

Bobby Baker's every decision about her performance work has a long pedigree sometimes stretching across a decade. In the interviews she reflects upon the reasons for the autobiographical content of her performance work, her very conscious political intentions and the devising process for both *Box Story* (2000) and for the work-in-progress *How To Live.*

The autobiographical

When and why did you make the decision to use the autobiographical in your performances?

I knew I could only speak for my own experience. That's a decision I made back in 1972 about my work – that I could only speak with my own experience and voice – that I couldn't put myself in someone else's shoes. I couldn't work like that. I made that decision very early on when I was studying at Goldsmith's College (London): I felt that I couldn't, with integrity, work in any other way. I applaud and love work that's done with another voice and obviously a great deal of the best work is, so I'm not saying that autobiographical work is essential, but my decision was bound up with a feeling that I had gone through a period when I'd made a lot of work that I was very excited about that wasn't autobiographical. I didn't make the decision that I was going to do autobiographical work. I made the decision that I was going to work from ideas and interests that preoccupied me at that stage of my life. I didn't look ahead at that stage – I was interested in food, meringues and what have you, you know, women and so on. That's what I decided to make work about – I couldn't go off and make work about the Third World, I had no experience of that.

I was very, very absorbed with the notion of integrity at that stage. By this I mean integrity in its widest sense, as much to do with the form, the integrity of the shape and form of a performance as to do with a sense of something being decent and good.

Is there a sense of the integrity being based on a truth?

I suppose a sort of *truth to me* which seemed to be the only way I could operate. The other thing that I didn't clarify for a long time was that I seemed to find myself making work that made people laugh and I found that very distressing – really distressing, because I was feeling very serious and I couldn't stop making audiences laugh and I couldn't think why this was happening. Then I realised that it was just part of the way I operated. I mean I think Marina Warner's[1] piece about women using humour in a very rebellious way actually puts her finger much more on why, historically women have used humour. Within my family that is the way women have coped with their frustration. So humour was part of it, but I remember sitting on a train, and I had this moment of thinking, 'I can't do that. I can't make work about this or what have you.' It was a sort of physical feeling within my body and my brain and the decision to make the work I do grew from there.

An Edible Family In A Mobile Home was autobiographical in a more oblique way. I think when I'd made it I realised how autobiographical it was and how appalling it was but when I made *Packed Lunch* (1974) that was when I became clear that I would like to explore the model of working from my personal experience using the details of my daily life.

When I made the decision – in 1972 or 1973, no it would have been more like 1974 that I made that decision – I remember thinking this could be seen as being very selfish or self indulgent and I thought, 'Well, I'm doing it! I have to do this work for myself, if it's of interest and relevance to anyone else then that's a wonderful advantage.'

You know there is a drive, a kind of craze, an urge, when you get an idea. You want to communicate it to people but the very starting point for me is to resolve issues, resolve things – thoughts, intellectual notions – for myself and that has to be part of a decision about what kind of work to make.

Is there a sense in which using your autobiographical details can be too self revelatory? For instance I am thinking of the use of your father's death in Box Story?

There was a kind of self-awareness of that and Pol and Jude [2] who were working with me, endlessly reassured me. I was just so conscious that the piece could be seen as being *about* me and it had got to the point with *Box Story* that I didn't want a performance of that sort of size to be just some kind of personal development strategy. There was a point at which all the stories within the performance were decided on and I did a very crude version in the church. Some friends and colleagues had come and heard the stories for the first time and saw what I did. What was so exciting was that we spent the next hour and a half sitting, the three of us, in the church talking about *their* lives and *their* experiences of tragedy. One said she remembered thinking, the first time she heard the stories, the first two, she thought how wonderful, what a wonderful, contented, secure life and then when that happened [the story of Baker's father drowning] she suddenly sort of jumped up and thought, 'No, this relates more to me!'

At the British Psychoanalytical Society[3] *you mentioned that you were quite fed up with housewife/mother label. If you were going to label yourself what would it be?*

Artist. I mean I am an artist, that's what I always wanted to be from when I was a child. I'm labelled a 'performance artist' or a 'live artist', which is fine. People are obsessed with labels and categorising and fitting things in and making sense. I do perform, but I also do work in other media and I will increasingly work in other media. I am an artist who happens to work in many different ways and I can imagine that I will perform less and be less of a performance artist eventually. It's a bit of a double bind because it really does conjure up certain sorts of expectations and prejudices and I much rather be known simply as an 'artist'.

Is all of your art in other media as autobiographical as your performance art?

The paintings and drawings are. I did a whole series about a diary for a year, every day a drawing of my life when my children were small. It was about things that were going on at the time and about feelings. The drawings I've been doing since I've been ill over the last six years are about my experiences of my own mental health problems and they were done specifically in a way that would channel some of those ideas and images – so they are autobiographical yes.

The political

How intentionally political is your work?

It is very political. In the sense that my work has got this slightly impassioned aspect to it, in order to make some impact on the way people think and behave. Very often, well always these days, when I'm thinking of a show I like to think about how people will leave, how I want them to leave, a sort of state of mind that I'm trying to produce. With *Box Story* and *How To Live* it was very much a case of me wanting them to go away and sit quietly and reflect on their lives. With *Take A Peek* people decidedly left in a frenzied, overexcited state – a very bedazzled state hopefully.

I actually feel that my intentions are now more confident and clear. I feel more sure about what I'm doing and I know – I'm going back to

Drawing On A Mother's Experience now – that came from a very political feeling. The work that I'm doing now has the same driving edge as did *Spitting Mad* (1997). I really do feel very strongly about the subjects that I'm dealing with. I hope to make some impact but I think with *How To Live* I want to make a much more major impact potentially by creating work in this very, very flexible package. This is also what I did with *Kitchen Show* where there was a video version. So *How To Live* is like an amalgam of *Kitchen Show* and *How To Shop* but with hindsight and experience and having also moved into a slightly different phase of my life. So there will be versions in other media – much more complete than the *Box Story* book – which will be sent winging out to people.

For *How To Live* we've come up with a great series of elements which are produced elegantly in packaged form and then we will have a touring version which is very adaptable for all sorts of spaces. This stems from a kind of driven attempt to get out there – I do feel concerned that so much of what's happened to me is, as with *Drawing On A Mother's Experience*, not spoken about or made clear. With mental health, if people don't behave in a certain way then the implication is that they become ill, but this isn't actually said. In all the books you read about mental health it's sort of written about but it's hedged around, because obviously people don't then want to go out in public and say that it was because of what someone did to them that they are ill. But that is the truth in a great many circumstances – not with all illnesses – but there is an element of it bound up in a great deal of illness from my observations. So I want to make a much wider stance in performance: 'You, you and you and you up there! You in that building, in your position of power! This is what we should be doing! But you in your small kitchen, this is the consequence of what you're doing.' So in that sense, yes, my work is very political. It has an element of innocence in the fact that one would attempt to do something in such a kind of bizarre way. But I'm very knowing, I'm very aware of that – the absurdity of it. It's part of the performance, that ironical slant. What's so fascinating, what so delights me, is that these mental health gurus are mostly American. They've set up these self-help guru packages and do present themselves quite unknowingly as these wonderful people. Their web sites have big photographs of themselves and they're all called Doctor and they're all pompous and so, in *How To Live*, I will take all of this kind of cultural package – it's got such potential – and then undermine it and twist it. It's about so many things, this show, but it is very much going back to being focused on minute aspects of daily life – using those as the sort of key.

I was beside myself because I'd been working from the outside-in for a long time, on all the different layers and aspects of the performance. Then I got to the actual kernel of it which is what is it actually going to be about – these things kind of click on like a series of cogs connecting with movements happening. How did it present itself in my mind? As something to do with 'God is in the details', that's what sprang to mind. And then I looked it up everywhere and I couldn't find any reference to it and my son was very kind of 'but mother that expression doesn't exist you just made that up', and I wasn't sure whether I had or not and then I found Blake: All the world in a grain of sand/to see heaven in a wild flower/to hold infinity in the palm of your hand and see eternity in a hour. Anyway, something like that! And I was just kind of, 'Yes, yes that's it!' So that's the core of the new piece.

This is very much what *Kitchen Show* was putting forward particularly with the first action which involved peeling this carrot, it's not the first action in the performance but it's actually the first one that I thought of. So I'm going back to that moment which had a very impassioned aspect to it, with the same kind of sense of absurdity. When I first thought of that idea for *Kitchen Show* I wanted to get an international satellite link worldwide of me peeling a carrot – what more could one want? Why not? It seemed to be the most important thing in the world. I think *Box Story* was very much a returning to *Drawing On A Mother's Experience*. It was using those stories in a sense that the stories in *Kitchen Show* are me relating habits and forms of behaviour.

If I could pursue the politics for just a little bit longer – it's always struck me that, in your performances, the political element is very much about women.

I think in a sense that I'm a woman who has come from a background where the focus was being put on the injustices of a woman's role. There is an historical background to where I arrived at that age, leading to changes that are now taking place in our society, but I would hate my work to be exclusive. I do get quite edgy if it's seen as being just about women's politics because nothing in life is a simple as that. We're all bound up with each other and changes in our lives impact on men's lives and their lives impact on ours – so women's politics is not at the forefront – yet I am who I am! My life has revolved around aspects of a daily life which is not necessarily one that men would share: some aspects of it, some of the details are feminine, some are universal – we are all a mixture of everything anyway.

How To Live is not about women's domestic lives although of course there is a political and gender dynamic – it is women who tend to become mentally ill, diagnosed as mentally ill in the face of injustice. I suppose the show is about *injustice* and *abuse* and how we treat each other. So I wouldn't say that it's particularly to do with a woman's perspective anymore than it is a man's. I am certainly not so concerned with my domestic role – my role as a mother. I'm not sure at the moment whether *How to Live* might be based on other people's behaviour – actually it's quite likely it will be, so I'm branching out into other people's modes of operating.

Devising *Box Story*

Could you describe the process of making of Box Story?

I decided to use the same model as *Drawing On A Mother's Experience* which was a structure involving a set of stories, so I knew there was a set of stories and I knew – because then I spent a period of time thinking a great deal about misfortune, tragedy and life – that I wanted it to be about that and I knew I wanted it to be about misfortune as it applies to us. I am middle-aged woman, a middle-class woman, living in Islington – a pretty privileged life in many ways – but actually personal misfortune and tragedy have an impact on all of us in different ways and it is inevitable that we compare, contrast and judge.

I did think that I had covered a lot of things in *Kitchen Show* in a quite fleeting way and I wanted to go in to them more deeply in other shows. So I thought that I would do five shows in different sites which I came up with very early on in the process. It seemed that the ones that I chose were inevitable and I knew that *Box Story* would end up in a church because it would focus on death and be more of an exploration of spirituality or Christianity – that was in 1991.

I started thinking about *Box Story* very early on. Throughout the 1990s I was thinking about it with a sense of longing because the more I got into the *Daily Life*[4] series the more bogged down I felt and frustrated by the limitations of the work. I do have a tendency, which is very irritating for the people who work with me, of becoming absolutely absorbed and delighted with something which is five years hence – it's so much more interesting and so much more magical and everything's possible!

It's difficult to say at what point I knew but I knew that it would involve a box. I remember very clearly being in Cairo at a theatre festival. Judith Knight and I went down into the bowels of a pyramid and we were standing by this sarcophagus and it had a sort of ceiling that was painted in blue. It was quite a magical experience with just one guy guiding us, just the two of us on our own on a British Council tour. There was this sarcophagus and I had one of those explosions, one of those trains of thought that I find it difficult to articulate, sort of connected with an image of boxes, the significance of these coffin-shaped objects in so many aspects of our culture. This connected with a fascination with a fridge freezer box, those giant boxes. I've always been very interested in packaging and boxing things up. It was at about that time that Andrew got a fridge freezer delivered upstairs and I remember I ran out into the road and said 'I want the box!' – I was frenzied with excitement at having my hands on one of these boxes that I'd been thinking of and then it gradually mouldered in the garden shed!

I can quite often remember the moment when I have had an idea. I was driving down the Camden Road and I got the idea of me being put in the box. That was the early stage. I would be put in the box by a group of children and it would be very solemn and ridiculous and absurd and that was as far as I got – for a very long time the idea was just this fabulous box in a church with a choir. The idea of the choir came very early on. But some of the elements got separated off into *Grown Up School* (1999). *Grown Up School* and *Box Story* were sort of fused in a way. I did *Grown Up School* and then *Box Story* clarified over a period of some years and it got to the point where I knew much more. I knew which church I would use.

That's your regular church?

Yes, I go there and don't think about – my God I think about my shows!! Then I got more focused on the choir and I realised very much, yes, in fact I did want to have the children's choir in *Grown Up School* and I wanted to work with a composer. I gradually realised that the choir was much more appropriate in the church and would be an adult choir and for about five years I was sort of pursuing the composer Jocelyn Pook – I'd heard her music and it was perfect. It was not essential, but I was very interested in using a woman composer and it was particularly wonderful that I discovered Jocelyn's work – I went to see various concerts and then went through a process of negotiation. I think she was a bit bewildered at first, I was very unsure about lots of things which were going into the performance. The title had come a very long time before – the titles are always my most enjoyable bit. I make these rather absurd rules about titles for my work. The point of them is to be absurd but they're sort of delightfully arbitrary. One of the rules was that each part of *The Daily Life* series would have a number attached to it and for some reason I decided, because I'd done *Kitchen Show*, every title had to have three syllables. I liked the elegance and they've got different intonations and so *Box Story* was such an obvious title.

I got the idea of the music and I'd got the ending and then I realised I couldn't have children putting me in a box. For ages I just focused on the ending and I realised that I would have to put myself in the box which changed the dynamic and then – this is going back a very long way – I think probably the very first idea I ever had was the idea of carrying the box on.

I very often think of that very first image. I did with *Drawing On A Mother's Experience.* I knew with *Box Story* that I would exit wearing it and come on carrying it. I couldn't work out the relevant number for a while and then I realised that I had thirteen with *Drawing On A Mother's Experience* and with *Kitchen Show*, seven with *How To Shop*, nine with *Take A Peek*, three with *Grown Up School* and so it had to be eleven. And I included the giant box as one of the eleven, so I knew there would be ten other boxes. Most systems are arbitrary and obscure and complex and bizarre so why not have eleven boxes? Why not have three sections? So I had the eleven and I knew there would be packaging. Gradually I got at the framework and that is always the way. I very often come up with the beginning and the end, the overall structure, the context and the kind of general meaning behind it.

That's the bit I'm not talking about – I mean the feelings and the ideas. Where Pandora came in it's hard to say but it was very early on that I'd realised I'd be opening this box. It must have at some point come pinging into my brain that this was an image of Pandora – actually I was in a psychiatric institution at the time and was very friendly with lots of the staff. I was putting together a funding application and this guy, who's amazing, an amazing guy I was friends with there, asked me about Pandora.

When I did *Drawing on a Mother's Experience* I felt that I'd so exposed myself and there's always this anxiety about being self indulgent so then I sort of backed away from that with *Cook Dems* and other pieces and the disastrous *Chocolate Money* (1990) and then I did *Kitchen Show* which again was more personal and then backed away somewhat. Then I came back feeling that I would look at the whole of my life. It finally got to the point that I would use ten stories and the piece would be about misfortunes that had happened to me.

I remember having conversations with work colleagues and friends about putting in the story of my father's death and feeling worried about it being too manipulative of the audience. I hadn't worked out what the stories were but I knew the stories would be triggered by the box. So then it was just like a process of searching through the supermarket shelves for those boxes that connected. All the stories had to be connected to a box but I worked out the ingredients and then I used some and I didn't use others. I found stories to fit some and some to fit others and I sort of made the stories fit the theme and the theme fit the stories.

I hadn't ever told Pol what had happened with my dad. I have rarely talked about it and this is what's so bizarre. It's ridiculous really but the psychologist who's been treating me for quite a while – I'd never told him. I mean he knew it had happened but I'd never talked about it and the most he's ever heard about it was through coming to see the show.

Work in progress: *How To Live*

You've said that your latest project involves looking at issues around mental health.

Yes, I go with whatever stage I'm at – one day I'll be making geriatric art! Now I'm very bound up, obviously, with mental health concerns because I have had so much experience of them. *How To Live* is based on behaviourism, Cognitive Behavioural Therapy, but it's also touching on therapy in the wider sense. I use the self-help ethos and look at the impact of psychology and psychologists on our current thinking. I'm inventing my own sort of therapy but I'm realising, increasingly, it's much bigger than that. *How to Live* looks at values and morals and at the way we live – it's about emotion, a great deal about emotion. So it is autobiographical but much less personal. There might be the odd personal anecdote wound in with it but it won't be obviously about me. It's not a performance for mentally ill people particularly: it's meant to be a very accessible show because it will take the form of a seminar. So it can actually go into any kind of context. Ideally there will be a web site and a video and a book.

How To Live is not going to be about my problems *per se*. It's going to be my invention of a therapy – with lots of twists and turns. It is related to my experiences but it's not going to be structured around stories. It's based on things that have happened to me but it's more like *How to Shop*, only less surreal. It isn't an examination of mental illness but a look at mental health. It's a look at a potentially healthy sort of society rather than at dysfunctional behaviour. *How To Live* is very much at the early stage at the moment but it is quite useful to try and think about it. The show is not based on the fact that I have been mentally ill so much as it is based on the treatment of mental illness so prevalent in our society. I've been treated with a Cognitive Behavioural Therapy called Dialectical Behavioural Therapy, which is actually very much steeped in all our everyday thinking in the form of self-help television programmes. I mean it's everywhere, this way of thinking, this way of analysing thoughts. While I've been subjected to treatment I have actually been thinking about it in relation to other ways of training us to think. *How to Live* uses my synthesised version of many, many different ways of operating, including religion. I'm currently working on the bare bones of it and I've got one section complete now – I'm now beginning to step back and look at that and think about what it implies.

Do you see *How to Live* as a performance in the way that you have done other performances?

Yes, as a performance in the style of a kind of guru. I'm going to be the self-help guru whose mission is to travel the world teaching people how to live and the show is going to have all the kinds of merchandising and marketing tools that run alongside it. I mean for instance the performance at the Barbican will be a very theatrical event. It will be styled as the launch of a new therapy and it will use film to start with. The screen will project a very large version of myself, a sort of grand straddling of the stage but then there will be the whole talk which will be interspersed with theatrical effects. And there is a very, very spectacular finale which is entirely more theatrical than anything I have ever done. This will make use the Barbican's technology although there is a problem in that it is all massively expensive.

What's thrilled me about it is that we've got a whole week at the Barbican so we can film. We have created a theatrical effect but we will film it so I can do a very small touring version. What we will design and build is a smaller version that can go to smaller performance spaces and so it can be just like *Box Story*, very flexible. In fact much more flexible than *Box Story* in the sense that I can do it in a classroom or an office with all the theatrical effects on a monitor, or I can do it in a small scale theatre with a scaled down finale or I can do it in massive spaces.

Most of your performance work has been fairly intimate. Is the Barbican's main stage a very imposing space?

It seems very appropriate. I have performed in bigger spaces several times before when touring abroad in theatres of about 900 seats but I think once you get beyond 500 it doesn't make that much difference it's just big: it's the size of the stage which is so exciting because it's very wide and deep and the potential is exciting.

You talked about the self? Can you elaborate about that a bit more?

Yes. I'm really interested in change and this 'focus on the self' which has happened historically. I've read quite a lot about it but I'm terribly bad at remembering facts and details – I've got a kind of general impression that the self didn't exist as a concept five hundred years ago. Diaries weren't being written until three hundred years ago. I know they might not have lasted but there wasn't that kind of focus – it was much more channelled through religion. Whereas if you look back over the last hundred and fifty years or if you look back since Freud, you see this increasing attention to the inner world, the unconscious, intention and behaviour. And I just find Cognitive Behavioural Therapy entirely fascinating in a sort of infuriating and intriguing way given that its historical roots are stoicism and a Pavlovian analysis of behaviour. It's a much more focused way of trying to alter behaviour than say psycho-dynamic therapy but it's all part of the same package. It's part of a whole movement to subtly impact on the ways in which society functions. That's why the show will reflect aspects of Cognitive Behavioural Therapy but also aspects of self-reflection that come from analysis, or spiritual concerns. I think they are all versions of the same thing. So it's my take on it, my idiosyncratic take on the whole thing. Part of the treatment I have received has been an attempt to teach me mindfulness, a version of meditation and I am spectacularly bad at it!

To some extent Cognitive Behavioural Therapy is about making oneself into a sort of 'self-engineer'. You're in charge and the relationship between the therapist and the patient is much more of an equal one, like in counselling where you are part of a project together – you are working on yourself. The methodology for this self-examination is empowering – essentially you are in charge whereas with psycho-dynamic therapy for example, there is the extraordinary dynamic of transference, which is of course all about power imbalance.

We have these very powerful therapists who have 'the knowledge', like a priest or a god, and they impart very little of it. I've had analysis and they sit there in silence – it's quite extraordinary. I wrote a diary for a Gulbenkian project (2002) and the artists who had taken part were invited to go on a panel at The British Institute of Psychoanalysis with an analyst interviewing us. There were all these famous analysts there and a lot of regular decent therapists and some of the public. It was absurd! At the end we had question time and there were these very, very arrogant people asking complex intellectual questions entirely, as far as I could see, with the purpose of increasing their status within this milieu. So it was like, 'I'm more important than you, I'm cleverer than you and I'm more obscure than you.'

So I do favour CBT over analysis. I think there are a lot of grey areas in between where you get psycho-dynamic therapists who actually do have an inclination to teach. I think there is a movement towards them all coming together but I think it's very difficult to make sense of your thinking unless you do have some kind of reflection on the past. That kind of insight is very helpful. We are changing.

So How To Live *is optimistic although it's got very dark side to it?*

It has a dark aspect to it but I think everything I do has. It's has a certain ambivalence but also celebration and joy at the same time as agony and despair.

Are you going to use the same performance persona as you have used in your earlier performances?

I know the kind of body stance I will use but won't talk to my director for quite some time other than about the bare bones of the piece. She'll come in at some point next year when the show is fully made and we'll develop the performance. At the moment I can see it being a sort of a version of *How To Shop.* I was watching Rosemary Connelly the other day – it's that kind of persona I want to create and the woman who invented Dialectical Behavioural Therapy which is the one I got treated with – photographs in her books have her looking over the top of her big moon-like glasses – very intimidating and academic, a clever looking woman. I will use that kind of body language. I also have the shoes she will wear – they came very early on in the process.

Jocelyn Pook is going to collaborate with you again?

Yes. I loved watching what she did so much in *Box Story* and I love her music. I love other work that she does and wanted to develop the relationship rather than starting another relationship with another composer. Jocelyn now has much more understanding of my work and I've got a good relationship with her so we can actually develop it as we go along. The music, when I first thought of it, was very much a finale but I'm now thinking that it might run right throughout the show. I'm not sure of whether it's going to be vocal or instrumental.

In Box Story *the choir acted as a commentary on the stories – the heavenly chorus – angels – a Greek chorus. Will the music have a similar purpose in* How To Live?

No. I think it is too early to know. The music is coming from hidden speakers – part of the magic! When you get a guru coming on you don't *see* things. It's all part of the show – wonderful banks of speakers – all part of the indoctrination.

This is the first time I've talked about *How to Live*, apart from my impassioned presentation – I launched into this speech at the Barbican. We were meeting to plan the run that I'm doing now and I said, 'Oh by the way I've got this idea!', and at the end of it there were all these people looking astonished and they said 'Yes!' It was extraordinary because there are so many different layers to it and so many different angles and perspectives and if you start from scratch there's an awful lot to talk about. It's a show for a supposedly mentally healthy society, which inherently our society isn't. That's what slightly takes me aback when I realise that actually I'm inventing a therapy which people only turn to if they see there's a problem – so that's quite interesting. I really think the idea of an individual inventing a therapy is so absurd that it will grab people's imaginations. That's what I think *Box Story* didn't have but *Kitchen Show* did. It had that idea – here's somebody opening their kitchen to the public – it's just that little sort of spin which gets people in. The idea of a person inventing a therapy is so wonderfully grandiose that I hope that will be the twist.

There is one last question that I would like to ask: given absolutely carte blanch and unlimited resources what kind of performance would you like to devise?

Oh God! I would do a television series!

Selected performance and video bibliography

Those marked with an asterisk are available in video form from Arts Admin, Toynbee Studios, London, E1 6AB, UK. Tel: 020 7247 5102. email: admin@artsadmin.co.uk

An Edible Family In A Mobile Home (1976)
Drawing On A Mother's Experience (1988*; 2000*)
Kitchen Show (1991*)
How To Shop (1993*)
Take A Peek (1995*)
Spitting Mad (1997*)
Grown up school (1997*)
Box Story (2001*)
How to Live (scheduled for the Barbican Theatre, November 2004)

Notes

1 Marina Warner, 'The Rebel at the Heart of the Joker', in N. Childs and J. Walwin (eds), *A Split Second of Paradise: Live Art, Installation and Performance* (London: River Oram Press, 1998), pp. 68–87.
2 Polona Baloh Brown, Baker's artistic collaborator and performance director. Judith Knight, Producer and Director of Arts Admin.
3 Talk given by Baker at the British Psychoanalytical Society, Maida Vale, London, 24 May 2002.
4 *Daily Life Series* was commissioned by LIFT (London International Festival of Theatre) in 1991. It was comprised of five performance pieces: *Kitchen Show* (1991), *How to Shop* (1993), *Take a Peek* (1995), *Grown Up School* (1997) and *Box Story* (2001).

With huge thanks to Andrew Whittuck for provision of and permission to reprint photographs.

INDEX

Lightning Source UK Ltd.
Milton Keynes UK
UKOW030659180212

187495UK00003B/13/P

9 780719 063336